THE BIRMINGHAM POLITICAL MACHINE

WINNING ELECTIONS FOR JOSEPH CHAMBERLAIN

Andrew Reekes

Published by West Midlands History Limited
Minerva Mill Innovation Centre, Alcester, Warwickshire, UK.
© 2018 West Midlands History Limited.
© All images are copyright as credited.

ISBN: 978-1-905036-42-4

Cover images: Mary Evans Picture Library and iStock.

Caric Press Limited, Merthyr Tydfil, Wales.

To John Beasley, Late Modern confrère

ACKNOWLEDGEMENTS

I am very grateful to Mike Gibbs for seeing the potential in a first full-length study of Chamberlain's unique political operation and then for commissioning me to set about researching, and writing it. I am equally grateful to my editor, Jenni Butterworth, for her infectious enthusiasm for the project and the emerging text; and for her invariably pertinent and imaginative critiques of early drafts. Malcolm Dick has been a reassuring and supportive presence throughout the writing of this book. The History West Midlands team has been a pleasure to work with: Janet Sullivan has been an imaginative and rigorous picture editor, sourcing some excellent images to illustrate this book, and David Beattie has been a precisionist proof-reader. I am also indebted to Alison Goodfellow for her help with formatting the draft manuscript.

Over the years I have greatly appreciated the advice of, and conversation with, Peter Marsh, the doyen of Chamberlain studies. More recently I have benefited much from stimulating discourse with Stephen Roberts, especially with regard to Chamberlain's time on the Birmingham Town Council.

It has always been a great privilege to work in the Special Collections at the University of Birmingham, where the atmosphere is so conducive to scholarship and where the team of archivists has been invariably helpful. I am also appreciative of the assistance given by the staff at the Library of Birmingham, who have remained cheerful despite the vicissitudes of public service cuts in the city. I am much obliged to the University of Birmingham which, by appointing me an Honorary Research Associate in the School of Cultures and History, has allowed me beneficially to utilise its library and research facilities.

Patrick Derham has read every word and been hugely encouraging, as has Lynne, who has brought an unerring eye to any inelegant expression and over-complex construction obscuring the text's clarity, and who has remained remarkably tolerant of the long periods of pre-occupation which have accompanied the completion of this project.

CONTENTS

INTRODUCTION

Joseph Chamberlain's power base in the West Midlands was like no other in British political history. Its finest hour came in the 1906 General Election when the Unionist party suffered crushing defeats across the country. Yet all Birmingham seats held fast for the Unionist party, remaining faithful to Chamberlain and his colleagues. No politician has had an enduring electoral fortress like his, which encompassed Birmingham and many of its neighbouring Parliamentary constituencies. Statesmen from Benjamin Disraeli and William Gladstone to Lord Salisbury, Arthur Balfour and David Lloyd George, enemies and allies, acknowledged that it was both a unique and a formidable phenomenon. His hegemony outlasted his death in 1914, and not till 1945 was his spell truly broken. Control was exercised by whichever party he backed, at first Liberal, later Unionist and – after him – Conservative. It encompassed many of the organs of municipal government as well as Parliamentary representation.

His Birmingham political organisation was likened by many contemporaries to a Machine. Chamberlain himself used the image: 'The fact is,' he wrote to his old friend J.T. Bunce, 'the Machine is running very well in the old groove.'[1] The Machine concept was particularly appropriate for Birmingham, city of James Watt and Matthew Boulton, where precision craftsmanship from jewellery making to the engineering of large machinery commissions had made it a world industrial leader. For Chamberlain's Machine had some of the qualities evoked by the metaphor; it was an orderly mechanism, reliable and remorseless. Henry Crosskey, minister, educational reformer and dedicated Liberal, caught just that metronomic quality when he wrote of Chamberlain's Birmingham praetorian guard, the Liberal Association: 'The discipline of this electoral body was perfect; the forces at the disposal of the Birmingham Liberal Association were not hordes of wayward freelances, but they were armies of disciplined men well accustomed to stand side by side and move in unbroken battalions.'[2]

This book is about the successive phases of that political machine and the men who operated it; it campaigned both in local and national politics – for example in the 1870s in the Town Council and the Birmingham School Board while at the same time it engaged as a country-wide pressure group, the National Education League. It well exemplifies the sort of extensive and influential network identified recently by Niall Ferguson in *The Square and the Tower*. For more than thirty years it continued to maintain these twin focuses concurrently. At the time of Chamberlain's enforced retirement in 1906, the Machine was crusading to secure Birmingham and the Duchy for Tariff Reform, whilst also directing the fortunes of the Liberal Unionist party in the country and effectively running the national campaign against Free Trade.

The early incarnation of the Birmingham Machine pre-dated Chamberlain, for Thomas Attwood's Birmingham organisation (the Political Union), demanding the reform of Parliament in the 1830s, was a template for others all over England. Under Chamberlain it was refined and rendered formidable. When Moisey Ostrogorski, the Russian founder of political sociology, wrote a pioneering study of political organisation *(Democracy and the Organisation of Political Parties)* in 1902 he devoted much of his time to a detailed analysis of Birmingham and the 'Caucus', his name for Chamberlain's operation there.

Contemporaries were in no doubt about its effectiveness: Herbert Gladstone, the Liberal chief whip and a leading opponent, commented: 'Chamberlain shows us how to do it.' An earlier Conservative rival, Lord Randolph Churchill, wrote admiringly of how 'the whole governing power of Birmingham is in the hands of (Chamberlain's) Caucus… which owns the gas works, owns the water supply, controls the lunatic asylum and the grammar school as well as the drainage farm'.[3] He might have railed against it but Churchill then set about reforming the Conservative Party by founding the National Union of Constitutional and Conservative Associations to extend party democracy; it was closely based on Chamberlain's pattern.

The Machine created a political monopoly and it was all-embracing, even extending to appointments to the magistrates' bench, and to the selection of council officials. Its enemies understood and resented this versatility, a caustic article in *The Yorkshire Post* remarking that:

> 'There are various expressions of this Caucus. In its municipal aspect it is the Town Council. In its political aspect it is the 800 (the ruling committee of the Birmingham Liberal Association). In its religious aspect it is the Central Nonconformist Union. If some municipal job is to be perpetrated or some piece of extravagant expenditure saddled upon the ratepayer, the Caucus acts through the medium of the Town Council. If the Caucus wishes to dictate on the Bulgarian Horrors, to vilify the Tories, the lungs of the 800 are set at work. Dissenting chapels within a considerable radius of Birmingham are for the most part subservient sub-centres of Caucism.'[4]

And always, behind the scenes, critics discerned the manipulative hand of Joseph Chamberlain; consequently, a sceptical Liberal MP, A.J. Mundella, believed he 'was creating a phalanx of marionettes with the wire pulled by himself from Birmingham'.[5] For even when Chamberlain fashioned wide-ranging national movements like the National Education League, the National Liberal Federation, the National Radical Union and the crusade for Tariff Reform, the heart of their operations remained in Birmingham. Ostrogorski observed of one moment at the Caucus's height that 'The whole process of agitation, all the resolutions, all the circulars, emanated from three or four persons with Mr Schnadhorst as the driving wheel.'[6] He might as well have been writing of C.A. Vince, the presiding master a generation later, for the centralisation on Birmingham offices continued unbroken until 1914.

Birmingham had been at the forefront of professionalising politics and Chamberlain learnt much from William Harris, who created the democratic structure of the Birmingham Liberal Association in the wake of the Second Reform Act in 1867. This Act dramatically increased the electorate, challenging politicians to reach out to them (chapter 1). A common theme running from Harris right up to the later incarnations of the Machine in the tariff debates of the Edwardian era is that of democratic involvement. Much of the Machine's success involved educating prospective supporters. From the 50,000 leaflets pouring from the National Education League's presses in Ann Street in Birmingham in 1870 (chapter 2), to the observation about Birmingham's Tariff Committee in 1903 that 'it is the busiest and most effective leaflet agency in Britain' (see chapter 7), Chamberlain and his team exploited the printed word. In just the same way, 20 years' support from the editor of the *Birmingham Post* (and its proprietor John Jaffray) ensured column inches and favourable coverage of education policy, of Mayoral strategies and of Birmingham School Board battles. The Machine was always at the forefront in embracing innovations in communication technology from new lithographic posters, the electrograph, the movie film and the picture postcard. Their Birmingham offices and warehouses bombarded voters for more than 30 years.

Caucus politics dictated that the Machine organised democratic party structures to involve all members. Birmingham's Liberal Association pioneered the pyramidical system in the late 1860s, whereby ward meetings elected ward committees, which in their turn chose representatives for a general committee that nominally determined candidate and policies. For Chamberlain and his allies this was the essence of democratising politics – not only in extending the vote to a wider electorate, but also in breaking the suffocating control exercised by the propertied classes over the nomination of candidates. This committee grew from the 400 to the 600 and eventually numbered 2,000; it was widely imitated. A generation later, Chamberlain established a very similar arrangement when he created the Midland Liberal Unionist Association in the late 1880s; local committees represented all Liberal Unionists in the thirty-three constituencies and they sent delegates to a central committee to nurture Liberal Unionists in the diurnal round between elections as well as supervising the elections themselves.

Chamberlain was an inveterate founder of new political organisations, either when he felt blocked by institutional inertia or when his political survival was threatened. These were invariably based on Birmingham. After the failure of his Education League he wanted to rejuvenate the Liberal party and so conceived the National Liberal Federation to add Radical 'ginger' to party affairs. In the wake of his damaging rebellion against Gladstone's Home Rule Bill in 1886 he summoned up the National Radical Union; when Birmingham itself was in danger of slipping away to Gladstonians he created the Birmingham Liberal Unionist Association; when his reckless tariff gamble precipitated new party splits, he devised the Birmingham Tariff Committee. But equally he had an incurable predilection for new committees; the Machine functioned through efficient committee work and he was a chairman who knew his mind and dispatched business peremptorily. He admired those qualities in others of his team. The Mayoral revolution of the 1870s (chapter 4) was enacted by a flurry of full Council meetings but their decisions were effected by committees he had created – Gas, Water, Sanitation and Improvement committees, all peopled by his close allies.

The Machine also involved the generality of its supporters by utilising historic methods. Early in its life it employed petitions as Thomas Attwood had done a generation before when calling for reform of Parliament. The Birmingham Education Society, the National Education League, and the National Liberal Federation all collected thousands of signatures on petitions to be presented to Parliament. If the petition became less fashionable across the Machine's lifetime (although it still has its place in the twenty-first century), the use of public meetings did not. Chamberlain, William Harris, George Dixon, C.A. Vince and others had started out in politics with the memories of the huge crowds calling for Parliamentary Reform in 1867 and – the same year - chanting for George Dixon in his by-election campaign. Attending vast popular meetings (with crowds of 200,000) was part of Birmingham's DNA. The Great Reform Act of 1832 had resulted from the peaceful popular pressure expressed through huge rallies in the town. And meetings great and small punctuate the history of the Machine. They were the means by which the National Education League conducted mission work, carrying the good news of free, compulsory education beyond Birmingham. Meetings rallied enthusiasts for municipal, School Board and parliamentary elections; it mattered that Chamberlain, Henry Crosskey, Robert Dale, J.S. Wright and Jesse Collings were renownedly good speakers. Meetings continued to fortify the faithful and to convert the waverers, through the battles over Home Rule, and then into the era when Tariff Reform was pitted against Free Trade.

Equally, there was a more sinister side too. The corollary of holding one's own meeting was, for the Machine, the disruption of the rallies of one's opponents. From Liberal violence perpetrated in support of George Dixon against Sampson Lloyd in the 1867 by-election contest, and outside the Town Hall against Anglican supporters of the Church party on the Birmingham School Board (chapter 3); to the riot at Aston Manor in 1884 (chapter 5), the assault on Lloyd George's supporters in 1901, and the attack on Free-Food spokesmen, Winston Churchill and Lord Hugh Cecil, the Machine showed a regrettable inclination to employ physical force to get its way (chapters 6 and 7).

Caucus machinery had another more manipulative side. It was famed for its management of potential voters. Harris was the first political manager to find a way to maximise his party's vote under the terms of the minority clause of the Second Reform Act (see chapter 1 for details). He directed Liberal voters in 1868 as to how to cast their two votes for the town's three Liberal candidates. He and his successor Schnadhorst applied the same techniques to the Birmingham School Board election in 1873 (chapter 3). The return of all three candidates in 1868 was a triumph of intelligent planning. His broader legacy was that of an organisation (the Birmingham Liberal Association) that had mastered the detail of voter registration, that had devised means by which ward committee members metamorphosed into an army of canvassers at election time, and that had established the value of paid agents to nurse constituencies and wards in the down-time between elections.

The experience of C.A. Vince, Chamberlain's right-hand man from the 1890s to 1914, illustrates how the Machine's political methodology was transmitted. As a young boy he posted news - on behalf of William Harris - of the latest Liberal poll standings during the election of 1868, which fired his enthusiasm for politics; later as a retired headmaster, in 1892, and keen to learn the political ropes in the Birmingham Liberal Unionist Association, he was inducted by Powell Williams, a veteran campaigner; he trained on to become an acknowledged electoral expert. Between 1903 and 1914 he was masterminding a deluge of tariff literature and posters, organising agents, canvassers and party workers, calling political meetings, all recognisably in the early Machine tradition. The only novelties were his use of the latest technologies, and the mass employment of women from WUTRA (the Women's Unionist Tariff Reform Association) as educators and canvassers, an initiative very much prompted by Chamberlain himself.

One important component in the Machine's successful operation was that of the accumulation of statistical evidence. In this it reflected both the painstaking eye for detail of William Harris and – more – the business-like efficiency of the successful entrepreneur, Joseph Chamberlain. From the time of the Birmingham Education Society in 1868 when Chamberlain and Robert Dale quartered the streets of Birmingham to determine the number of school-age children and see their home conditions for themselves, Chamberlain and his colleagues showed the value they placed on factual evidence to strengthen their case. Mastery of the detail helped J.S. Wright and Chamberlain fight their battles for new schools on the Birmingham School Board (chapter 3); equally Chamberlain, and later Powell Williams, made a scientific analysis of constituencies and their peculiar electoral characteristics which was invaluable, from the time of the National Education League right through to the mid-1890s when the two of them piloted the national Liberal Unionist Association (chapter 6). The Tariff Commission in 1903 (chapter 7) was founded expressly to furnish Chamberlain with statistical ammunition.

All these components were brought to life by their operators. This book profiles eighteen important members of his team with biographies appended to the chapters that follow. Some clear conclusions can be drawn about Chamberlain's political friends and colleagues.

Sensibly he relied on the tried and tested. So, family members like Arthur, Richard and Austen Chamberlain as well as the Nettlefolds, and the Kenrick and Martineau clans – closely intertwined through multiple marriages with the Chamberlains – are ubiquitous in the history of the Machine. Their names recur on the Town Council and its committees, in the National Liberal Federation, on the Birmingham Liberal Unionist Association, on the Free Libraries Committee, on the council of the Birmingham and Midland Institute, and in the administration of the Arts, of Birmingham's schools and the Central Library. Chamberlain's sons proved able and articulate champions of Tariff Reform and Liberal Unionism in the Machine's final phase.

With the family nexus at its heart Chamberlain built a formidable team of loyal adherents. They were bound by a common vision – educational, social, municipal and political – and by admiration for their leader. Many shared a Nonconformist background, attending chapels led by George Dawson, Robert Dale or Henry Crosskey. Many had absorbed ideas, as Chamberlain had, about their obligation as successful businessmen to serve the municipality and to bring about social reform. Commercial accomplishment was an excellent preparation for managing municipal projects. Attendance at Edgbaston, or Birmingham, Debating Society was a training for public articulation of policy and for School Board, Council and eventually Parliamentary debates.

What impresses is their versatility and their sheer stamina. Some of them must have spent a good portion of their sentient lives in committee or on municipal or party affairs. One explanation might be a deep sense of religious obligation to work for the betterment of others, a response encouraged by Birmingham's Nonconformist ministers. Equally, many – having succeeded in securing their financial independence – will have seen politics as a new challenge, and even as the means of expressing a strong inclination to exercise power.

Chamberlain operated on the principle that if someone proved reliable, was – in the modern idiom – 'a completer finisher', then it was only advisable to ask him to do something more. So, the Machine was peopled by multi-taskers. Three examples will serve. Jesse Collings (chapter 2) successively belonged to the executive committees of the Birmingham Education Society and the National Education League, was persuaded to be President of the National Liberal Federation, became Birmingham mayor (two years after Chamberlain), joined Chamberlain on the Liberal Unionist benches in the Commons after 1886, and helped launch Chamberlain's Rural Labourers' League in 1888. At every stage he was Chamberlain's loyal friend and intimate.

William Kenrick, Chamberlain's brother-in-law, served on the executive of those same education pressure groups as Collings, sat on the Town Council for over 40 years, was chairman of the general committee of the National Liberal Federation, governed the Grammar School as one of the nominees after the Council's coup overturning the ancient Anglican monopoly, sat on the Free Libraries Committee, Chamberlain's pet project the Improvement Committee and chaired the Council's Museum and School of Art Committee. He followed Chamberlain out of the Liberal party, sitting as a Liberal Unionist MP for Birmingham North (chapter 4).

Finally, Joseph Powell Williams (chapter 6) was the honorary secretary of the Birmingham Liberal Association, the original caucus, sat on the Town Council, was a key player in the executive of Chamberlain's National Liberal Federation, worked with the boundary commissioners to secure a favourable re-drawing of Birmingham's constituency boundaries in 1884, became first a Liberal, then a Liberal Unionist MP, ran the national Liberal Unionist Association and once again followed his political master when in 1903 Chamberlain embraced tariffs.

All three men typify the varied talents of the Chamberlain team. Their loyalty was rewarded by their leader; both Collings and Powell Williams were awarded ministerial posts in 1895. But occasionally there were rifts in the team. Francis Schnadhorst and William Harris deserted Chamberlain over their support for Gladstone and Home Rule, while brother Arthur Chamberlain proved a bitter enemy over tariffs and over local licensing issues in Birmingham. They found that Joseph Chamberlain could be an unforgiving enemy.

As we briefly saw in the case of C.A. Vince there was a sort of collective wisdom which accrued in those who operated the Birmingham Machine. Methodology was learnt and was refined across time and experience was passed through the generations. But the one constant factor was its animating spirit, the energy, the drive and the will of Joseph Chamberlain for whose benefit the entire operation was conducted.

The absence of women among the eighteen profiles of Machine members demands some explanation. Nineteenth-century British public life was monopolised by men, with the honourable exception of the Monarch herself; women were unable to vote, to sit in Parliament or to exercise municipal authority. Towards the end of the century a movement for women's suffrage was stirring, but the Vote was not to be won until 1918, and even then it did not apply to all. Nevertheless, several women intrude into the inevitably masculine narrative of Chamberlain's Machine. For example, Elizabeth Sturge, niece of the renowned Birmingham Quaker Joseph Sturge (see chapter 1), was an early member of the 'Liberal Eight' on the Birmingham School Board (from 1873 onwards) where she loyally supported the party's drive to expand the school building programme and to ensure rates were not deployed to subsidise Anglican schools. Millicent Fawcett, widow of a Liberal MP, was an important national figure from the late 1880s and by persistence, articulate advocacy and quiet networking did more to bring about the eventual enfranchisement of women than the Pankhursts; a prominent Liberal Unionist and a central figure in the Women's Liberal Unionist Association, she shared a platform with Chamberlain in Birmingham in 1889 at the annual meeting of his National Radical Union.[7] She would continue supporting Chamberlain and his Liberal Unionism until she recoiled in horror at his espousal of tariffs in 1903; she felt so strongly that she resigned from the WLUA. Yet these two figures could by no stretch be thought of as team members of his Machine; indeed, Millicent Fawcett was at no time based in Birmingham.

She used every opportunity through the 1890s to persuade Liberal Unionists to embrace the cause of women's suffrage. She made absolutely no headway with Joseph Chamberlain. He opined in a speech to Birmingham's WLUA branch that: 'It is quite true you have no votes, and I believe it will not be a good thing for women to be mixed up in the rough and tumble of our political agitation. They can exercise their influence in a more legitimate sphere in their own homes and in their social circles.'[8] This was the authentic anti-suffragist argument of the 'separate spheres' inhabited by the sexes. Still, as is made clear in the last chapters of this book, he was innovative in employing women as canvassers and in promoting Liberal Unionist and Tariff Reform policies, especially at election time. The number of women involved in campaigning in the 1906 General Election in Birmingham was deemed worthy of comment in the Press, while Chamberlain encouraged Liberal Unionist candidates from 1903 (especially after the Oswestry by-election setback; see chapter 7) to engage with local women sympathetic to the party. Across the course of time, then, women came to assume marginally greater significance in the political process. But Chamberlain, his son Austen, and indeed most of his team members featured in this book held resolutely reactionary attitudes to the central issue of women's suffrage and to the extent to which women should be involved in what they deemed 'high politics'.

BIRMINGHAM BEGINNINGS

T he Birmingham electoral machine reached maturity in the 1870s and was so renowned that the Conservative Prime Minister, Benjamin Disraeli, in conversation with Queen Victoria ruefully attributed his election defeat to 'the organisation the Liberals had (modelled) on the American system called the Caucus, originated by the great Radical Mr Chamberlain'.[9] Based on Birmingham, this Liberal organisation concerned itself not only with influencing national elections. Joseph Chamberlain himself boasted to his life-long intimate Jesse Collings of 'a Liberal tyranny (in Birmingham) with a vengeance – Council, School Board, Guardians are ours – never was such complete and absolute supremacy'.[10] He might have added the Council of the Midland Institute and the Grammar School Governing Board for good measure.[11] To less friendly eyes, like those of Conservative champion Lord Randolph Churchill, Chamberlain's mature system was 'Tsarist despotism ruling every public function, with all the resources of terror and intimidation, dispensing patronage to maintain 25,000 servants and to employ none but the blindly docile as *tchinovniks* (bureaucrats)'.[12]

There was a higher aspiration than simply the pursuit and monopolisation of power and doing down the Conservative opposition. Rather it was 'to provide for the full and efficient representation of the will of the majority', a democratic reflection of a new reality, the necessity to engage all Liberal voters of whatever class after the 1867 Reform Act had enfranchised urban working men.[13]

Yet despite the plaudits and the brickbats which personalised the achievement Chamberlain was not the concept designer of this Birmingham political machine; instead, he inherited the blueprint and brought it to perfection, reassembling and fine-tuning pre-existing components, whilst employing and learning from those who had pioneered Birmingham's Radical campaigning in the first part of the nineteenth century.

Chamberlain's avowed intention to democratise, for example, his plan to federate local Liberal Associations from all over the country in 1877 – 'the Caucus' to which we saw Disraeli refer above – had been uncannily anticipated by Thomas Attwood fifty years earlier when he announced the formation of his Political Union in Birmingham to campaign for Parliamentary Reform. Just as Chamberlain justified his new National Liberal Federation (NLF) 'to secure a perfect representation of the opinion of the people of the party', so Attwood had aimed in 1829 'to collect and organise the peaceful expression of public opinion so as to bring it to act upon the legislative functions in a just, legal and effectual way'.[14] In many other ways, too, both the Birmingham Political Union (BPU) and Thomas Attwood himself would anticipate Chamberlain and his methods.[15]

Thomas Attwood, 'King Tom', had national stature before Chamberlain ever came on the political scene and made his name. For if Chamberlain made Birmingham an insistent presence in national politics, and Gladstone observed in 1877 that 'Birmingham has acquired a kind of primacy in organisational leadership', then Attwood had briefly already made it so before. [16] When Attwood's biographer wrote that 'the provincial challenge to London's dominance was unceasing, and distinctive, and so pervasive that no government could ignore it', he might as well have been describing Chamberlain's legacy half a century later.[17] Where Birmingham's Liberal Association was widely imitated (outside London) in the late 1870s, Attwood's Birmingham Political Union, so evidently effective in directing the charge against the old unreformed Parliament, was widely emulated a generation earlier as 130 new unions were formed from Leeds to Stow-on-the-Wold in 1831-2. In Chamberlain's time the Birmingham Liberal Association sought to unite working and middle classes; the very title of Attwood's novel organisation proclaimed his goal of 'Union' to win Parliamentary Reform.

Attwood made much use of monster petitions to keep pressure on the Whig government, a technique Chamberlain was to employ in his education campaigns. If he did not address mass meetings of over 200,000 people as Attwood did, in other ways he followed. Attwood had a talent for publicity, inviting local journalists to attend his committee meetings to ensure a favourable understanding in the Press, and painstakingly recording all public meetings before sending carefully crafted reports to local and national papers. Chamberlain equally understood the importance of a friendly Press, maintaining a close alliance with John Jaffray (owner) and John Thackray Bunce (editor) of the *Birmingham Daily Post* and, to the end of his days, bombarding national and local newspapers with letters trenchantly justifying his position; he, like Attwood, had an eye for the appropriate image, the eye-catching poster, the striking pamphlet and the telling jingle.

Chamberlain may well have been familiar with the history of the Birmingham Political Union and, if so, aspects of Attwood's management of his organisation would have resonated, for they closely foreshadowed his own methods. Thomas Attwood was a brisk and summary chairman, ruthlessly cutting contributions short and side-stepping areas of disagreement by dispatching them to the long grass of sub-committees. He centralised decision-making by empowering the executive committee of the BPU with unlimited authority to speak for the Union. He also established discipline in a potentially unwieldy body by enacting that 'individual members were to obey strictly all the just and legal directions of the Political Council'. 'The organisation was to be kept in his hands as far as possible.' [18] Chamberlain, too, was always instinctively autocratic in controlling his Machine.

The Birmingham Political Union, after winning a landmark measure of parliamentary reform in the Great Reform Act of 1832, subsequently had a chequered history, a brief revival in 1838 marking Birmingham's important contribution as the venue for the launch of the Chartists' campaign to enact the six points of the Charter of Parliamentary Reform.[19] This time however Thomas Attwood's appeal for unity between middle and working classes, and for wholly peaceful tactics, foundered in a welter of acrimony. Many Birmingham working-class men and women felt bitterly betrayed when the town was incorporated in 1839 and – as they saw it – the BPU's middle-class leaders abandoned them, joined the establishment and became enthusiastic advocates of law and order.[20]

Joseph Sturge revived mutual trust and confidence between the classes when he founded the Complete Suffrage Union in Birmingham to promote Parliamentary, and Corn Law, reform in 1842. This clear evidence of middle-class support for further reform, allied to a shared deep faith in Liberalism, brought artisans – who had dallied with Chartism – and middle classes together in Birmingham. The Complete Suffrage Union (CSU) anticipated Chamberlain's democratic Caucus in several ways. For example, it drew on local Nonconformist Radicalism's frustration and resentment; so, at a CSU conference in 1842 Thomas Swan, a Baptist minister, called on the middle and working classes to unite against a common enemy, 'the tyrannical and overbearing aristocracy'. [21] Chamberlain would harness just this Nonconformist sense of injustice; that resentment at being excluded is evident in the National Education League, in his Birmingham School Board, and in the National Liberal Federation. Furthermore, in its utilisation of tracts, letters, manifestos and the drafting of resolutions, the CSU anticipated at least some of the modus operandi of the Birmingham Liberal Association, the National Education League and the National Liberal Federation.[22] In its targeting of the Town Council to win its support for complete (universal) suffrage the CSU antedated the strategy employed by Chamberlain and other education reformers at the end of the 1860s of forming a cadre of Liberal sympathisers on the Council.

From 1842 to Joseph Chamberlain's emergence in 1868 - and the new intense and more energetic phase in Birmingham's campaigning and political systemisation he brought – there was a steady advance of class cooperation, all of it in the Liberal cause. T. Tholfsen in an influential article anatomised the stages.[23] Although the Complete Suffrage Union failed to achieve its goals in the mid-1840s, the dream of enfranchising the working classes lived on in the creation of a Committee of Non-Electors in 1849. These working men organised their own Town Hall meeting to interrogate prospective Liberal Parliamentary candidates, finding G.F. Muntz and W. Scholefield reassuringly sound on universal suffrage. Once the candidates were approved, workers vigorously campaigned for their (successful) election, through the medium of large public meetings. Here was the sort of cross-class cooperation to which William Harris aspired when he democratised the Birmingham Liberal Association in 1868.

It also proved to be a precedent for what happened when John Bright was invited by influential Liberals to consider standing for a vacant seat in Birmingham in 1857. An open meeting of all Birmingham Liberals was held to support John Bright's candidature. As a subsequent Liberal pamphlet put it: 'A new feeling had arisen that the whole party, non-electors as well as electors, ought to have a voice in a matter so deeply affecting their interests.'[24] The election of the acknowledged national champion of democratic reform inspired a decade-long focus by middle and lower classes on winning the vote for working men in Birmingham. That process of endorsing John Bright also reinforced the allegiance of working men to the Liberal Party. Thus, the Birmingham Reform Association founded in November 1858 proudly announced that 'it embraces men of all shades of Liberal opinion, enfranchised middle class and non-electors'. So, too, in the 1859 General Election artisans actively campaigned for the Liberal candidates. And in the attritional struggle to extract the vote from Derby's Conservative government in 1866 and 1867, Birmingham artisans formed a local branch of the National Reform League and organised two monster meetings of over 200,000 supporters at Brooks Fields (with financial backing from the local Liberal Association). Tholfsen commented that 'they illustrate well the careful organisation and planning that was soon to be enlisted in behalf of the Caucus'... 'and the constant invocation of Liberal principles... made Liberalism more than ever the uncontested political creed of the working-classes'.[25]

Such examples of cooperation are significant because it is on these foundations that a strong and far-reaching Liberal organisation would be built in the late 1860s and early 1870s by Joseph Chamberlain and his close associates. His political structure was further underpinned from an entirely different direction. For a small group of Nonconformist churches in Birmingham was notably important in enabling him to develop an effective political organisation. One of them, the Church of the Saviour, was the platform from the late 1840s for the charismatic preaching of its founder George Dawson, and his influence on Chamberlain, whom he met through the Birmingham Education Society, and on his circle was profound. Firstly, he popularised the idea that the city was established by divine will to be responsible for providing a healthy and stimulating environment for its citizens – both sanitary but also culturally and intellectually nourishing. He then challenged Birmingham's entrepreneurial class to wrest civic leadership from unimaginative incumbents and become engaged in municipal government, bringing their business know-how to bear on the problems of an overcrowded, sometimes toxic urban environment. His inspiration drew businessmen like Joseph Chamberlain onto the Town Council, providing him and others with a mission cause.

Several of Dawson's congregation would become central figures in Chamberlain's Machine, notably William Harris and Jesse Collings, their names recurring through Town Council membership lists and executive committees of the National Education League, the National Liberal Federation and the Birmingham Liberal Association. Other less well-known attendees at Dawson's church who lived out his civic gospel, like W. Shammon, C.E. Mathews and G.J. Johnson, were Council members of long duration, and served on committees concerned with free libraries and education. Dawson's vision of literature improving the minds of working people was evidently so compelling that for thirty-one of its first thirty-three years the Free Library committee was under the chairmanship of a member of Dawson's church.[26]

Without Dawson's ministry and church it is sure that the shape, activity and manning of Chamberlain's Machine would have been radically different. Chamberlain himself was equally influenced by his attendance at the Unitarian Church of the Messiah, where teaching in its Sunday School in the late 1850s first awakened his interest in education. Around him grew up a tight-knit group of fellow congregation members, several being close relations by blood or marriage. As in Dawson's church, they were to give unstintingly to municipal service, his brother-in-law William Kenrick being a councillor, then alderman, for over 40 years, while Chamberlain's brothers Arthur and Richard were councillors; his Sunday School colleague, R.F. Martineau, served on the Council from 1874-1909.[27] They were for many years overwhelmingly loyal supporters of Chamberlain's schemes.

These men were commencing their engagement with educational, then municipal, reform in the 1860s, before Joseph Chamberlain emerged to invigorate Birmingham political organisation; in the course of trying to educate Birmingham's workers through the agency of voluntary (church-based) initiatives they were drawn into politics, for they discovered how desperate were the living conditions, how unsanitary was the environment, in which these people were struggling; as the Quaker George Cadbury would put it: 'How is it possible for a man to cultivate ideals when his home is a slum?'[28]

One last and very important preliminary structure was to be put in place on the eve of Chamberlain's emergence into local politics in 1868. It was largely the handiwork of William Harris, Dawson's disciple, a Birmingham architect and surveyor. He seems to have had an innate talent for committee work for, by 1865, he had already been the Honorary Secretary of the Public School Association and had led the campaign to prise endowments from the Grammar School for the benefit of the town's elementary schools;

he joined the Town Council in 1865. It was presumably these experiences that taught him how to organise, persuade and manipulate others.

He was one of the initiators of the Birmingham Liberal Association (BLA). Francis Schnadhorst later recalled its beginnings at a Committee Room in the Town Hall in February 1865 where a meeting was convened by a circular signed by George Dixon, John Jaffray and William Harris. 'It has, for some time, been a matter of regret,' it read, 'that the Liberal Party in Birmingham has had no recognised organisation. We desire to see some course taken which would unite all Liberals in the town and provide them with a regular and efficient method of exercising legitimate influence in favour of their political principles.' [29] Joseph Chamberlain would echo just those sentiments when he summed up a new national Liberal organisation in 1877.

The inauguration of the BLA was prompted by disappointment at the defeat of the Liberal candidate, P.H. Muntz in the North Warwickshire election of 1865. Philip was the brother of George Muntz (see above). A post-mortem concluded that the party needed to have an organisation which was permanent and effective. [30] Harris became its Secretary and set about establishing that permanence and creating a structure of ward committees which had until then been intermittent, merely being resurrected as and when an election was called. The new BLA proved its worth in the by-election that returned George Dixon to Westminster in 1867. Then the Liberal Association collaborated closely with working men from the local Reform League to ensure Dixon's victory. This congenial alliance no doubt helped convince Harris of the possibility of greater democratisation in the Association.

Not all BLA officers saw the organisation as simply about projecting party power. Henry Crosskey, later to be a most influential member of Chamberlain's circle, reflected more philosophically in his Memoranda in 1877 that: 'The Liberal Association is an agency through which men who believe in the possibility of a higher state of civilisation than now exists have attempted to carry out clear and definite plans for the culture, happiness and prosperity of the community.' [31]

Nevertheless in 1867 it was the severely practical which preoccupied most Birmingham Liberals when the Second Reform Act reached the statute book in 1867. The new constituencies were larger, with many more voters. As these comprised mainly working-class householders it became important to recognise their aspirations. Schnadhorst explained: 'The primary motive for the change was that Liberal leaders were wise enough to recognise that the extension of the right of voting to the working men still carried no right to selection of the men for whom they would be asked to vote.' [32] Beyond that, Clause 9 of the Act was especially pertinent to Birmingham –

nicknamed the 'minority' clause it determined that, in the three parliamentary seats the Act awarded the town, each elector should have two votes, its Conservative authors hoping that in addition to the election of the inevitable Liberals at the top of the poll, a Conservative candidate might gain the final seat.

It was Harris who shaped Birmingham Liberals' response. Chamberlain dubbed him the 'Father of the Caucus'. 'The whole credit of having initiated and carried out the new machinery belongs to my friend Mr Harris.'[33] He made the Association more accountable by devising a structure whereby representatives were selected from the ward committees to sit on a central committee of 400. In 1868, he refined this; the ward committees would elect their 24 representatives at open ward meetings, 'mere adherence to objects of the Association (being) sufficient' qualification to participate in the process.[34] This democratic system would be a template for Chamberlain for thirty years, for he replicated it in the National Liberal Federation, the Birmingham Liberal Unionist Association, and in the Midlands Unionist Association from the 1870s through to the late 1890s.

It was Harris, too, who directed this new apparatus towards the General Election of 1868 when local Liberals, motivated by a sense of grievance about the Tory chicanery of the minority clause – Dixon called it 'an insidious and mischievous device' – sought to achieve a clean sweep in all three of Birmingham's seats.[35] Harris himself explained his strategy to Edgbaston Liberals. 'It was plain after the selection of the candidates that, with three Liberals and one Tory going to the poll, and the electors being allowed to vote for two candidates only, the nicest calculation and the utmost subordination would be necessary to carry the three Liberals.'[36] Birmingham Liberalism was 'regimented', wrote J. L. Garvin, Chamberlain's biographer, and 'wards were canvassed to the last man'. 'A scientific distribution of votes was contrived.' 'In some wards electors were asked to vote for Bright and Dixon; in others for Bright and P.H.Muntz; in others again for Dixon and Muntz.' 'The thing worked like clockwork', as can be seen in the evenness of the poll, with Dixon accumulating 15,198 votes, Muntz 14,614 and Bright 14,601.[37] Predictably this became known as the 'Vote-as-You're-Told' election.

Schnadhorst subsequently boasted that 'by this process Birmingham had revolutionised political organisation in Britain'.[38] Certainly by 1868 the Association had refined a number of electioneering strategies which Joseph Chamberlain and his Machine would make their own as they developed a formidable monopoly on power in the different institutions – municipal, national, and pressure group – across future years. Ward committees set up originally for parliamentary elections were to become central to the politicisation of municipal elections in the 1870s. Canvassing, and cultivation of individual electors in wards, became a staple for Chamberlain and his allies; he even learnt lessons from the Association's dubious recourse to violence in George Dixon's by-election campaign (the *Gazette* alleged that the BLA hired 150 roughs at sixpence an hour to wreck the meetings of Sampson Lloyd, the Tory candidate).[39] The suspicion that he indulged the tactical use of thuggery clung to Chamberlain in 1884's Aston Riots, in the assault on Lloyd George in 1901, and right on into the 1906 General Election.

The Birmingham Liberal Association was to be the still centre of all the later manifestations of the Chamberlain Machine. It provided the leadership of the National Education League, the know-how for the School Board elections, and an enlarged 400 (Chamberlain extended the governing committee to the '600') provided the support and manpower to campaign aggressively in the 1873 municipal elections which ensured overwhelming Liberal dominance, on the eve of Chamberlain's legendary mayoralty.[40]

The Second Reform Act profoundly changed politics in Britain, more than doubling the electorate. It seems appropriate that one of the burgeoning industrial towns which benefited from it should first develop an effective response to the challenges of reaching out to a new electorate. Chamberlain was not a part of Harris's revolution in 1867 and 1868 but he was to be the foremost national politician in exploiting the Machine's potential. His journey into politics was just underway, but initially through the channel of education reform. Prompted by George Dixon and the Birmingham Education Society, Joseph Chamberlain commenced a rapid apprenticeship in the mysteries of campaigning and electioneering, which would draw on the collective wisdom and experience of those Birmingham pioneers of the preceding fifty years.

William Harris

William Harris is not a well-known figure beyond Birmingham; for instance, unlike several of his contemporaries in Midlands politics, he was not considered important enough for an entry in the Dictionary of National Biography. Those who really knew him, however, valued him greatly; when the Birmingham Liberal Association presented him with a book case furnished with a small library of books in 1883 Chamberlain wrote to Francis Schnadhorst that 'there is no man who has given more loyal, more devoted and more valuable service than our late President'. Indeed, William Harris had been the designer and the father of the electoral organisation which made Birmingham politics famous. His work was generally undemonstrative, for he seems to have been happiest operating in the shadows, devising schemes, mastering detail – perhaps these were appropriate qualities for the architect and surveyor who for many years headed the firm of Harris and Harris he had founded on Birmingham's Colmore Row. Occasionally he made telling public contributions to the Liberal cause. At the inauguration of his brainchild, the National Liberal Federation, he memorably distinguished between the limitations of the single-cause pressure group like the National Education League and his new vision of 'a federation which, by collecting the opinions of a large majority of the people in all the great centres of political activity, should be able to speak on whatever questions arose with the full authority of the national voice'.

A local man, he was inspired to use his talents in public service by George Dawson at the Church of the Saviour and he involved himself in an impressive range of enterprises from the 1860s. In almost every theatre of activity he rapidly found himself an integral part of the executive, a recognition of his appetite for committee work and for mastering the minutiae of the brief. So, he was Honorary Secretary of the Public School Association, Clerk to the Birmingham Tame and Rea District Drainage Board, he was a town councillor, he chaired the Birmingham Free Libraries Committee (being Honorary Secretary of the committee which campaigned to introduce the Free Libraries Act to Birmingham in the first place), and for many years he was a member of the Council of the Birmingham and Midland Institute. His obituary in the Birmingham Mail *in 1911 also made much of his abiding interest in the Library, in the Shakespeare Memorial Library, in the Art Gallery and Museum – this enthusiasm surely reflected the passionate advocacy of improving literature for the working classes of Harris's charismatic teacher, George Dawson. Undoubtedly the quiet influence he developed through this impressively wide-ranging voluntary work would have helped his political activities in the town.*

His talent and experience as a committee man was repeatedly called upon by his party. He had already done much for Birmingham Liberals when, with J.S. Wright, he had summoned a meeting of Birmingham's working men to ratify John Bright's candidacy as replacement for George Muntz. He went on to become one of the founding fathers of the Birmingham Liberal Association in 1865 and as its Secretary he was the man who shaped the ward and central committee structure, a model which became hugely influential in the Liberal party after 1868. While he continued to serve the Association he was also a founder member of the National Education League, for he was a persistent advocate of a national system of secular education. He took charge of its finances and later of its Parliamentary sub-committee. When it had exhausted its useful life he – with Joseph Chamberlain – recognised the potential for a Radical grassroots federation of local Liberal parties to shape national policy and priorities. He was to become the Chairman of the Central Committee of the new National Liberal Federation and an articulate advocate for its involvement in the policy-making of the Liberal government after 1880. His work in the Liberal cause extended to a term on the Town Council from 1871, where he was a close ally of Chamberlain's in his municipal revolution, and to journalism. He and George Dawson became part proprietors of one of the first daily provincial newspapers, the Birmingham Daily Press, *and Harris became editor. Later he would write extensively for the Liberal daily, the* Birmingham Daily Post, *as its leader-writer.*

For many years he was a loyal supporter and close ally of Joseph Chamberlain, meeting him through their mutual membership both of the Town Council and the founding committee of the National Education League in 1869. Chamberlain relied on him for the efficient running of the several organisations which formed his power base. Things changed after 1886, when Chamberlain split from the Prime Minister, William Gladstone, over his policy of Home Rule for Ireland. Harris followed Schnadhorst into Gladstone's party, and helped commandeer the National Liberal Federation for the Liberal cause in opposition to Chamberlain. Harris at one point tried to broker peace between the two sides of a badly-divided Liberal party, but concluded he could not follow Chamberlain in his new Unionist dispensation. Thereafter, until his death in 1911, he withdrew from active politics.

George Dixon

George Dixon was for a number of years Joseph Chamberlain's close ally. Unlike William Harris, Francis Schnadhorst or Powell Williams who acted in a largely subordinate role to the great commander, Dixon was an equal, and a sometimes opinionated and awkward one too. Nevertheless, he was part of the Chamberlain circle, and a founding member of the Machine.

Born in Yorkshire in 1820 he came south to Birmingham. There in the circles in which he moved he was unusual in that he was an Anglican; so many of this Liberal set were Nonconformists, motivated by a keen sense of exclusion from an establishment club which monopolised educational opportunity. Like Chamberlain he was a successful businessman, in his case not in manufacturing but as a merchant, then a partner, in Rabone Bros. in Birmingham, specialising in oil lamps, cutlery, garden forks and increasingly in guns; the firm flourished during the American Civil War, arming the North. A wealthy man, he became a generous philanthropist, with St Asaph's church especially benefiting. He also followed the pattern of so many Christian upper middle-class Victorians in a commitment to worthwhile public service. He became a Poor Law Guardian in 1861, the same year he became a Vice-President of the Birmingham Chamber of Commerce and he would go on to be a Birmingham delegate at the national meeting of the Association of Chambers of Commerce in 1867.

By 1864 his reputation had been made by his contributions to the Edgbaston Debating Society (also the training ground of Joseph Chamberlain) and as a result he was made a borough magistrate, and elected to the Town Council. In 1866 he was – briefly – Mayor of Birmingham, a tenure marked by his successful and decisive action to bring calm to the town during the Catholic riots of 1867. His political involvement commenced at about the same time, for he attended a meeting to support the election of John Bright and William Scholefield as Liberal MPs in 1865. Concurrently, his membership of the same committee to which William Harris belonged – the Free Grammar School Association – awakened in him what would be a life-long interest in educational reform. The sum of this activity made him a man to be cultivated; predictably he joined a group of concerned Liberals organising a meeting in 1865 to found the Birmingham Liberal Association. He became its first Honorary Secretary and he spoke at the first annual meeting in 1866. It was then understandable that he should be selected to take Scholefield's seat in Parliament in 1867 on the latter's death.

It is remarkable that he had the time and energy for the campaign of educational reform he initiated and led in Birmingham. He was drawn to act on the matter partly by an appeal made to him by the Manchester Education Aid Society, but as much by his own observation of scores of rootless and unschooled children in the town, and by his experience in business, which identified the need for a skilled workforce in an increasingly competitive world. He invited local worthies to a meeting at his home, 'The Dales', to help found the Birmingham Education Society in 1867 with the intention of extending school provision and paying the fees for poor children. George Dawson and Joseph Chamberlain were among the committee members under Dixon's presidency. All three were central to the decision to create a very different, more ambitious body, the National Education League in 1869, which was a pressure group based in Birmingham and founded to promote agitation for a national education system. Once again Dixon's home was the venue for the inaugural meeting. Dixon was the Chairman and parliamentary leader; Chamberlain was the Vice-Chairman and ran the executive while Dixon was away at Westminster. This proved to be Chamberlain's apprenticeship in committee work and in campaigning.

George Dixon led the NEL's ultimately unsuccessful fight to amend Forster's Education Bill; many Nonconformists represented in the NEL objected to the preservation of Anglican schools in a new national system. One of the Act's provisions was to set up local School Boards chosen by ratepayers. He was elected to the Birmingham School Board in 1870; after 1876 he would become its Chairman.

That year he was hurried into resigning from the Commons. Although he suffered from overwork and concerns about his wife's health, he had not determined to step down until the Birmingham Post *announced his departure, so facilitating his replacement by its champion, Joseph Chamberlain. 'The town,' it wrote, 'turned instinctively to Mr Chamberlain.' Although Dixon had much admired Chamberlain ('he is a better speaker than I,' he conceded) he felt rushed, and observers detected a tension between them which descended into acrimony, firstly because Chamberlain insisted on still trying to determine policy on religious education for the School Board after Dixon had assumed the chairmanship. Secondly, they differed in 1878 over the issue of Council nominees for the Board of King Edward's School. Chamberlain excluded Dixon, who had some claim as the Chairman of the town's School Board, and livid, Dixon took to the pages of the School Board Chronicle to vent his spleen: 'It seems as if the terms of Mr Joseph Chamberlain and Birmingham are becoming synonymous. Mr Joseph Chamberlain is Birmingham, and Birmingham is Mr Joseph Chamberlain. He represents himself in the Town Council and he also represents himself in the House of Commons.'*

Dixon was unusual – a member of that Chamberlain Circle who showed rare public dissension at its acknowledged leader's often high-handed and Olympian disregard for others. Yet amicable relations were duly restored. They worked together in the Birmingham Liberal Association, Dixon becoming its President in 1882. In 1885 Dixon became an MP again for

Edgbaston, a new constituency created by the Redistribution Act of that year. In the Liberal schism of 1886 over Home Rule he supported Chamberlain and became an active Liberal Unionist, being a vice-president of the Birmingham Liberal Unionist Association. In his last decade he assumed a prominent role in the Round Table Conference in 1887 which unavailingly sought to bring the fractured Liberal Party back together; he continued an active member of the Birmingham School Board; and he fought hard against Sir John Gorst's Education Act (1896) which increased public funding of voluntary (Anglican) schools, at the expense of school boards. When he died in 1898 Chamberlain, reflecting on Dixon's life-long dedication to the cause of public education, on his stalwart opposition to Home Rule and his support for Birmingham Unionism, talked of George Dixon having been: 'a tower of strength to us'.

CHAPTER TWO

THE BATTLE OVER EDUCATION AND CHAMBERLAIN'S EMERGENCE

The implications for politicians of the 1867 Second Reform Act were profound and various. With 700,000 new voters in the boroughs in the new dispensation, an increase of 138%, the scale of the electorate was transformed in places like Merthyr Tydfil (a ten-fold increase from 1866), Birmingham (a tripling over these years) and Leeds (an increase of 400%).[41] Reform of the old style of open voting was inevitable, and John Bright's long-held nostrum, the secret ballot, was urgently adopted in 1868 by a Cabinet sub-committee of Gladstone's First Government before becoming law in 1872. Disorder and undue influence at elections were to be banished. Now a larger electorate had to be understood, managed and enthused, and historians have discerned from 1867 a great change in the way that politics was conducted, with the emergence of party machines and of public speaking.[42]

We have already seen that in Birmingham the new Liberal Association established a permanent structure, replacing the old ephemeral organisation which only appeared at election time. This was mirrored in the North too, in Salford, Broughton, Rochdale amongst other towns, for all – in both major parties – recognised that their terms of trade had been revolutionised by the arrival of a mass electorate. Liberal associations across the country applied a simple formula, that a more volatile electorate would be swayed over to whichever party had the most effective organisation. Leafleting, canvassing, registering likely party voters, tracking removals in the year between registrations – these became the familiar activities of associations, with the Conservatives following hard from the mid-1870s.[43]

The Second Reform Act did not simply pose an organisational question; in a more fundamental sense it marked the elevation of urban working man, for the Act enfranchised borough householders, and over 60% of males in the large towns could now vote. Disraeli recognised that his election defeat in 1868 was 'the verdict of the people' and promptly resigned, ushering in a new constitutional practice – governments were made by elections not by Parliamentary chicanery. To Chamberlain it was clear that no longer could a great constituency's representation be secured 'for the nominee of a few gentlemen sitting in private committee… The working class are now the majority in most borough constituencies, and no candidate and no policy has a chance of success unless their good-will and active support can be secured.'[44] That response to the new mass electorate justified, for him, the creation of the caucus in the late 1870s. It was the consciousness of the potential of working-class voters which explains Chamberlain's decision to embrace

22

national Radical policies, not just for their intrinsic value, but also to head off the emergence of an independent, anti-capitalist working-class movement disaffected, because ignored by mainstream politicians.[45]

The fact that many urban working men now had the vote both coincided with, and prompted other, associated developments. The literate were able to take advantage of a newly confident and rapidly expanding Press, because the repeal of the Stamp Duty Act in 1855, capped by Gladstone's removal of the tax on paper a few years later, greatly lowered the cost of newspapers and opened up the prospect of a much wider readership. New publications proliferated, especially in the provinces; from 400 different provincial newspapers in 1858 the number had grown to 900 by 1874.[46] 'The role of newspapers both as reflectors of public opinion and mouthpieces of party policy assumed much greater prominence as literacy levels grew.'[47]

Many of these papers were Liberal, while the Conservatives held the whip hand in the metropolitan Press. Out in the provinces the link between Liberal politicians and the newspapers was openly acknowledged, for example, in Oldham, Leicester, Newcastle and Manchester, where officers in Liberal associations wholly or partially owned local weeklies.[48] In Birmingham too that relationship was apparent with John Jaffray, proprietor of the *Birmingham Daily Post*, and Thackray Bunce, its editor, both prominent supporters of the Liberal Association, the National Education League and thereafter a sequence of other Liberal causes. The *Birmingham Mail* also provided 'Liberalism for the masses interspersed with police matters and news of monstrous births'.[49] Chamberlain understood the opportunities afforded by control of the means of broadcasting to a new electorate. In 1875, he was writing to his great friend Jesse Collings of his (unfulfilled) plans to become proprietor of the *Birmingham and Midland Review*, 'an organ pledged to all our little capers.... I shall preserve despotic control in my hands, though not intending to interfere with the management unless necessary'.[50]

The rise of the Press was linked to a new prominence of outstanding orators after 1867. Speeches by national figures were faithfully recorded by reporters, who had been forewarned of the imminence of a notable event. Orators like Bright, Chamberlain, Gladstone, Lord Randolph Churchill, following in the wake of Attwood, were aware of the possibilities and ensured that provincial and metropolitan papers received full transcriptions of the speech to follow hard on the heels of its live delivery. 'The Press virtually raised the great public orators to national thrones', wrote John Vincent in his seminal work on the Liberal Party.[51]

Editors and orators assumed that columns devoted to closely, and invariably lengthily, argued political exposition would be welcomed by their readers. They assumed both patience and education in the readership; that might be present in a middle-class readership, but these orators were appealing just as much to working men. In the debates about Parliamentary Reform in 1867 many MPs, influenced by Samuel Smiles' widely-read book, *Self-Help*, had assumed that the new working-class electorate would be both interested in, and capable of, exercising the vote with discrimination. In truth, there was no evidence at the time for the assertion – it was based on guesswork or profound optimism. Although they passionately approved of the democratic principle, Chamberlain and his circle –Birmingham industrialists and employers - knew better than many blithely insouciant Parliamentarians.

These keener observers observers – including Chamberlain, Dixon, Dawson and Harris amongst others in Birmingham – recognised that the vote had been granted to many who were ill-equipped to use it intelligently and it was this insight that spurred them to embrace the cause of education reform. They concurred with the spirit of Sir Robert Lowe's famous remark in the House of Commons on the passing of the Second Reform Act that 'we must educate our masters'.

Lowe and others recognised that the arrangements for educating a rapidly expanding population were woefully inadequate. The middle classes could send children away to one of a number of recently established public schools, or were able to take advantage of inexpensive ancient grammar schools as in Birmingham, where the richly endowed King Edward's School provided a keenly sought-after academic education. The working classes, if they were interested in their children's schooling (and perhaps up to a half were not, given the numbers of parents in Birmingham who failed to ensure their children attended school even when they had been given a place), were reliant on voluntary schools, overwhelmingly Anglican.[52] There clung to these schools and their clergy 'a faint sentiment of social pre-eminence on the part of the Establishment, an irritating consciousness that it has the Sovereign and the aristocracy among its members', in the words of a contemporary Birmingham observer, W.L. Sargent.[53] The National Society promoted and resourced Anglican schools; it was imbued with the idea of the inalienable right of the Church to provide children's education and of its being a charitable boon, granted by the wealthy to the needy. Its aim was to communicate to the poor such knowledge and habits as would be sufficient to guide them through life in their proper stations and to teach them the doctrine of religion according to the principles of the Established Church.[54]

Its attitude to the suggestion of a Conscience Clause, which would permit children of Nonconformists to opt out of religious teaching in voluntary schools, was predictably hostile and unsurprisingly many Nonconformists, like Chamberlain and Collings, took grave exception to such intolerance. But for them and other campaigners a far more serious dereliction was the sheer inadequacy of the number of schools nationally. The Church was losing its battle to fund new schools in rapidly expanding towns and cities – the old parochial divisions were unfit for purpose. Anglican organisations responded to this evident crisis; the Manchester Education Union, for example, campaigned for 'the judicious supplementing of the present denominational system of national education'. This would become known as 'filling the gaps', and the aim was to persuade the government to extend grants it had been making for decades to Church schools to enable the building of more.

There was also an element of genuine fear in the reaction of the Anglican Church to calls for educational reform: the Anglican Birmingham Education Union in 1869 articulated its belief that such reform would be the precursor to disestablishment. After all, Gladstone's First Ministry in 1869 had just disestablished the Irish Church; was it not feasible that the policy could cross the Irish Sea? Certainly, the apprehension of what havoc vengeful militant Nonconformity might wreak on voluntary education explains the vitriolic attacks by churchmen on School Boards across the land in the 1870s.

Would-be reformers focused on several shortcomings in national education provision at the time of the Second Reform Act. An early pamphlet of the National Education League (1870) expressed disgust that after 'thirty years of subsidies, for 4/5ths of the scholars about to leave (voluntary) school no account, or a wholly unsatisfactory one, is given by an examination of even the most elementary kind'. This situation was deemed 'lamentable and deplorable'.[55] For the Association of Chambers of Commerce what was especially alarming was the absence of technical education, an area in which trade rivals in Germany were far ahead. But of far greater importance was the emerging evidence that the number of school places was insufficient, and that even so, many of those places remained unfilled as parents found reasons to absent their children from school. With the Factory Extension and Workshops Act of 1867, the hours which children could work was delimited; as a result, many were simply left to roam the streets unprovided for. There was evidence in some towns of a miniature crime wave, and Parliament debated in 1870 the proliferation of 'street arabs' spawned by reduced employment and too much undirected leisure time.[56]

This study is primarily concerned with the creation and operation of Chamberlain's Machine, and its genesis lies in the Birmingham Education Society (BES), the brainchild of George Dixon, with help from the Principal of Saltley Church of England Training College, Canon Gover. The Birmingham Education Society was created in part to gather information, to determine the true extent of the derelictions in current educational provision alluded to above.

Its first meeting on 13 February 1867 at Dixon's home, 'The Dales' in Edgbaston, gathered a select group of local worthies, men with a known interest in education reform.

It included a future Archbishop of Canterbury (Frederick Temple, then Head Master of Rugby School), the Chief Inspector of Midlands Schools (Rev H. M. Capel) and others both Anglican (Dixon among them) and Nonconformist. There were from the start tensions between the denominations which were to be a harbinger of long-running divisions in Birmingham between an identifiable Church party and increasingly militant Nonconformist Liberals. The purpose here is not to record every instance of this, but rather to trace the emergence of a distinctive Birmingham Political Machine and to identify the methods and insights that its members learnt even in its early years.

The Society was partly 'a statistical, partly a philanthropic, body'.[57] Its objects were the advancement of education in Birmingham, the collection and dissemination of evidence, campaigning for local rating powers, the payment of fees for poor children, and finally, fundraising to enlarge, to build and to maintain schools. Chamberlain, Dale and others walked the streets, knocked on doors, asked questions about the whereabouts of the household's progeny and contributed to detailed research on Birmingham's school-age children. They found that of 65,000 children ranging from 5 to 13 years old, 25,000 were in school, 16,000 at work and the rest were at liberty. Some 4,720 places were funded (by the Society and other philanthropists) but barely one quarter were being taken up. Although subject to the derision of Anglican supporters, the validity of those statistics was attested by government-appointed inspectors, J. G. Fitch and D. R. Fearon who told the Commons that: 'We regard the statistics collected by the Birmingham Education Society as of the deepest significance and eminently worthy of the attention of the House.' Fitch went on to comment that the fact that only 8,700 of the 25,000 scholars actually passed an exam was truly 'melancholic'.[58]

The statistical exercise convinced Chamberlain and others in the Society that no voluntary agency could transform parental attitudes to education, whereby many saw schools as depriving them of their children, who might otherwise make a vital contribution to the family's weekly income. It was a seminal experience for Chamberlain; the Society's research uncovered the depth of ignorance in a sample of 26 workforces in Birmingham, and the extent of poverty in Birmingham's slum areas where over 1,000 children could not attend school for lack of proper clothing. It radicalised him. He concluded that only State power could compel attendance. Only rate-funding could hope to pay for a greatly enhanced school system, for charity simply could not cope. Only local authorities would have the necessary overview to consider the needs of a whole town or city; no voluntary gap-filling could adequately solve the scale of the problem. Indeed, his new friend Jesse Collings calculated that there was but one place available for every 12 children of school age in the Borough of Birmingham.[59]

The Society's Committee gave Chamberlain his first taste of political committee work, and it brought into politics alongside him a small group of largely Nonconformist, philanthropic individuals who would form the key personnel in Chamberlain's Machine for many years to come. George Dixon was the President, Robert Dale, a Vice-President, Jesse Collings was the Honorary Secretary and J.T. Bunce, John Jaffray, George Dawson, Charles Vince and William Kenrick sat alongside Joseph Chamberlain on the committee. Although he was to fall out with Dixon in the mid-1870s, Chamberlain was to win the admiration, friendship and loyalty of this embryonic cadre of Birmingham Liberal reformers. As well as appreciating, as a businessman, the collection of statistical data, Chamberlain learnt the value, too, of a professional secretariat with James Freeman appointed to be a paid secretary.

The Society was a local agency, not a national pressure group. However, it had become clear from the research carried out in Birmingham that its own efforts at fee-paying and fundraising for the town's poor could not hope to solve Birmingham's educational problems. Only a national legislative solution would do, and the Society therefore gave place to a new national campaigning structure.

Jesse Collings might justifiably claim to have inspired the creation of this new national pressure group. He records in his autobiography how in 1868 he wrote a pamphlet, *The American School System*, in which 'I strongly advocated the formation of a society, national in its name and constitution, refusing all compromise but adopting as its platform national secular (or at least unsectarian) education, compulsory as to rating and the attendance of children, with no fees, with State aid and inspection, and local management'.[60] After a conversation with George Dixon about this prospectus, the two men determined to call another meeting at 'The Dales' in February 1869 'to consider the advisability of organising a National Association, for the purpose of agitation'.[61] A familiar team of Birmingham allies attended, now habituated to action by their experience in the cause of the BES. As a result, a circular was issued and a public meeting was called; 2,500 people responded. A resolution there was passed to establish the National Education League and the new programme, Collings complacently recalled, 'was that suggested in my pamphlet, namely national free schools, universal school boards, secular or unsectarian teaching, compulsory attendance of children, local rates, and State aid and inspection; and, finally, local management'.[62]

At the outset, a provisional committee was formed, which would later be made permanent at the First General Meeting of Members of the National Education League, on 12 and 13 October 1869. Dixon was the Chairman, Chamberlain his Vice-Chairman, and Collings, the Honorary Secretary. An Executive Committee was appointed with

Chamberlain as its Chairman, and because Dixon was that summer to become one of Birmingham's MPs and so became preoccupied at Westminster, Chamberlain assumed virtual leadership of the League. The make-up of the main committee reads like a *Who's Who* of the later Birmingham Political Machine, for it included J. Jaffray as Treasurer, J.T. Bunce as Chairman of the Publishing Committee, C.E. Mathews as Chairman of the Parliamentary Committee, and R.F. Martineau as Chairman of the Branches Committee. William Harris, already so experienced in shaping the Birmingham Liberal Association, was nominated to be the Chairman of Finance. Other committee members included the ministers, Dale, Crosskey and Dawson, Chamberlain's brothers-in-law, William and Thomas Kenrick, Charles Vince and J.S. Wright. Because many of these men were already engaged in Liberal electoral activities (reinforced by their involvement that summer of 1869 in the campaign to ensure George Dixon's victory in the by-election) the League from its inception became another expression of Liberal politics.

The aim was to campaign actively for government action to create a national education system. It sought to build a large membership, involving working men if possible; so, instead of insisting on a standard subscription, forms for giving simply asked 'What amount are you willing to subscribe to League funds?' In fact, wealthy businessmen on the committee like Dixon, Chamberlain, the Kenricks and John Jaffray, headed the subscription lists with sums ranging up to £1,000. By the time of that First General Meeting there were 3,000 members, and the ample funds they contributed were needed for an attritional battle which would be based at 47 Ann Street in Birmingham, with Francis Adams, a local solicitor (and later the movement's historian) as paid secretary. This was to be the nexus for a national organisation, with 430 branches by 1872; yet it was always firmly centred on Birmingham.

The strategy announced at the First General Meeting in 1869 was to rouse the public in support for an education bill to Parliament which would embody League principles. It was overtaken almost immediately by the proposals for education reform of W.E. Forster, the Vice-President of the Privy Council, responsible in Gladstone's Cabinet for education. Although Dixon claimed credit for the effect of the League's agitation, that national educational reform was at last firmly on a government's agenda, the Forster Bill at the end of the year was a profound and shocking disappointment to the League. Some tensions within the League emerged when the Bill was announced. Chamberlain was bitterly disappointed at George Dixon's lukewarm response to Forster's proposals in the debate in the House. 'Strong exception was taken to the first paragraph of your speech in which you are alleged to have said that the country would receive the Bill with satisfaction,' he wrote from Birmingham.[63] Dixon's measured and judicious approach didn't always appeal to his combative and belligerent Vice-Chairman, but Dixon had at least recognised that Forster's Bill represented a major step forward. It was government's first, albeit imperfect, attempt to create a comprehensive national education system.

Objections to Forster centred on the Bill's basic premise that voluntary schools were to be allowed to continue; new state schools (Board schools) were only to be permitted to fill in the gaps left by voluntary schools. There was to be no compulsion, and fees would continue to be paid. New Board schools were to be built, out of ratepayers' taxes, under the aegis of boards elected by ratepayers rather than being appointed by Town Councillors as the League proposed. As the Bill progressed through the Commons, amendments made it barely more palatable. One clause, which seems to have been included without its full implications being realised by any party, became a *cause célèbre*. Clause 25 permitted School Boards to educate children at voluntary schools, funding them on the rates, in areas where there were no Board schools for children to attend. This was additionally painful, rubbing salt in Nonconformists' wounds, for they had already had to contemplate the comprehensive triumph of the Anglican Church, whose schools the Bill protected. Now, despite the sop of a Conscience clause, which might permit a child to be temporarily withdrawn, the prospect loomed of Nonconformist children receiving religious instruction in Anglican schools. It determined the manner of the League's campaigning for years.

From the start a twin-track approach emerged. George Dixon, having conceded that the League should drop its own bill, fought the good fight against the government's version, introducing amendments to Forster's Bill in the Commons. Sadly, for the League, none were adopted. Back in Birmingham, Chamberlain assumed effective leadership. He and his team imparted urgency to the campaign. Commencing with the publication of Forster's Bill a relentless programme of pamphlets followed. With print runs ranging from 20,000 to 50,000 copies they advocated school boards, free education and compulsion, and railed against the iniquities of Clause 25 and of propping up a voluntary system which had let down generations of children.

Regularly, communications to branches encouraged local committees to provide copy for the provincial press publicising the League's programme and activities. Some pamphlets were designed to solicit cooperation of working men, others were copies of supportive letters from correspondents enthusiastically endorsing the work of the League, such as that from J. MacNaught, Minister of Laura Chapel, Bath which averred that 'this League which proposes a prompt remedy for our country's crying evil of ignorance is just the machinery that a man is longing for'.[64] They all emanated from the League's Ann Street Birmingham presses, and reflected the League's centralisation on Birmingham, and Chamberlain's own predispositions – 'It is certain that we (in Birmingham) are the only people who know what we want and how we mean to get it,' he would later boast to Collings.[65] All the leading officers were Birmingham men, as were 20 out of 49 members of the National Executive Committee.

The aftermath to the publication of Forster's Bill provides an object lesson in the League's methodology and tactics. Within two to three hours a circular was on its way to 138 branches of the League requesting their views of the Bill, and also setting out the Executive's own objections in full. Within days a League circular from Francis Adams was being dispatched from Ann Street giving further precise instructions. Branches were required to send delegates to join a deputation which was off to see the Prime Minister. A door-to-door canvass was to be initiated to drum up signatures to the League's accompanying petition.

Furthermore, a meeting was to be summoned in the branch's immediate area to generate support. Local Nonconformist ministers were to be consulted, while the constituency MP was to be importuned for help for the League's programme.[66] As Chamberlain put it in a letter to Dixon: 'We have sent out an inflammatory circular to all branches urging large delegations, also public meetings and petitions.'[67] Here, long-standing constitutional remedies, like petitioning Parliament (the favoured tactic of those complaining about government injustice for centuries), were complemented by more contemporary campaigning, the use of pamphlets being reminiscent of the methods adopted by the Anti-Corn Law League in the 1840s.

There seems little doubt that the hectic pace, the pugnacity and sense of outrage of the Executive Committee came from Chamberlain. His first biographer Garvin articulated its dynamic character: 'All his qualities as a man of action, and the defects of his qualities now came out – swift and punctual in dispatch; prompt in decision; fibrous in tenacity; over-sanguine; full of venture; but full of resource; too blistering in attack and retort; but never fumbling nor shrinking. He is for fighting to the last.'[68]

To maintain the pressure on the government, in the days before the deputation's departure for London, the Executive Committee widened the assault. Crosskey, Dale, Dawson and Vince arranged for a public meeting of Nonconformists from all over the country to meet at Carr's Lane Chapel (where Dale ministered). Nonconformists felt themselves frozen out by the distinctly Anglican character of the Bill, and the result was to establish a Central Nonconformist Committee 'to watch over specifically Nonconformist interests'. It too would petition Parliament, in March 1870, ensuring that all over the country ministers placed a copy of a petition against Forster's proposals in their chapels – 8,000 congregation members signed in four days, and later on the Committee petitioned Parliament over the Birmingham School Board's bye-law enabling it to use rate-payers' money to pay for children at Church of England schools in the town.

The Central Nonconformist Committee encouraged those same congregations to continue petitioning, to demonstrate, and to urge local MPs to support. Like the League it sent a deputation, led by Dale and Crosskey, to see Gladstone a month after the League had done. This national organisation was but another adjunct of the Birmingham Machine, whence it originated and where it was to be based. Dale and Crosskey were the honorary secretaries, and they unearthed a hitherto undiscovered organisational talent in the Birmingham draper, Francis Schnadhorst, who became the Committee's secretary before going on to become the secretary of the Liberal Association. It worked hand in glove with Chamberlain and the League; the former occasionally appeared at the Committee's meetings. In October 1870 he chaired one of its meetings, no doubt responsible for its impatient conclusion that 'the Committee were of opinion that they had previously been a little too moderate'.[69] Later he would attend its protest meeting against the application of Clause 25 in Birmingham, contributing a fiery speech from the floor to stir up those present, in which he said that 'the new bye-laws were a revival of church rates', and that there was 'no right to make the ratepayer pay for religious instruction'.[70]

With Nonconformists organised for a flanking attack, the preparations for the deputation to Gladstone continued. Their thoroughness and meticulous eye for detail exemplify the League's planning and organisation. Circulars to branches now asked for the names of delegates and urged 'all boroughs where we have branches' to ensure that their Mayors attended too, 'in order to make the League deputation as impressive and influential as possible'. For Birmingham delegates, a circular announced: 'the provision of a saloon carriage for use of the deputation to Mr Gladstone, the train leaving New Street station at 9.30 am.'[71] On the day itself some 400 delegates and 46 MPs gathered at Westminster Palace hotel, then making their way to Downing Street to see Gladstone and Forster. That meeting established Chamberlain as the coming man, for it was clear to Gladstone even then that, although Dixon was nominal leader of the deputation, Chamberlain was its most articulate spokesman who, said the Prime Minister to the assemblage: 'I may consider as in some sense your chairman – the representative of you all.'

Chamberlain set out the League's case: that at many of the 114 branches of the League large meetings had been held, clear evidence of the League's strength and popularity. That it had considerable volunteer and trade union support; that it embodied Nonconformist sentiment in the country. That 96 branches were represented in this deputation from Newcastle to the Isle of Wight, Ipswich and Falmouth. That its members objected 'to permissive compulsion, to permissive secularism' and 'to a Conscience clause which would be absolutely unsatisfactory'.[72] Although a success in that the League had been able to reflect its strength of feeling by directly communicating with Gladstone himself, and with Forster who was present, the net result was that the government changed nothing in the wake of the meeting.[73] The campaign went on.

In October 1870 the Executive Committee 'resolved to influence public and parliamentary opinion by meetings, publications, petitions and all other available means in favour of a national, unsectarian, compulsory and free system of education'. The blizzard of communications continued unabated, Dixon boasting of 800,000 pamphlets produced in 1870 alone. Many were concerned with money; although Dixon might brag in 1870 that the League had subscriptions of £70,000 and a fighting fund of £10,000 it was never enough with a professional secretariat, a prolific printing press, and expenses of speakers and agents to support. Sometimes the Chairman of Finance, William Harris, would himself hand-write letters (examples of which survive to Bristol, Bradford, Devonport, the Isle of Wight, Dewsbury, Leicester and Wednesbury) to branch chairmen: '... requesting immediate help in canvassing for, and collecting, additional subscriptions to support a vigorous agitation throughout the country in support of the parliamentary actions of Mr Dixon. This necessitates additional funds to be placed at the disposal of the Executive Committee.'[74]

Those expenses were incurred when, from the League's inception, its leading figures travelled from Birmingham on missionary work round the country. Collings, Dixon, Dale and Chamberlain set out in the autumn of 1869 and journeyed the length and breadth of the country via the railways, addressing wildly enthusiastic meetings. So, regular a feature did this become that a carriage was retained in a siding at New Street for the specific and emergency use of an NEL speaker when it was needed. The Executive Committee had already established contact by letter with every parliamentary borough in England and Wales encouraging local sympathisers to establish a provisional committee to hold a general meeting, from which sprang an embryonic branch. Once that had happened a formal meeting would be called, to be addressed by one, but usually two, of that quartet of leaders. Dixon travelled to Leeds and then Manchester in the first days of December 1869, while Chamberlain helped establish Leicester's branch in the previous November. The effects of this were several-fold. The League was spreading its influence, and senior officers were honing their speech-making skills. But the impact was also to identify even more firmly in the eyes of the rest of the country that Birmingham was the centre of the elementary education movement. Just as the Birmingham Liberal Association was establishing itself as a model political organisation to be imitated by others, so the Birmingham branch of the National Education League was an archetype.

What went with this leadership was an autocratic spirit, expressed by Chamberlain when he wrote to Charles Dilke in 1871: 'We want a distinct understanding that adherents be loyal while they adhere and shall leave us when it becomes necessary, without disturbance.' [75] So, they must toe the line, or woe betide. Nothing in this regard would change in thirty years; this was the relationship Chamberlain expected in all subsequent incarnations of his Machine. It had been evident right back at the First National Meeting in October 1869; the painstaking preparation that saw reception rooms and information centres at railway stations to help travelling delegates bound for Birmingham had as its corollary a suffocating control of the meeting's proceedings. 'It was made clear that (members') business was only to listen and to rubber stamp decisions once taken. A precise and definite creed was promulgated and ordered to be embodied in the League's Bill; there was no loophole left for compromise and none was intended.' [76] Predictably some branches rebelled, as they would in the National Liberal Federation a few years later, kicking over Birmingham's traces. The local staffs of London, Merthyr, Ipswich and Sheffield resigned in due course over the controlling character of the Executive Committee.

One gets a flavour of its sense of urgent expectation from the League's pamphlet no. 311 urging branch officers to support (yet another) resolution in the House of Commons on the subject of Clause 25's iniquities. The manner is imperative:

> 'Hold public meetings to submit Mr Dixon's resolution, then send the meeting's resolution to your local MP; telegraph brief reports of the meeting to London papers especially *The Times* and the *Daily News*; bring direct influence to bear on your members of Parliament for some do not understand the question; and when MPs address the constituency, call a branch meeting and arrange that education questions be brought forward. For MPs declining to support, their failure to reflect constituents' feelings should be brought home to them. As well, send reports of Branch committees to local journals for publication. Try and obtain new members.' [77]

This pamphlet exemplifies the League's awareness of the importance of the Press. The Executive Committee's Chairman of the Publishing Committee was J.T. Bunce, the *Birmingham Daily Post* editor. Not only did he commission that flood of literature pouring out of Ann Street offices, but he also sought to place favourable stories across local and metropolitan publications. His own paper, naturally, lent strong support to Chamberlain, Dixon and the League. When Forster secured his Bill unamended in 1870 it opined of him: 'Never was a man more self-satisfied. He cannot keep his satisfaction to himself… He needs something sobering and saddening to chasten him. His irrepressibility requires to be taken down a peg or two.'[78] In another example, over the Anglican Church's bitter opposition to the School Boards that the League espoused, the *Post* was partisan, warning readers to be on the look-out for Church attempts to thwart champions of Board Schools in their justifiable attempts to build new schools in their area.[79] No doubt strong Press support in the League's home provided it with solid foundations.

Pamphlet no. 311 above also betrays a new League strategy: direct electoral pressure on members of Parliament. In 1873, its militant leadership determined to bring pressure to bear on Gladstone's government through the ballot box, running a League candidate (Cox) against a Liberal at the Bath by-election. Mundella, a leading Radical and articulate critic of Chamberlain's wrote: 'I appealed to Dixon to stop Cox. Chamberlain's fanatics have the mastery and mean to gratify their vanity and magnify their importance by showing their power to do mischief.'[80] After some unseemly violence, the Liberal candidate Hayter agreed to support League education policy and Cox withdrew. To Chamberlain and others on the Executive Committee it was a successful experiment, and initial coyness over an electoral strategy which discomforted rank and file Nonconformist Liberals was shed in favour of an overtly aggressive stance, justified by the Liberal government's shabby dismissal of Nonconformist concerns. It is revealing that this new militancy was never debated by the membership. It is of a piece with the dictatorial tendencies of Chamberlain's executive Machine, from its inception.

After Bath, the new strategy of opposing Liberal candidates who did not support repeal of Clause 25 was implemented at East Staffordshire, Shaftesbury, Dundee and Greenwich. It was intended to show that the Liberal Party could not win without Radical and Nonconformist support, and to illustrate the power of the League, although it could have the unfortunate side-effect of allowing Conservatives to win a seat. That meant paradoxically reinforcing support in the Commons for Gladstone's policy, for Conservatives – the party of the Established Church – were more committed to the Anglican settlement enshrined in Forster's Act than were many Liberals.[81]

The campaign was suspended in 1873 when Gladstone brought John Bright into the Cabinet. League leaders hoped – unavailingly – that the presence of their local Birmingham MP and colleague would initiate a revision of Forster's Act and, especially, repeal of the totemic Clause 25. Yet even if the campaign was halted the fact was that at the 1874 General Election over 300 of 425 Liberal candidates agreed to support the League in revising Forster's Act. In the Liberal wreckage, after the Conservative landslide that followed, a clear majority (167 of 251) Liberal MPs favoured repeal of Clause 25. In a Conservative/Anglican-dominated House that repeal was never going to be carried.[82] Still, the story of this electoral strategy is important in illustrating Chamberlain's rapidly expanding horizons; he had gone from Birmingham new boy to a player on the national stage by 1874, and perhaps Mundella was right to see the aggression as a simple expression of burgeoning Chamberlainite ambition.

The League's electoral approach would not have been possible without another organisational innovation borrowed from Cobden's Anti-Corn Law League, that of professional agents. By May 1872, that master operator William Harris was chairing a new sub-committee of the Executive, the Electoral Committee, which controlled twelve full-time agents, who constantly peregrinated round the country, their work supplemented by part-time assistants. Every Parliamentary borough and county seat was canvassed in 1873, an essential prerequisite to Chamberlain's aggressive electoral strategy. There were now thirteen agents, each with a designated area. Their instructions were dauntingly comprehensive. They were to visit branches to keep them up to the mark, form new branches, revivify dormant branches, arrange public meetings, collect subscriptions, distribute League publications, correspond with local newspapers, urge League members to harass local MPs, generate local campaigns to initiate School Boards, report on local educational disputes to the Executive Committee, canvass the whole district, seek interviews with local Liberals and interview, and report on, locally influential people. The significance of these agents lay both in their success in the dissemination of League ideas and, in a longer perspective, in tutoring Chamberlain and his inner circle in the minutiae of how to build a party and how to win an election.

Members of the League's Executive Committee and of its secretariat gained invaluable experience in the seven years that it fought its educational battles. Bunce and his Publications Committee learnt the effective use of pamphlets, hundreds of different titles of which were produced, including reports of debates, policy position papers, and assaults on Church iniquities; they also developed the judicious placement of pro-League copy in provincial and metropolitan newspapers, at times on a weekly basis. That understanding of the unique power of the printed word, in an age before radio and television, would be replicated by every incarnation of the Chamberlain Machine, until its last manifestation in the Tariff Reform campaign of 1903-06.

If it utilised the potential of print technology to the full, it also understood the value of personal missionary work, and we have seen how in the early stages the inner circle of Chamberlain, Dale, Collings and Dixon travelled widely on the rail network from Birmingham to address new branches. Chamberlain never forgot the impact a visit could make, persuading an audience by personal advocacy. Even in the League's first year he was a star turn, Garvin writing: 'As a speaker and organiser he was the soul of the fight and he was becoming every day a more clean-cut speaker and adroit tactician.'[83] What he learnt in 1870 he applied thereafter in proselytising the Radical Programme in 1885, in fighting the Unionist corner in the 1892 General Election, in articulating the Unionist programme in 1895, and in carrying the fight to the pro-Boers in 1900. His last great national tour in 1903-4 encompassed Scotland and the South as he made the case against Free Trade.

This final phase of the League's struggle was especially educative for Chamberlain and his team. His biographer believed that:

> 'The League served him as an admirable "short model". It had enabled him to furnish himself with his register of political facts about all the industrial constituencies. Already he knew the names of all the local lights, and was in touch with agents and adherents in every one of them. The electoral map of democracy, plainly demarcated and minutely lettered, was alive in his mind. Thus equipped, he and his Birmingham men made themselves missionaries and guides to other Liberals in a hundred places…' 'Chamberlain applied himself to (this new kind of work) with minute attention,' Garvin elaborated. 'He soon obtained a closer knowledge of the constituencies in detail than any statesman of his time. With agents everywhere he kept his deadly little notebooks in his precise hand. Entries included: "Peterborough, the Nonconformists are much divided, but if they agreed on a candidate they have influence to carry him… Dewsbury is a very Radical place (where) the working class is 75% of the constituency… Cardiff, our Welsh agent reports that several boroughs with the Ballot could be carried for Radicals against the present representatives." [84]

The mind map of the country's electoral geography he had built up would prove invaluable for decades to come. He remained a keen student, even after the new single member constituency reforms in 1885, which radically altered electoral cartography. In his communications over Liberal Unionist candidacies, and over the fight for Tariff Reform, his understanding of the granular detail of constituency profiles is very evident.

He was not the only member of his team who was gaining experience and knowledge. William Harris, in frequent communication with branch secretaries over finance, J.T. Bunce, distributing League literature, Robert Dale, like Chamberlain an intrepid speaker and traveller, and Francis Schnadhorst, in his role as secretary of the Central Nonconformist Committee, the League's close ally - all built up an intimate knowledge of the social and economic character of the regions.

There seems little doubt that Chamberlain led the way when it came to implementing the ultimate lesson of the National Education League; that, in his words to his friend John Morley: 'There is not enough force in the education issue to make it the sole fighting issue of our friends.' [85] To Charles Dilke he was even blunter: 'I don't think the League will do.' [86]

To the historian Patricia Auspos what he meant was clear: he had become aware of the limitations of the pressure group, for a single-issue organisation lacked a comprehensive notion of reform. She and H.J. Hanham argued that Chamberlain had had a revelation by 1873-4: for Radicals to implement reform they had to do so from within the Liberal Party rather than campaigning outside it. The solution was to broaden out the programme from its narrow focus on education, to embrace reform of church, land and labour, aiming to achieve it by re-structuring the Liberal Party. So, the League formed a vital apprenticeship for Chamberlain, helping him develop from being a single-issue provincial pressure group campaigner to a national politician pursuing a wide-ranging Radical programme of reform.[87]

Henry Crosskey

Born in Lewes in 1826, eldest son of a prominent Unitarian draper, Henry Crosskey entered Manchester New College Oxford in 1843 before becoming a pastor, ministering firstly to a congregation in Derby (1848-1852) where he became interested in the cause of free, compulsory, secular education. As a result, he helped to establish the National Public School Association; he then moved on to become pastor of the Unitarian Church in Glasgow.

In 1869, he was asked to take over the leadership of the Unitarian Church of the Messiah in Birmingham, instantly involving himself in the Church's own education day school provision, and in the newly established National Education League, in the words of R.A. Armstrong, his biographer, 'flinging himself with immense ardour into the movement, serving on the Executive of the League, writing fly-leaves for it and soon becoming known as one of its most fiery orators'. He regularly attended the Executive's meetings and took part in all its work, attending the debates on Forster's Bill in the House of Commons through early 1870, and with Dixon drawing up amendments to that Bill.

To Crosskey, the atmosphere that he found among his immediate friends at his new Church was exhilarating and almost intoxicating. The arrangement seems to have been a perfect fit, a minister of developed radical views with a dynamic and creative element in its congregation. Furthermore, his brand of Unitarianism seems to have chimed with that of Chamberlain and several others in his circle – he was a rationalist, reflected in his wide scientific and geological interests, and he stood like Chamberlain for a sort of humanistic theism, seeing his duty in practical social reform and scientific research rather than in debating theological niceties. So, he was attracted to the municipal gospel propagated by Robert Dale from the last years of the 1860s, which inspired the Chamberlainite revolution in the Town Council from 1873 onwards.

Armstrong tells us that although as a minister he could not stand for the Council, Crosskey campaigned 'November after November in the municipal contests, pleading with pathetic earnestness for Liberal reform; when the contests were on he attended two or three meetings, night after night, in the obscurest parts of the town, appealing for the election of the right man'. He became a renowned orator. Dale was, it seems, alluding to him when he wrote: 'Sometimes an adventurous orator would excite his audience by dwelling on the glories of Florence and other cities of Italy in the Middle Ages and suggest that Birmingham too might become the home of great literature and art.' This high-minded desire to elevate, to raise the expectations of his audiences, was captured by his biographer, who wrote of Crosskey 'addressing 80 to 100 working people in badly lighted rooms, his speeches did them good, just as if they were to look up from their narrow courts and see the constellations moving over their little patch of sky'.

Henry Crosskey stood for election to the Birmingham School Board in 1870 but lost. He eventually became a prominent figure on the Board after success in 1876's elections. He went on to be the chairman of its Sites and Buildings Committee, an important role as new schools were erected across Birmingham in the wake of the Education Act of 1870. He was afterwards Chairman of the School Management Committee. Even before becoming a member of the School Board Crosskey had campaigned vigorously against the Church party's overbearing behaviour from 1870–73, and most especially against its policy of implementing Clause 25, using the rates to fund places at voluntary schools.

In 1870, when the fight against the Gladstone government's education policy was gathering momentum, Henry Crosskey was a leading member of the new Central Nonconformist Committee, founded to focus national Nonconformist outrage at the terms of the Forster Act. Crosskey, with Robert Dale, was a joint secretary. Again, the role gave scope to his oratorical and organisational powers. His work for this Committee complemented his role on the executive committee of the Liberation Society. Both bodies were set up to protest against the privileged position of the Established Church. Crosskey argued consistently and passionately for the disestablishment of the Church of England, and for its endowments to be restored to the nation and applied to public purposes like education. Ultimately this campaign failed.

For twenty-five years Crosskey was a central figure both in Birmingham affairs and as a member of Chamberlain's cadre. His loyalty to Chamberlain is seen by his support for Chamberlain's stand against Gladstone over Home Rule in 1886. Like so many of his friends he had to make the agonising decision to abandon the Birmingham Liberal Party on whose behalf he had devoted years of dedicated campaigning.

His involvement in public works was remarkable; it exemplifies the commitment of Birmingham's influential citizens to the municipal ideal propounded by Dale and Dawson. In addition to the roles already mentioned above he was a governor of King Edward's School and a member of the Technical School Committee, town bailiff, President of the Birmingham Natural History Society, President of the Birmingham Philosophical Society and Chairman of the Women's Hospital. Meanwhile he continued to advocate Old Age Pensions, universal manhood suffrage, and the vote for women (he was President of the Birmingham Women's Suffrage Society) at a time when these formed a distinctly radical prospectus. He remained equally radical in his support for a different and modern approach to the curriculum in schools, promoting science classes in elementary schools, technical education, and merit pay for teachers. He died in 1893 before he was able to witness the fulfilment of his dream of a Midland university; his good friend and colleague Joseph Chamberlain established the University of Birmingham at the turn of the century.

Jesse Collings

Perhaps no other member of Chamberlain's Circle, with the exception of J. Powell Williams, was as close to Joseph Chamberlain as was Jesse Collings. They holidayed together on the Continent throughout the 1870s, and Chamberlain's letters in the Special Collections at the University of Birmingham are characterised by a warmth and intimacy he reserved for nobody else but close members of his family. Collings was quite evidently invaluable after the death of Florence, Chamberlain's second wife, her widower writing: 'I miss you very much. I am often dull and depressed and wish I had my good friend to talk to.' And where so many friendships were fractured by the events of 1886 – the Home Rule crisis – Collings and Chamberlain remained loyal friends and allies until Chamberlain's withdrawal from active politics.

Jesse Collings was born in Exmouth, Devon, in 1831 and became a commercial traveller in the ironmongery trade. He came to Birmingham to work for Booth and Co. in 1850, whereafter he became a partner in 1864, on Samuel Booth's retirement, the firm being renamed Collings and Wallis. His subsequent success in business freed him to pursue philanthropic and political interests in Birmingham. Before he had left Devon his conscience had been awakened by teaching in a Ragged School in Heavitree, Exeter, and visiting the slums whence these children came. As he wrote in his autobiography: 'I was struck by the deplorable, poverty-stricken condition of many both mentally and physically.' 'These people all seemed to be steeped in ignorance and want.' He therefore initiated a committee to establish an industrial school, which came to fruition in the building of the Devon and Exeter Boys' Industrial School in Exeter; later it moved into more rural surroundings at Exminster, and Collings was instrumental in fundraising for it.

Once he was settled in Birmingham it seems inevitable that he would pursue these educational enthusiasms there. Evidently reports of his Devon experiences had reached George Dixon by 1867 who invited him to join initial meetings which established the Birmingham Education Society. Collings became its Honorary Secretary. He took part in house-to-house research to build up a statistical picture of the state of Birmingham children's education; he was habituated to this sort of work by his slum visits in Exeter. In 1868 he published his influential text An Outline of the American School System *in which, he later wrote: 'I strongly advocated the formation of a society, national in its name and constitution.' He can be credited with inspiring the foundation of the National Education League; he became its Honorary Secretary. He joined Chamberlain thereafter in 'spending some weeks addressing the working classes in several towns, and being received with enthusiasm everywhere', with the aim of generating wide support for education reform. He himself felt that 'there is no doubt that the actions of the League in parliament and the country forced the government to bring in the Education Act'.*

Not only was he a prominent member of the National Education League's inner circle, he was a loyal ally of Chamberlain's on the Town Council; indeed, he preceded him, being elected for Edgbaston the year before his friend, in 1868. He immediately joined that element on the Council who might be termed the 'awkward squad', continually opposing the ruling party (in his own words) 'men who governed the town and were totally unable to deal properly with the state of things (regarding sewage and sanitation)'. Chamberlain's election inaugurated a new chapter of 'marvellous administration… the secret of his success (being) his trust in the people'. Collings became Chairman of the Free Libraries and Art Gallery Committee in 1872. He fought a hard and successful battle against the Lord's Day Defence Association when he resolved to introduce Sunday opening for the Reference Library and the Art Gallery so that working people could benefit from cultural and intellectual stimulus on their one free day a week, his argument being that: 'Art must not remain the perquisite of the few.'

In 1877, he became Honorary Secretary of a fund to support Samuel Plimsoll's campaign to reform Merchant Shipping; he hosted a meeting at the Town Hall addressed by Plimsoll, and it was Collings who presented the meeting's resolutions that there was a multitude of ill-founded, rotten, and unseaworthy ships and that an enormous number of over-loaded vessels left British ports. This campaign was one close to Chamberlain's heart too, for he would go on to introduce a Merchant Shipping Bill when he was President of the Board of Trade.

In 1878 Collings was elected Mayor of Birmingham, establishing the Mayor's Distress Fund in his first winter in office to raise money for working people thrown into temporary unemployment by three months' continuous frost. Relief came in the form of food, fuel, clothes and blankets. Whilst Mayor he also initiated a series of 'high class concerts' for ordinary people, in the belief that 'Mendelssohn will beat Champagne Charlie'. It was of a piece with his devotion to the idea of elevating the cultural and intellectual horizons of working people. Affordable concerts were a sell-out and inspired the creation of the Birmingham Music Association.

As a loyal apparatchik within Chamberlain's Political Machine, Collings was a committed Liberal, and as he had been central to the success of the Birmingham Education Society and the National Education League, and as he was a prominent Liberal Town Councillor, it was inevitable that he should assume a key position in Chamberlain's National Liberal Federation, that of President. In 1880, he consolidated his advance in the national ranks of the Party, by becoming MP for Ipswich. Increasingly he became more involved in campaigning for agricultural reform. He had always seen himself as springing from Devon yeoman stock. He had supported Joseph Arch's Warwickshire Agricultural Labourers Union from its inception at Leamington in 1872, when he became a member of its Finance Committee. He spoke at the foundation of the National Agricultural Labourers Union that same year, attending a meeting of 2,000 to 3,000 people, amongst whom was George Dixon. His theme in that speech did not vary over the next forty years; he saw the need to repopulate the rural districts by re-establishing a peasant proprietary class and by assaulting the iniquity of current land-holding in England. Representing a constituency in rural Suffolk only sharpened his focus. As he became more engaged in drafting and promoting bills connected to agricultural reform, so his friend and leader, Joseph Chamberlain, took up the cause of land reform, of votes for rural workers, and of allotments, adopting the phrase coined by Collings as shorthand for his demands, 'Three Acres and a Cow'. Collings carried an Allotments Extension Act in 1882, permitting charity trustees to release land retained for the poor from Enclosure Acts to be parcelled out into allotments for the rural poor. He established an Allotment Extension Association to advise county and parish authorities on the possibilities afforded by the Act. He went on to draft a bill to promote agricultural education in village schools and later another to initiate Peasant Proprietary in the country. Both failed. But he was successful in his campaigning for the enfranchisement of agricultural labourers when he joined Chamberlain in speaking on the cause in the Commons, and at huge meetings round the country, in 1884. The Third Reform Act gave the vote to county householders. He was also successful in persuading the government to pass Acts to extend Allotments and Small Holdings between 1887 and 1892.

By now the shape of national politics had dramatically changed. In 1886 the Liberal Party split over Home Rule. Collings, having been unseated at Ipswich, became a Liberal Unionist MP for Bordesley in Birmingham, one of the successful seven Unionist candidates in the town. The acrimony between Gladstonian Liberals and Liberal Unionists saw him voted out as President of the Allotments Extension Association in a Gladstonian coup in 1888. In reaction, he and the ever-combative Chamberlain founded the Rural Labourers League to improve the material conditions of rural labour. He then showed what he had learnt from the campaigning of the National Education League, employing agents of the League to address meetings in villages about the details of the Small Holdings Act he had inspired in 1892.

When Chamberlain embraced Tariff Reform in 1903 he had no more loyal a disciple than Jesse Collings who addressed many meetings on the evils of Free Trade imports and how Chamberlain's tariffs would boost employment.

Jesse Collings was there from the start of Chamberlain's active political career in 1868 and outlived him, dying only in 1920. In nearly every manifestation of the Chamberlain Machine we can find him a central figure, from National Education League, Town Council, National Liberal Federation, Birmingham Liberal Unionist Association, Rural Labourers League, and Tariff Reform League. It is an impressive testimony to friendship and loyalty over a period spanning four decades.

THE MACHINE BATTLES TO CONTROL THE BIRMINGHAM SCHOOL BOARD

A s we have seen, a key proposal of the National Education League was for the formation of nominated School Boards to supervise a new national education system. Forster's Act was in this – as in much else – a disappointment to League leaders, stipulating not nomination by local councillors but election by ratepayers. That rather defeated the object for men like Chamberlain and Collings, who had got themselves elected to the Town Council in confident expectation of their subsequent selection for the School Board. Nevertheless, once Forster's Act was in place in 1870, the League leadership concluded that Birmingham, as the heartbeat of the education campaign, should be in the vanguard of the operation of the Act.

Chamberlain, as Chairman of the League's Executive Committee, was determined that a Birmingham School Board should be the model for the rest of the country. An application to the Education Department to be permitted to elect a School Board in Birmingham was made in August 1870, with Chamberlain arguing in the Council debate that the League was certain to have the majority, and that it was therefore important to get on with it and use a base in Birmingham to campaign for the amendment of Forster's hated Act. There had been considerable discussion in Parliament as to how these new School Boards should be constituted. Men like Dixon had argued for nomination by Town Council. Forster had insisted on elections whereby local ratepayers would be given as many votes as there were vacancies on the School Board. The Education Department was therefore setting out on uncharted territory when it was asked by the League to devise a system for an election in Birmingham, which was in the vanguard of implementing the terms of the Forster Education Act for creating a School Board.

By mid-September the Department had worked out details of a Birmingham Board election, and a November date was set. Meanwhile a League directive to its branches sought to counter what the organisation believed to be the malign intent of clergy everywhere to obstruct the implementation of this part of the Act; to many churchmen, convinced of the importance of voluntary schooling, especially for the morally rootless lower orders as many saw them, School Boards were positively dangerous intrusions. Chamberlain, who prepared this pamphlet, instructed members of the League to inform themselves as to the true state of their local school's accommodation, and so to arm themselves with the statistical ammunition to challenge any rearguard action by churchmen against the expansion of school places through Board schools.

That same pamphlet of October 1870 went on to restate the League's central argument against the patchwork of voluntary schools in the country. 'In urging the universal establishment of school boards we are supporting the principles of popular government and local control and we are resisting the extension of a system by which national funds are entrusted to private agencies for distribution.' Here Chamberlain took a side-swipe against public subsidy for the Anglican church, and showed a characteristic faith in the local democratic process which, he was confident, would return an overwhelmingly Liberal Board membership at election time.[88]

The Birmingham Liberal Association took as keen an interest in these elections as it did in every other contest in Birmingham. Just as it would come to do in subsequent municipal and Board of Guardians elections, the Association decided to intervene in the impending School Board elections. In reality, the Association was also synonymous with the National Education League, and appears to have done its bidding, and when the Liberal Association's 400, the ruling representatives of Birmingham Liberalism, met in the Town Hall on 7 November 1870, to nominate the candidates, they were voting on the names of men approved by the League. From a list of 38, 15 were chosen, one for each available seat on the Board, although it was rumoured that not all present agreed with both the conduct of, and the final choices in, the meeting, no doubt a reflection on Chamberlain's relentlessness. The ultimate aim was to sweep the board, so to speak, by taking all 15 places on the School Board, and therefore to consolidate a Liberal domination of the town, recently demonstrated in the parliamentary elections.[89]

The published list of candidates contained many by now familiar faces, important cogs already in the emerging Chamberlain Machine. At the head of the list were Chamberlain and George Dixon, but the remaining thirteen were all League men. Of them, several would make a mark for themselves in different Birmingham manifestations in later years; so, J. Collings, J.S. Wright, H. Crosskey, R.W. Dale, Rev C. Vince, and G. Dawson were all central figures in the Liberal revolution in the town. Only George Dixon, and Archdeacon Sandford, were Anglicans in what was otherwise a Liberal Nonconformist phalanx; and this is important, for nationally and as reflected in Birmingham's School Board, education politics came to be divided along religious lines, with the establishment of new Board Schools, and the implementation of Clause 25, as particular *points d'appui*. Certainly, the Birmingham School Board election of November 1870 resolved itself into a contest of Nonconformists against the sponsors of traditional voluntary education (Anglican and Catholic).

The League relished the forthcoming contest, entirely sure of its ability to score an overwhelming victory; the campaign, Chamberlain argued, would in itself stimulate debate and excite the public mind. In the event, however, it was to be the only significant setback that Chamberlain's Birmingham Machine ever really suffered. In its overconfidence, and it seems that in this Collings and Chamberlain were especially guilty, it believed all 15 seats eminently winnable, despite the fact that the franchise was that of the cumulative vote, whereby each ratepayer had the same number of votes as there were candidates. So, in theory, the voter could 'plump' his votes, in other words apply all 15 votes to one candidate. Although the League had seen these dangers, and fought against the idea of cumulative voting when the Bill was debated, it was so positive it would dominate Birmingham that it ignored warnings of the foolishness of fielding so many candidates. The Labour League, to whose working men Chamberlain and Collings personally appealed for support, pointed out cumulative voting's unpredictability, especially in light of evidence of Parliamentary and municipal elections suggesting that one third of Birmingham's electorate did not support the Liberal Association. The Labour League's advice, to limit the number of candidates and so concentrate the Liberal vote, was ignored.[90]

It did not help the Liberal-League cause that in the lead-up to the election it should be put on the defensive over the nature of the religious education it advocated in future Birmingham Board Schools. The logical position, held by Charles Dilke and by Robert Dale among others, was the 'secular' one, that is that there be no religious content – not even the Bible – in educational provision. This would avoid quarrels over the extent to which a teacher was leaning towards one denomination rather than another in his or her interpretation of a Bible reading. But even Chamberlain, privately sympathetic, thought this too radical a step for the moment, being a gift to opponents; he compromised by supporting a plain Bible reading.

What would stick in the Liberal craw, as a final irony, was that their Church party opponents took a leaf out of Harris's book of 1868 and conducted a 'vote as you are told' election, dividing the town into eight sectors, issuing instructions in the Churches to electors to give two votes to each of seven candidates, and one to the eighth, the eighth name being different in each sector. This strict discipline worked as effectively for the Conservatives – the Church party – as it had for the Liberals. It was a striking tribute to the effectiveness of Birmingham Liberal electoral methods.[91]

Election day, 27 November revealed the extent of Liberal hubris. Canon O'Sullivan, a Catholic priest who was later to prove a useful ally for Leaguers against the Anglicans, topped the poll. Being the only Catholic candidate enabled him to garner the Catholic vote. He was followed by five Churchmen. Indeed, all the Anglican candidates were elected, becoming known as the 'Church Eight'. From an anticipated Liberal Fifteen, the Leaguers were reduced to the 'League Six' – Chamberlain, Dixon (highest placed), Dale, Dawson,

Vince and Wright. There was no room for Collings. The Conservative/Church strategy of concentrating cumulative votes on a few candidates had triumphantly succeeded.

In a series of exhaustive postmortems the *Birmingham Daily Post* extracted a moral victory for the Liberals. They achieved the majority of votes cast (220,637 to the Church party's 153,703) and attracted more individual voters (14,702 as opposed to 10,245). 'The cumulative vote has we will not say spoiled, but damaged, the new School Boards… enabling the minority to override the majority, being a contradiction of common sense. The result all over the kingdom is a triumph for partisans and sectarians,' it thundered. It attributed the defeat to the absurdly early poll (voting closed at 3pm unlike London's 8pm) whereby many working men were denied the chance to vote. It also blamed dirty tricks, ignoring evidence reported by its rival *Birmingham Daily Gazette* that a handcart of spare and duplicate voting papers had been spotted rolling down New Street to the Liberal Association offices during the course of the morning. The *Post* preferred to highlight Church iniquities: 'We do most certainly believe the charges made against the Conservative canvassers and agents for falsifying voting papers, and we do so because the evidence in the hands of the Liberal committee is too precise and abundant to leave a shadow of doubt.'

Here once again is that indispensable element in the Chamberlain Machine, that of the loyal mouthpiece in the popular press; the editor, J.T. Bunce's advocacy of League and Liberal causes was unswerving in its constancy, and extremely influential. Still, in this instance, all its support for the League cause in the School Board elections was unavailing. A sympathetic *Post* tried to draw some lessons from the debacle. 'So far as the Liberals are concerned,' it opined, 'we honestly think it will do them good. Uninterrupted success is not wholesome for parties. Adversity has very potent and salutary lessons.' It went on: 'Owing to divisions and to lukewarmness, which ought to have roused (men) into action, education in Birmingham is placed under the control of the Established Church… and the very home and origin of Liberalism is made to appear before the country as willingly submitting to the Conservative Party.' Chamberlain, Dale, Vince and the rest of the League Six, with Collings in close attendance, certainly learnt important lessons from this humiliation. Never again could charges of complacency, ineffective canvassing and half-hearted electioneering be made against the Machine.[92]

Now the task of the League minority was to challenge the triumphant Church Eight at every turn. In consequence, as Francis Adams, the first historian of the Birmingham School Board, put it: 'The fortnightly meetings of the School Board (at the Parish Offices on Paradise Street) were looked forward to with the greatest interest and zest, partly because of the principles at stake, partly no doubt also because of the intellectual enjoyment they afforded. They were always inconveniently crowded by the public.'[93] What made them compelling viewing for these spectators – and absorbing reading for many others in the *Post*'s columns – was that the Liberal minority contested the ground with the Conservative majority foot by foot, believing the Church party to be in power only by a temporary fluke. One observer quipped that the meeting-room was like the Black Hole of Calcutta, so poisonous was its atmosphere. Joseph Chamberlain was in the vanguard – 'always his torrential energy and debating skill dominated the assembly'. 'In tactics, in arrangement in private counsel of the plan of the battle and, above all, in the scheme concocted on the spur of the moment to avoid checkmate on a sudden and unexpected contingency – in these things, Chamberlain was supreme,' wrote Garvin quoting an eyewitness.[94]

However, he was by no means on his own. He had a talented team: Robert Dale was at least as combative and as persistent in the battle, George Dixon showed himself an articulate ally and at times Charles Vince could prove the equal of them all as a thorn in the side of the Church party. Dale set out to debate education policy at every turn; he became a master of filibuster, goading William Sargant, the (Anglican) chairman, and S. S. Lloyd of the Church party to introduce a motion in 1871 establishing a guillotine on debate. Popular disavowal in Birmingham of such repression defeated the proposal, but the League Six were unsuccessful on a much more fundamental matter, that of the payment of fees and compulsion. Dixon himself had contributed funds to the Birmingham Education Society to ensure the town's poor children could receive an education, but he balked at the School Board taking over this role; after all, the issue was the use of public funds applied to voluntary schools, denominational education.

Dixon, Chamberlain and Dale fought a protracted battle, first to resist the adoption of bye-laws which would empower the School Board to pay the fees of the poor, and to compel children to attend local schools. They resisted because the children would land up in Anglican (voluntary) schools. Chamberlain, seconded by Dixon, moved unavailingly that before anything else, more school places should be found, through building schools or adopting existing school buildings. Only late in 1871 were these enabling bye-laws carried, with Chamberlain, Robert Dale and Jesse Collings taking the argument to a large Central Nonconformist League protest meeting where Chamberlain and Collings denied the Board's right to make the ratepayer pay for religious instruction. Henry Crossley, not on the School Board but a member of Chamberlain's circle, proposed a motion expressing irreconcilable hostility to the proposal of the Birmingham School Board to pay the fees of indigent children at voluntary schools.[95] Indeed, in tactics which would become all too familiar to observers of the Machine in years to come, they fired up a crowd (some 3,000) to surround the Town Hall and intimidate Birmingham Union (Anglican) supporters who were meeting inside.

Whilst the campaign on fees and compulsion was being fought out in 1871 Chamberlain was doing other more constructive work as Chairman of the Committee of Inquiries; a survey of the borough was initiated and a development plan to increase school accommodation was published. Dixon and Chamberlain worked on Forster in London to persuade him to agree to build schools for 5,000 children. Here are the origins of Birmingham's Board Schools, the first of which, Bloomsbury, opened in March 1872 to accommodate 1,000 children. Chamberlain also sought to persuade the majority on the Board to accept an offer made by Nonconformist churches in Birmingham (those, as it happened, of League members like Dale, Dawson, Crosskey and Vince) that the School Board should take over their schools, subject only to the proviso that the nature of their religious instruction was perpetuated. This the Church party would not accept.[96]

The strength of opposition to the idea of compulsion, when it involved children being forced into voluntary schools – the only available type of school until non-denominational School Board schools could be commenced – had led the dominant Church party to agree to hold off implementation until a choice of school could be brought about. In late November 1871, it went back on this commitment, so provoking a furious reaction from the League Six. Chamberlain threatened to lead the Town Council into open defiance, by refusing to honour the precept, which meant refusing to permit the rates to be used to fund places in voluntary schools – the Church party's employment of Clause 25 smacked to him of a revival of the old Church Rates controversy. Jesse Collings, on the Council but not on the School Board, was a veritable firebrand for confrontation. In the event Dixon and Dale negotiated a temporary truce after a promise that the Board would hold off paying the fees. A year later, with Sargant and his supporters refusing to renew their undertaking, the League-dominated Town Council once again refused the precept.[97]

In the absence of any movement on either side, the Board took the case to the highest legal authority in the land and briefed the Attorney General to apply to the Queen's Bench for a mandamus. The court duly ordered Birmingham's Town Council to pay; it reluctantly did, murmurings of resistance, non-payment and distraint from militants like Chamberlain notwithstanding, but in some ways this was an empty victory. The Board shied away from putting into effect its own bye-law on compulsion; and before the year was out, another set of School Board elections would overturn the Church majority.

One further controversy dogged these years when the Church party reigned. It concerned the nature of the religious education which should be provided in Board Schools. In 1872, the Anglican majority presented regulations providing for a hymn and the Lord's Prayer in morning assembly and for the Bible to be read and taught daily. Bible teaching was to be such that 'it did not tend to attach children to any particular denomination'.

Anglicans like F. S. Dale (no relation) argued that Board Schools were the only chance for working-class children to learn about Christianity. Robert Dale contended, on the other hand, that a neutral, unsectarian teaching of the Bible was impossible; indeed, that the likelihood was that the teaching could detach (my emphasis) from a particular denomination. Chamberlain agreed and he wanted the wording on the religious instruction to be qualified to specify that the teaching should not only not seek 'to attach to' but must also not 'detach from'.[98] He and Dale could envisage the difficulties teachers would have in trying to be strictly impartial when expounding on the Bible in class. And he – a Unitarian – feared that children with a Dissenting background would be actively discouraged away from their Nonconformist roots by an Anglican teacher.

The whole issue would come up when teachers were appointed. It gave rise to an unintentionally diverting episode, faithfully reported in four full broadsheet columns in the *Post* in January 1873, when Chamberlain, Dawson and Vince joined Church party members to interview candidates. One hapless candidate, a Mr Ball, was pressed by Chamberlain as to how he would teach the creed to children whilst he adhered to the Board's Regulations, which were not to seek to attach his pupils to any particular denomination. After Ball had been altogether too orthodoxly Anglican in his response, Chamberlain told both interviewee and the rest of the panel that 'it appeared to him that no Unitarian child could attend a school, and be taught by Mr Ball, without being subjected to an attempt to detach him from his religious belief'. Mr Hayman, the next to run the gauntlet, incautiously assured the interview panel he would explain only those parts of the Bible which were universally received. That did not save him from a remorseless Chamberlain, keen to know exactly what these were.

Another candidate, Mr Cooper, averred that 'he would teach the plain words of the Bible'. to be challenged by Charles Vince of the League Six to explain what precisely 'the plain meaning of the words' meant. Flailing around for an answer, Cooper said that he would look for guidance in the works of the great divines. Chamberlain, and the Catholic O'Sullivan, both pressed him – 'What great divines?' With Cooper's response, 'Why, the great divines of the Church of England', they had effectively exposed both an inexorable bias towards the Established Church's teachings and the impossible demands made by the Board's Regulations on its teachers. George Dawson asked a candidate 'whether he does not think in his judgement it would be much better if the Board had settled these things and given (precise) instructions upon them – and then questioned him?'[99]

The episode achieved national notoriety, featuring in the columns of the *Daily Telegraph*, which thought the interviews' gladiatorial nature rendered the town's Bull Ring an entirely appropriate venue for future meetings. On that paper's letters page, Chamberlain sought to draw out the significance of these interviews; that was, to show the inconsistency or insincerity of the Church party when it purported to be able to secure undenominational teaching at the public expense. Such was the uncertainty and variety of response from the candidates that he concluded: 'The most opposite and irreconcilable views of religious truth will be taught in the Board Schools at the public cost.'[100]

The whole interview saga illuminates the way that religious division bedevilled the education debate. And the three years from 1870 to 1873 when the League Six fought a long rearguard action against the ascendant Church were an important apprenticeship for the political machine which Chamberlain and his close allies were forging. We have seen in the last chapter how the experience of the National Education League helped develop campaigning skills, and the opposition years of adversity on the School Board proved equally formative. Chamberlain, Dawson, Dale, Wright and Vince (until his untimely death in 1874) became a close and loyal team. Dixon was often an equally intimate collaborator, but both geographically (Westminster-based) and temperamentally (he disapproved of some of Chamberlain and Dale's more militant behaviour) there were times when he was semi-detached.

The School Board elections of November 1873 changed the dynamic entirely. This time the Birmingham Liberal Association, with its new secretary Francis Schnadhorst, was fully prepared. Indeed, the School Board elections were part of a comprehensive strategy to take over the commanding heights of Birmingham governance, which that month also included the municipal elections. In March 1873, the Association had agreed to Chamberlain's suggestion that: 'In consequence of recent action by the Tory party in Birmingham in reference to the municipal elections (of 1872), the Liberal Association should in future take part in such elections, and that whenever a Liberal candidate is opposed by a Tory candidate, the support of the Association should be given to the Liberal.'[101] The implication for the forthcoming School Board elections was plain; the full weight of the Association would be put behind Liberal-League candidates. Henry Crosskey explained: 'It was decided that the Liberal party should if possible secure a working majority on every representative body connected to the borough.'[102] November 1873 saw a bitter mayoral contest between advocates and opponents of Joseph Chamberlain (see chapter 4). Pro-Chamberlain Liberals were widely adopted by ward committees with the Association canvassing and pamphleteering in support. A decisive Liberal victory was won on the eve of the School Board elections.

Here too the Association had meticulously planned for the contest; eight Liberal candidates had been selected well in advance, in July 1873, by the 400, the Association's ruling body, a lesson having been learnt from 1870 about the necessity of concentrating the vote. The League Six were to be joined by Jesse Collings and Elizabeth Sturge, niece of the local hero Joseph Sturge (see Introduction). Garvin recorded that: 'Drilled was each ward to give its vote to a particular portion of the whole group of Liberal candidates. With 15 votes at the disposal of each elector this, at first tackling, seemed an involved affair; solved, however, with a thoroughness looking like simplicity.'[103] In fact, Schnadhorst had decreed that each of the wards should have three candidates allotted them and electors were told to give five votes to each of the three in their wards. Voters were to resist the temptation simply to plump their votes for Chamberlain, which would have endangered the election of other candidates.[104]

The run-up to election day witnessed a fevered debate on education and political issues. Clergy fulminated, many preaching political sermons, on the Sunday (16 November) before the contest, with the vicar of St George's colourfully claiming that 'the angels in Heaven were waiting for the decision'.[105] Calm appears to have descended on the day itself; Anglican hysteria seems to have been counter-productive. In any case Schnadhorst's meticulous corralling of Liberal voters safely overturned the Church Eight and installed a new Liberal majority. It was a hugely significant victory which was reported as such in the national Press, with the *Daily Telegraph* commenting on 'the size of the poll and the concomitant enthusiasm, showing Birmingham wanted a national and consistent system of education'.[106] After all, the aberration of 1870 had been reversed; Birmingham, the home of the National Education League, at last had a Board which reflected the dominant sentiment in the town. Equally, the School Board elections augmented the hold that the Chamberlain Machine was taking on Birmingham; every aspect of its governance was being politicised and Liberalised.

Huge crowds of Liberal supporters celebrated the results outside the Parish Offices and the Liberal Association headquarters. The announcement of those results was marked by the discharge of 'brilliant rockets and other fireworks', reported the partial *Post*. Loyalists were addressed by members of the Machine, firstly John Skirrow Wright and then Robert Dale, who commended the 'energy, earnestness and enthusiasm with which they had won a great victory for the Liberal Eight', while Jesse Collings sought to provide historical context, declaring: 'This day they had shown themselves worthy successors of the men who on Newhall Hill carried the Reform Bill of 1831.'[107]

Two days later a large crowd of working men met at the back of the Town Hall in honour of the Liberal victory, and Wright addressed them, claiming that 'all men of Birmingham should rejoice at this exhibition of their political strength'. He dismissed the criticism that the School Board elections should not have become a political fight; such critics were wrong – 'People would see that it was rather a question of (ending) the domination of priests and the Conservative party.' He went on to claim that this new Liberal-controlled Board would now discuss questions concerning the education of their children (my emphasis); Mr Lakin, the Labour leader, took up the theme saying that working men and their children had been ignored by Sampson Lloyd and his Tories. In scenes echoing those of other nineteenth-century Birmingham demonstrations in support of Chartists and Parliamentary Reform, and anticipating those for Empire and tariffs prompted by Chamberlain in later years, the crowds noisily surged – though peacefully enough – round Edmund Street and Congreve Street, taking in Dale's Carr's Lane chapel, where cheers were given for its popular minister, and finally along New Street and Paradise Street.[108] Chamberlain and his team certainly understood how to generate and direct mass public enthusiasm.

Joseph Chamberlain now assumed the position of School Board chairman, a role he had selected for himself three years earlier, only then to have the cup rudely dashed from his lips. J.S. Wright, from that inner circle Chamberlain had established, was elected deputy chairman, and he proved a doughty ally. When the *Post* memorialised Wright at his death in 1880 it paid tribute – among much else – 'to his perfect and comprehensive grasp of the minutest detail connected with the working of the vast and intricate machinery of the town… his thorough familiarity with the districts'.[109] This might as easily have been written of his chairman, for a study of Chamberlain's notebooks in the University of Birmingham's Special Collections shows an equally formidable grasp of the minutiae of Birmingham's educational system. Clear, bold and legible, and with scarce a correction throughout, column after column of beautiful copperplate and colour-coded lists record, for example, the population in the town's registration sub-districts, the school accommodation and the (invariably much lower) average pupil attendance, with reasons for absence entered. Similarly, for each Board School, every head teacher, and assistant teacher is listed, their names and salary recorded; the costs of all school buildings are itemised. Furthermore, recommended books – like Nelson's *History of England*, Chambers' *National Series* (for Reading) and Davis's *Graduated Arithmetic* – were dutifully chronicled. The notebooks diligently assemble the story of School Board battles from all over England – Swindon, Luton, Glasgow among others – to illustrate the ubiquity of the threat from vested interests.[110] In sum, these notebooks illustrate why Chamberlain and his team were so successful – they put in the hard yards, they mastered the detail, and could out-argue opponents because they knew more.

It helped that many of the schools which Chamberlain recorded had been built under his aegis. Designed by Birmingham architects, Chamberlain and Martin (the former, J.H. Chamberlain, being no relation), they expressed the civic gospel of this period, 'the projection of values into space and stone', in their own modest way as much as did the Venetian or Ruskinian Gothic of the Council House, the Museum and Art Gallery and the shops and offices of Corporation Street in the town centre. In red brick and terracotta, with their high pointed windows, their turrets and lofty ceilings, they sought to bring dignity, seriousness and a sense of style to Birmingham schooling. The distinctive tower, part of the 'air-conditioning system', indicated the Board's wish for the development of 'a healthy body and mind'.[111] The Board under Chamberlain, and then Dixon, differed from its critics in the Church by wanting large buildings because impressive and cheaper per head to build, whilst Churchmen disliked the inevitable comparison and competition with their own voluntary schools.

Even if several Board Schools have been demolished, and others changed their usage, the remaining buildings reveal much about the hopes and aspirations of the nineteenth-century educational visionaries who surrounded Chamberlain and are a tangible legacy of an extraordinary period in Birmingham's history. They had sought dignity for their schools just as churches and town halls were invested with nobility. At an address to the School Board at the end of his term as chairman Chamberlain argued that the school 'buildings were the outward and visible signs of the work going on within. The fact that our schools are ornamental has not added in any appreciable degree to their cost. If they are beautiful it is because the outline is noble, because the grouping is harmonious and pleasing, and because the general appearance is graceful; but not because they have been overladen with any superimposed ornament without meaning and use.'[112]

With the same alacrity he applied to establishing these new Board schools, after three years of foot-dragging by the champions of voluntary education, Chamberlain also moved sharply to resolve the issue of religious teaching in its schools. This was an issue which divided the Liberals on the Board. Chamberlain, supported by Robert Dale and by Henry Crosskey (before his election), pushed through the policy of secular education, abolishing even the plain unadorned Bible reading resolved on by his predecessors, Sargent, F. S. Dale and the Church Eight. Time would be set aside on Tuesday and Friday mornings, during which religious instruction would be given by outside agencies. Experience would show that there were insufficient good religious studies teachers, and that some had difficulties with discipline. *The Dart* harshly characterised it as 'the most melancholy farce ever perpetrated in political annals', and even Chamberlain's right-hand man, John Skirrow Wright, the deputy chairman of the School Board, was opposed from the start in 1873, whilst remaining an entirely loyal ally of his chief.[113] When Chamberlain had stepped down, it was Wright in 1879 who successfully moved that in future the Bible be read daily in schools without note or comment.[114] Henry Crosskey perpetuated the split in the Liberal

Machine on this issue, showing 'the strongest aversion to compromise with the Church party; he only accepted under great pressure from his colleagues'.[115]

Under Chamberlain's vigorous leadership on the Board, then, the Liberal Eight had a considerable impact on education in Birmingham in terms both of expanding school places by building new schools, and of settling, albeit temporarily, the debate on religious instruction. The years of that leadership, 1873 to 1876, exactly coincided with his mayoralty, an era famous for its historic and fundamental municipal reform; in the round, it was an extraordinarily rich legacy for Birmingham. What he achieved he did so because he had the support of George Dixon, J.S. Wright, Jesse Collings, Robert Dale, Charles Vince and others. Even where they differed, those disagreements were generally conducted civilly. But when Chamberlain and Dixon swapped roles in 1876, with Chamberlain assuming the parliamentary seat, and Dixon the chairmanship of the School Board, a rift occurred which for once became all too visible.

It perhaps reflected Dixon's unease at the unseemly haste with which he had been persuaded to cede the seat; or a temperamental difference between the two men, with Dixon resentful of Chamberlain's combativeness, ruthlessness and the cast-iron conviction in his essential rightness. Equally, what occurred showed Chamberlain's occasionally heroic insensitivity. After a protracted battle fought by members of his alliance over the previous decade to liberalise the King Edward's Foundation and so break the Anglican monopoly, he was presented in 1878 with the opportunity to nominate Town Council governors to the Governing Body. Strictly adhering to the Council's own rules he chose current councillors to fill the vacancies, ignoring the claims of George Dixon who, though not a councillor, was Chairman of the Birmingham School Board.

Normally long-suffering and patient to a fault, Dixon snapped, pointing out the importance of having someone conversant with Birmingham's lower grade schools on the King Edward's governorship: 'How is that system of graded schools to be filled and properly established unless there is continuous communication of the most friendly character between this School Board and the governors of the Grammar School?' Beyond an appeal to logic, Dixon succumbed to personal antipathy.

> 'Mr Joseph Chamberlain is a remarkably clever man, but he is undertaking a great work; he is undertaking to create the public opinion of the Town Council and of Birmingham. In fact, it seems as if the terms of Mr Joseph Chamberlain and Birmingham are becoming synonymous. Mr Joseph Chamberlain is Birmingham. He represents himself in the Town Council and he represents himself in the House of Commons.'[116]

The Dart devoted one of its weekly doggerel verses to the embroglio, imagining George Dixon declaiming of a dastardly Joe Chamberlain:

'I gave him my seat,

I laid all at his feet:

With his Statue and Street

His triumph is complete

And for me I was left a poor exile...'[117]

The combined evidence of Dixon's popularity, and of some significant local opposition to his own ambition, provoked Chamberlain to fury, in which he threatened resignation of his Birmingham seat, the town being evidently unworthy of his continued representation. Within a few months in 1879 the matter was smoothed over and amicable relations were restored. What *The Dart* dubbed 'The Liberal Schism' illustrated Chamberlain's imperiousness and his thin skin. It also showed that however impressive the unity and single-mindedness of the team, occasional tensions arose and usually because the acknowledged leader was insensitive to the feelings and opinions of his team.

The Liberal Machine would dominate the School Board after Chamberlain's *démarche* in 1876 to its demise in the next century. The Machine he and his colleagues had developed continued to operate smoothly to control and manage Birmingham's Board Schools; at no stage did the opposition challenge its domination. For 22 years George Dixon was its Chairman. With J.S. Wright he compromised on the vexed business of religious teaching in the Board Schools; in return for avoiding acrimonious elections, agreement was reached with the Church party to restore plain Bible reading (in 1879). Later in 1885 a similar arrangement was negotiated and Dixon conceded a daily reading of the Lord's Prayer, and allowed explanations of the Bible reading when confined to matters of grammatical, historical and geographical understanding in reaching out to Anglican opponents.[118] He also supported the ideas of his invaluable ally, Henry Crosskey, who devised a programme of education in morals, lessons in Birmingham Board Schools to be twice weekly, covering obedience to parents, honesty, truthfulness, industry, temperance, courage, frugality, thrift and keeping one's temper. Crosskey was a star witness of Cardinal Manning's Royal Commission on the teaching of morality apart from religion. Birmingham was in this a national leader, as well as being more than 120 years ahead of its time in anticipating the recent emphasis on PSHE (Personal, Health and Social Education) in twenty-first-century schools.

In other ways, too, the Birmingham School Board under Liberal auspices was groundbreaking. Crosskey was visionary in proselytising Science teaching in elementary schools, and equally far-seeing in championing the central importance of practical experiments.

Thanks to him a system was devised whereby Birmingham Board Schools shared a central laboratory and an expert demonstrator. Crosskey's School Management Committee (of which he was from 1881 the Chairman) also initiated a salary scheme in which pay rises were linked to classroom performance, not to an inexorable incremental pay scale.[119] This too was a forerunner of developments more than a century later.

Dixon made the provision of properly trained teachers a priority. He was determined to end the mid-Victorian reliance in schools on unqualified pupil-teachers. In this he too was in the vanguard of educational policy. He was also innovative in that he pioneered the idea of taking able senior (Seventh Grade) pupils from right across Birmingham 'to give the boys a more complete and effective instruction than they are able to receive when scattered in twos and threes over the Board Schools.' Dixon offered the site at Bridge Street himself rent-free, it being surplus to the requirements of his business (Rabone Bros.), and the burden on the rates was small. A school was opened which drew Government ministers from London to Birmingham to observe, for its significance was that here was an, albeit experimental and local, attempt to kick-start the public provision of secondary schooling, an initiative only to be formalised in 1902 with Balfour's Education Act. In a rich irony, that Act, which did so much to establish secondary education, also stipulated the destruction of the School Boards for which Birmingham's Nonconformists had fought so hard thirty years before, their local Board being acknowledged nationally as a model of good practice.[120] Dixon, Crosskey and Wright would not live to see that awful day although Chamberlain, so much the personification of the idea of School Boards in the 1870s, found himself an embarrassed member of the Unionist Government which planned the destruction, both of the Birmingham School Board in which he and his allies had invested so much emotion, time and effort, and the rest of the country's Boards as well.

Robert Dale

Robert Dale was one of Chamberlain's closest allies. In his own right he was a most important figure, in Birmingham and beyond, and that significance was not just confined to the education campaigning examined in chapters 2 and 3, but resulted as much from his reputation as being the foremost Nonconformist preacher of his age, and from his articulate championing of the civic gospel, for he was the inspiration and spokesman for the Birmingham revolution outlined in chapter 4.

Born in London in 1829, and then teaching in Andover, he there underwent a spiritual crisis, after which he became a Congregationalist and a preacher in 1845. He went on to attend Spring Hill College in Birmingham from 1847 to 1853 where he made a name for himself as an outstanding scholar, achieving first-class honours in a University of London Bachelor of Arts degree and winning a gold medal in philosophy. He rapidly became first assistant preacher and then minister at Carr's Lane Church in Birmingham, remaining there for thirty-six years until his death. Carr's Lane was renowned during his lifetime for the vigour of its ministry and because it influenced and shaped a number of Birmingham's leaders. They were attracted both by Dale's message and by the energy with which he propagated it. For he was one of the great English orators of the nineteenth century. His son, A. W. W. Dale, wrote in the biography of Robert Dale: 'His manliness and his eloquence materially strengthened his influence. He was literally a power on the platform; his voice could reach to the farthest limits of the largest audience.' Of Dale's arrival on one occasion on the stage at the Town Hall, he went on to write: 'The vigour with which he pulled off his overcoat as he rose to speak was a sure sign of what was coming. His one aim was to instruct and convince. When the meeting was tempestuous, he ploughed along through the storm with the steady rush of an Atlantic liner as it shoulders its way through the blustering seas.' In a professional sense, he used these powers of oratory in exposition of his evangelical theology in the pulpit at Carr's Lane. Yet, many of his great speeches were made in support of social, political and educational reform movements of which he was in many cases an integral part. No other Victorian clergyman was quite as involved in the cut and thrust of political campaigns.

The first cause which engaged him was that of national education, and he became an early driving force in George Dixon's Birmingham Education Society. Thereafter he was prominent in the foundation of the National Education League, advocating a national system which would be compulsory, free, and liberated from the influence of the Established Church. His passionate opposition to Forster's Act of 1870 expressed itself in his foundation (with Henry Crosskey) of the Central Nonconformist Committee in 1870, a national organisation set up to defend Nonconformist churches against what they thought to be a determinedly rapacious Church.

Joseph Chamberlain in later life, pencil sketch
by W Strang, 1903.

William Harris, key organiser in the early years of the
Birmingham Liberal Association, and one of Joseph
Chamberlain's early inspirations and allies, 1889.

Detail of Birmingham seats

West Midlands Constituency Map 1885-1914.
The enlarged detail shows the 7 Birmingham constituencies (after Pelling 1967).

MP George Dixon led the campaign for education reform in Birmingham and then at national level. He admired Joseph Chamberlain, but their relationship was sometimes strained.

Jesse Collings was a close friend as well as life-long political ally of Joseph Chamberlain. He became Mayor of Birmingham in 1878.

JH Chamberlain, Birmingham architect, leads a band including Joseph Chamberlain (second left) and Francis Schnadhorst (third left) bearing bags of money paid by city ratepayers for expensive council schemes, 1879.

George Dawson. His congregation at the Church of the Saviour in Edward St. (now demolished but, see photo below) included many of Chamberlain's allies who were deeply inspired by his preaching of the Civic Gospel.

Robert Dale was also renowned as one of the foremost orators of the age, and was minister at Carr's Lane Chapel for nearly 40 years.

THE REV. R. W. DALE, D.D., LL.D., IN UNION CHAPEL, ISLINGTON.

Clockwise from top right: Robert Dale, Charles Vince and Henry Crosskey. Three Birmingham Nonconformist ministers who each played a vital role in the campaign for education reform.

John Skirrow Wright. Liberal stalwart on the School Board, NLF member,
who parted with Joseph Chamberlain over bible teaching in schools.

Icknield Street Board School. Many members of the Machine learned their political
organisational skills serving on local education boards which controlled schools like this.

Teachers Names

Head Master — Edwin T Hart
Second Master (Class I) — Thomas Blaze
Assist do (Class II) — Joseph Cox
do do (do III) — J. C. Horobin
do do (do II) — John Shipton
Pupil Teacher (4 yr) — Thomas Dean
do do (2 yr) — Christopher Lucas
do do (Candidate) — Walter Hiatt

Head Mistress — Sarah Baldwin
Assist do (Class II) — Mary Ann Lowe
Pupil Teacher (Candidate) — Ellen Wilcox
do do (6 yr) — Adelaide M Harding
do do (5 yr) — Harriet M Wilson
do do (do) — Maria Walsh

Head Mistress (Infant) — Mary Jane Waldron
Assistant Mistresses (Class II) — Harriet Lines
Emma Wood
Pupil Teachers (Candidate) — Lavinia Wilcox
Sarah Ann Woolley
(Candidate) Hannah Anston
Isabella Hill

The success of Joseph Chamberlain's Machine was in large part due to his meticulous organisation and attention to detail, as illustrated by his notebooks, these pages relating to Board Schools.

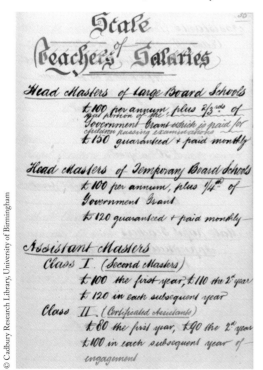

Scale of Teachers' Salaries

Head Masters of Large Board Schools
£100 per annum, plus 2/3rds of that portion of the Government Grant which is paid for children passing examinations
£150 guaranteed + paid monthly

Head Masters of Temporary Board Schools
£100 per annum, plus 1/4th of Government Grant
£120 guaranteed + paid monthly

Assistant Masters

Class I (Second Masters)
£100 the first year, £110 the 2nd year
£120 in each subsequent year

Class II (Certificated Assistants)
£80 the first year, £90 the 2nd year
£100 in each subsequent year of engagement

List of Books used in Board Schools

Reading Books (Boys)
1st Standard — Chambers National Series
2nd do — do
3rd do — Nelsons Royal Readers
4th }
5th } "The alternative series of Nelsons Readers known as the 'Junior Reader' part I, the 'Junior Reader' part II and the 'Senior Reader' and 'Technical Reader'" (extract from Clerk's Report)

Reading Books (Girls)
1st, 2nd, 3rd, 4th & 5th Standard — Nelsons Royal Readers
(same as Boys)

Reading Books (Infants)
Standard I Royal Readers
Royal Primers

Arithmetic (Boys)
Davis' Graduated Arithmetic up to part 4
Davis Arithmetic Part 1.

Not everyone was convinced that Chamberlain's improvement schemes to bring services to the city represented value for money, 1882.

Equally, he was a powerful advocate of disestablishment of the Anglican Church, joining the Liberation Society. Above all, it was the National Education League which gave him the outlet for this detestation, and he was one of its most belligerent leaders as well as being one of the four men tasked with travelling out from Birmingham to address newly-founded branches in the early months of the League's inception.

He was just as combative in the provincial theatre of the Birmingham School Board. Here he and Chamberlain fought the Church Eight majority on the Board between 1870 and 1873, doing all they could to frustrate its plans for Bible reading in the curriculum, and for the passage of bye-laws to facilitate the payment of fees out of the rates for poor children, enabling them to attend voluntary schools. Once the School Board elections were successfully negotiated in 1873 and the Liberals had won he became a formidable bulwark in support of the new Chairman, Joseph Chamberlain. He was a leading advocate of secular education, taking great pride in implementing this, with Chamberlain, in Birmingham's Board Schools after 1873. Equally, he was a strong opponent of the policy pushed through by Chamberlain's successor as Chairman, George Dixon, and his deputy, J.S. Wright, which was to re-introduce the Bible reading, and in the process offer an olive branch to their Anglican opponents. Dale was less generous-minded.

The closeness between Dale and Chamberlain was reinforced by their mutual faith in municipal government's capacity to alleviate the lot of the poorest classes and more than that, to elevate the entire city environment in terms of health and sanitation, as well as culturally and educatively. Robert Dale succeeded George Dawson as the most famous, and most coherent, expositor of the civic gospel. Dawson had identified the absence of the brightest and the best from municipal leadership, perceiving the generation of councillors before 1870 to be second-rate and unimaginative. Dale amplified the message. He sought to get compassionate, talented people into the Council, who had business sense and who had the confidence to be decisive. These men, he preached, 'ought to give their time as well as their money to whatever improvements are intended to develop the intelligence of the community, to reform local abuses, and to see to it that the towns and parishes are well drained, well lighted and well paved. They must not shrink from the roughness of local elections.' He was able to elevate municipal involvement into a noble vision. It was largely thanks to Dale and Dawson that Nonconformists, not just from Carr's Lane, but from the Church of the Saviour (Dawson's church) and the Church of the Messiah (Crosskey's ministry), stepped up to take responsibility as Dale had envisaged. So, Chamberlain, the Martineaus, the Kenricks, Collings, Harris, C.E. Mathews heeded the call and came to live a life which was more than simply focused on personal enrichment, but was more about public duty and the wider community.

Where the events surrounding Home Rule in 1886 divided friends and allies in the Birmingham Machine, so torn were they over conflicting loyalties to Gladstone and

Chamberlain, Dale never wavered. When Chamberlain fought for his political life on 21 April 1886 before the ruling Liberal committee of the 2000, Dale was prominent in his corner. And when, after an electric speech from Chamberlain, supporters of Gladstone led by Francis Schnadhorst tried to recover lost ground, it was Dr Dale with his own charismatic contribution who sought speedily to capitalise on the momentum achieved by Home Rule critics by insisting on a successful vote of support for Chamberlain's policy of opposition to the details of Gladstone's Bill. In all probability, that prompt action ensured both the survival of a Birmingham base for Chamberlain and of a national Unionist opposition to Gladstone in the coming years.

As a member of Chamberlain's inner circle, he was the most staunch and faithful of associates. If after 1886 he became less involved in politics it was not because any distance had grown between Chamberlain and himself, but rather that with a nice sense of circularity his interest in Spring Hill College - whence he had launched himself on Birmingham forty years earlier – revived, and in his last years he became chairman of its Council, negotiating its transfer to Oxford where it became Mansfield College.

John Skirrow Wright

Like Robert Dale and Joseph Chamberlain, John Skirrow Wright hailed originally from London, where he was born in 1822. Moving in 1824 with his family to Stourbridge, where his father managed the Birmingham, Stourbridge and Wolverhampton Canal company, thenceforward Wright was to spend his life in the Midlands. He worked his way up from the position of junior clerk to partnership and then sole proprietorship, of a company specialising in military buttons. He would become known as a leading figure in Birmingham's commercial life, being a member of the town's local industries committee, contributing to the same Samuel Timmins publication on the industrial history of Birmingham as that for which Joseph Chamberlain wrote a chapter. He later became president of the Birmingham Chamber of Commerce, organising a selection of Birmingham's products at the Paris Exhibition of 1867, representing it at the opening of the Suez Canal in 1869 and giving evidence on the need for science and technology education to the Commons select committee on scientific instruction the previous year.

While he was establishing himself in business he was also founding a small Baptist congregation, the People's Chapel, in Hockley, to the north of the town centre in 1848. As with Joseph Chamberlain, George Cadbury and Jesse Collings among others, his work with the Sunday school, where he organised evening classes for up to 150 young people, piqued a wider interest in the education of the working classes. He was an early member of the Birmingham Education Society, and rapidly became one of that inner circle of activists around Dixon and Chamberlain, which explains his appointment to the Executive Committee of the National Education League in 1869 at its outset. He was also one of the Liberal Six minority on the Birmingham School Board; he became its vice-chairman in 1873, being a loyal lieutenant to the charismatic chairman, Joseph Chamberlain. Additionally, he became chairman of the Board's General Purposes Committee. One letter in the Birmingham Daily Post *in 1880 when he died, commented on 'his perfect and comprehensive grasp of the minutest details connected with the making of the vast and intricate educational machinery of the town'. Another noted that 'his unfailing urbanity was not in the slightest degree affected during the whole time of his constant dealings with the Board,' of which for long (when Dixon was absent) he was effectively its chairman from 1876. That urbanity was tested by the strain of his holding a strong belief in Bible reading in the Board Schools, even when Chamberlain and Dale were vociferously opposed to it. One further educational issue preoccupied him for many years. He was one of the earliest Liberal critics to make reform of the governance of King Edward's School Birmingham a priority; he railed against the closed shop which Anglicans applied to the governance, the distribution of endowment funds, and the admission process. He took some wry satisfaction in helping force the Foundation to open itself to radical reform in the mid-1870s.*

His political activity went well beyond his involvement in education reform and administration. Witnessing the Chartist riots in Birmingham in 1839 made an indelible impression on the young man, and he became committed to peaceful change to release a potentially revolutionary build-up of pressure among the working classes, excluded from participation in the governing process. In 1848 he supported a petition for household suffrage, vote by ballot and the abolition of the property qualification, demands uncannily like those of the Chartists. He was in the welcoming party for Kossuth, the Hungarian revolutionary, who came to Birmingham in 1850. With William Harris, he helped organise the meeting of working men at which John Bright was nominated for the vacant parliamentary seat. Subsequently he became honorary secretary of the Reformers Union, the body dedicated to parliamentary reform, which was the antecedent of the Birmingham Liberal Association, of which he was elected President in 1863. He would follow Chamberlain's lead to become the first treasurer of the National Liberal Federation in 1877, establishing a name for himself, which explains his selection to contest the Nottingham seat in the General Election of 1880. His involvement with the Liberal caucus meant that he was a marked man and 'his candidature (wrote the Birmingham Post*) was met with unscrupulousness and the bitterest calumny'. The emotional strain he suffered – though he won the seat - may explain his shockingly sudden death a few days later, when he succumbed to an apoplectic attack in no.3 committee room of the Birmingham Council House on 15 April.*

The historian E.P. Hennock describes his influence on local Liberal affairs: 'In time he became something of a local boss in the poor district of north Birmingham in which his works and his church was situated.' He was therefore a part of that coup (inspired by Harris, Chamberlain, Collings and others) by which the incompetent old guard on the Town Council was, around 1870, replaced by more active, committed reforming Liberals like James Whateley, a pearl button worker, and William Cook, a pin manufacturer, who were elected to the Council to represent Hampton Ward, home of Wright's People's Chapel. They would play their part in the Chamberlain mayoral revolution from 1873. Equally, whilst never on the Council himself, he used his influence on neighbouring St George's ward to ensure the election of his son, Frank, in 1874. Hennock concludes: 'In the perspective of the municipal reform movement, Wright's place was without parallel.'

If he wasn't a councillor, that was one of the few local roles he did not fill with distinction. His sheer energy and dutiful involvement in a clutch of Birmingham institutions, as well as his philanthropy, is remarkable. He was variously a JP, vice-chairman of the Birmingham School of Design, chairman of the Prison Visiting Service, a Director of Lloyds Bank, a committee member of the Midlands Debating Society and the most active member of the finance committee of the National Agricultural Labourers' Union from its foundation in 1872. He made generous donations to the new Birmingham Art Gallery, to Aston Park and to scholarship funds. He epitomises both the voluntaryism and idealism of his class and his religion in the Victorian era.

Even allowing for the euphoria which inevitably permeates obituaries of the famous, the encomiums on the passing of John Skirrow Wright were strikingly generous. The Birmingham Daily Post *of 16 April 1880 wrote that he was '... in the truest sense a citizen of the town animated by its progressive spirit. No public work of any real value, of any real utility, was carried on without having at some time the benefit of his sympathy.' He was 'an educational reformer, municipal reformer, champion of popular rights, a teetotaller and a Liberal on principle'. Quite as importantly he was a vital, dedicated and utterly reliable human ingredient in the Chamberlain Machine for that first, very constructive, decade of its existence.*

CHAPTER THREE

Rev Charles Vince

The length of these biographical notes on Charles Vince reflect the comparative brevity of his contribution to Chamberlain's Liberal alliance in Birmingham. Born in Farnham, Surrey, in 1823, he became a Baptist and trained at Stepney College. In 1852, he was inducted as the minister of Mount Zion Baptist Chapel in Graham Street being, like Henry Crosskey, Robert Dale and George Dawson, a politically active Nonconformist pastor using his pulpit to further Birmingham's municipal and educational revolution.

He first came to public notice as sympathetic to the Dawson/Dale school of thinking when he made a widely reported speech at the mayor's luncheon in 1866. Robert Dale's son wrote: 'Mr Vince, a man of genial humour, who always fought smiling, reminded the meeting that the sailor's whole life was bounded by his ship. The ship was his home, and at the same time his prison, from week to week, from month to month. It was his Free Library and his Art Gallery. And if, Mr Mayor,' he continued, 'he wants to spend an hour in the parlour of the Woodman, the ship must be his Woodman too.' The Mayor of the day was generally understood to be one of the most frequent supporters of the tavern in question, and the sally was received with tumultuous laughter. Then suddenly the laughter stopped; the audience saw the reproof veiled in the jest, and with one impulse they began to applaud, steadily for several minutes. The significance of the demonstration was clear – the town had set up a new standard of dignity for its public men.'

Perhaps Dale over-dramatises but Vince undoubtedly expressed here an abrupt change in attitude to the town's councillors, which chimed with Dawson and Dale's aspiration for a new, business-like and idealistic class of municipal leaders.

Vince was an active Liberal as far as his vocation allowed. Being a minister he could not sit on the Town Council, but he could be nominated onto its committees and he was a member of the Free Libraries Committee, which did such good work to take culture and knowledge to the Birmingham working classes. He was a Poor Law Guardian until 1870, and spoke in 1873 to endorse Samuel Plimsoll's campaign against unseaworthy shipping. He could do much, also, to assist Liberal candidates in elections. In 1868 he took the platform to speak up for George Dixon in the hotly contested parliamentary fight that year and later, in 1872, he spoke publicly in support of Joseph Chamberlain in the municipal election campaign. The Birmingham Daily Post, *in its obituary of 22 October 1874 wrote: 'In politics he was a thorough Liberal and he never faltered. He was a great political speaker…' This was unsurprising for, as the* Post *continued, 'he was well known as an elegant, persuasive and most earnest preacher, in request throughout the country'.*

His importance to the Liberal organisation was greatest in the sphere of education. George Dixon identified him as a likely ally when he invited Birmingham's great and good to an initial meeting about forming a Birmingham Education Society in 1867. Charles Vince sat on the new organisation's committee, and similarly he became a founding executive committee member of the National Education League in 1869. He was one of the Liberal Six who survived the blow of the first School Board elections in November 1870 and thereafter, as the Post *expressed it, was involved in 'tenacious fights against the Church Party.' Those fights were in part personal; Vince took grave exception to an article by the School Board chairman, W. L. Sargent of the Church party, who had written a scathing assault on Dissenting ministers. Vince's hostility was fuelled by a strong belief in the Disestablishment of the Church. He was re-elected to the School Board in 1873 when the Liberals exacted their revenge for the humiliations of 1870. Thereafter he was a staunch adherent of Chamberlain's party line on secular education.*

His early death in 1874 shocked his Liberal associates. Bunce's Birmingham Post, *and Robert Dale in a separate tribute, lavished praise on him; they were but two contributions in a plethora of memorial sermons and obituaries. His funeral was a great public display. It may be that the unexpectedness of his loss led some accounts to be too emotionally highly coloured, but he was a formidable and highly respected figure who had achieved much but had a great deal more yet to give to Chamberlain's Liberal revolution.*

THE MUNICIPAL REVOLUTION

Chamberlain Square, Council House, the Municipal Art Gallery and Corporation Street today still vividly evoke the confidence and ambition of Birmingham's civic revolution, which made of it 'the best governed city in the world'.[121] The architecture also celebrates the mayoralty of Joseph Chamberlain, who re-defined that role in a way that resonated right round the country. By force of a dynamic personality he elevated municipal office, providing, with others, a new vision of the function and nature of the Corporation; in Asa Briggs's words: 'What Chamberlain and his associates had done in the 1870s was to light the fires of zeal in local government and to infuse collective vigour into municipal affairs.'[122] At the outset, it is important to clarify this. Birmingham was not the first city to take municipal control of utilities – Manchester and Glasgow among others had stolen a march earlier in the nineteenth century. What distinguished Birmingham was the coherence, and loftiness, of the philosophy which underpinned its transformation. And it was a 'revolution' also in the way that Chamberlain and his supporters brought a business-like attitude to executing new policy; it was a sharp, and transformatory, contrast to the more easy-going pace and diffused focus of their predecessors a generation earlier.

Chamberlain's mayoralty happily coincided with an extension of State powers – the Public Health Acts of 1872 and 1875, the Artisans Dwelling Act (1875) and the creation of the Local Government Board – which supplied him with the levers by which to introduce change. His term of office was innovatory in several ways. No mayor of Birmingham before had articulated the nobility of municipal action as he did: 'Local government will bring you into contact with the masses. By its means you will be able to increase their comforts, to secure their health ... to carry out a vast co-operative system of mutual aid and support, to lessen the inequalities of our social system,' he later said.[123] Nor had anyone before conjured such a vision of the Council's scope: 'I distinctly hold that all monopolies which are sustained in any way by the State should be in the hands of the people... and I am inclined to increase the duties and responsibilities of the local authority... and to constitute these local authorities as real local Parliaments.'[124]

Even his assumption of office was novel. Where traditionally gentlemen's agreements ensured a negotiated appointment, in Chamberlain's case in 1873 there was a bitter electoral contest, a fierce skirmish in a larger campaign fought by highly politicised Liberals in Birmingham. 'The Liberals have determined to run me as mayor; the result is that every ward in the town is to be contested. The air never was hotter,' he observed to his friend Morley.[125] He was already a councillor (since 1869) and his hands were full as the recently appointed Chairman of the School Board, as the executive chairman of the National Education League, as a member of the Council's Sewage committee and as an entrepreneur busy negotiating the sale of his screw company. Yet he agreed to stand for the mayoralty to stop a time-server, one of the Birmingham old guard, William Brinsley, from acceding to the position. Never before had an election of a mayor been a matter for debate and division in the wards. For many Liberals, this contest represented a watershed, inaugurating a new reformative regime after decades of drift and defensiveness in the smoke-filled committee rooms of local government.

Once in power he initiated a transformation, acting more as a Prime Minister than as chairman of a provincial board. Garvin, his biographer, asserted that 'into two and a half years he crowded more cleansing and reconstructive measures than before him had been seen in a lifetime'; here he emphasises the energy and relentless pace Chamberlain brought to the office, and to that he adds a touch of reckless daring by employing a phrase from Chamberlain himself which distilled his essence in these years, 'sagacious audacity'.[126] Many of the qualities he brought to the role were those which made him a successful businessman. He prepared his case thoroughly, he did his research, he knew what he wanted, and he worked out the best strategy to achieve it. Once he had prepared, alliances were forged, and speedy, often courageous, decisions were made. His mastery of detail, and his imaginative exploitation of the possibilities will be seen later, in his leadership with regard to the municipalisation of Gas and Water, and in the development of an Improvement scheme.

He was, according to Garvin, 'the pattern for a chairman in his art of getting the day's work done on its day, avoiding inconclusive adjournments, procrastination and arrears'.[127] Equally, he supervised the various committees of the Council tirelessly; he was 'the chief coordinating influence on the Council's work and its mediator and referee', for he attended all committee meetings. By the time he finished there were sixteen committees, three of which he had himself created. In fact, with regard to the new Gas committee, so confident was he that his expertise would be needed to guide the municipal project to a successful outcome, he had himself elected its first Chairman. By such close supervision, diligence and attendance, he alone was privy to the overall picture of the Council's scope and reach.[128]

The brilliant light shone by Chamberlain's mayoral regime has only served to cast his predecessors in still deeper shadow in most accounts of Birmingham's Victorian history. As early as 1885 an official, Liberal orthodoxy had emerged – in J.T. Bunce's *History of the Corporation of Birmingham* (published in 1885). It is an important and valuable work but its very existence reflects the town's new-found pride and sense of its own significance, for Chamberlain and his associates had commissioned it. Bunce writes of Joseph Allday, leader of the Council in the middle of the century:

> His course of proceeding excited a strong feeling of hostility, personal, political and municipal. He was violent in speech, prone to make personal charges and to engage in personal attack and his ideas of local government were embodied in the one desire to keep down the rates. The Council in this period had frequent discussions of a disorderly character, (involving) reckless imputations, unwise and even impossible projects of financial reform.[129]

Henry Crosskey in his *Memoranda* fleshes out this characterisation:

> The struggle to obtain the triumph of Liberal policy over the conservatism, timidity and prejudice of the rulers of Birmingham under the old regime – men accustomed to meet and arrange the affairs of the town at a well-known public house (the Woodman) – was fierce and laborious.[130]

The old regime was concerned with economy, with lowering rates, and lacked the necessary drive and imagination to invest in solutions to the perplexing problems of sanitation and clean water that Birmingham faced. Still, Liberal narrators in the nineteenth century were more polemicists than historians when they drew a Manichean distinction between pre- and post-Chamberlain eras. In truth, momentum for change was already building up before his mayoralty. Thomas Avery (chairman of the Finance committee in 1867) before Chamberlain was in many ways typical of the parsimonious economists of his generation, and a Conservative to boot. So, he remained suspicious of Council-funded street-widening and amenities, like public baths. But in the face of hard facts, these being the legal actions taken against the Council in 1870 over Birmingham's utterly inadequate measures for sewage disposal, he became an advocate of radical reform.

The opposition he then led against a complacent Birmingham establishment prepared the way for Chamberlain and his associates. Thomas Avery started to improve drainage, widen streets and open libraries, and his creation of a Sewage committee in 1871 involved Chamberlain (temporarily), Collings, Harris and other Chamberlainites in their first municipal crusade, initially so to organise sewage disposal that it would satisfy the law courts. Beyond that – as they learnt more – they would move on to target the Council's Public Works committee, which was responsible for drainage, paving and street-widening, and was run on unimaginative lines. In other words, before Chamberlain ever became Mayor of Birmingham, he and his allies were gauging the extent of the problems regarding utilities in the town, as well as formulating some solutions.

Those early historians of Birmingham's civic efflorescence tend to personalise it, celebrating Chamberlain at the expense of others. But Briggs is surely right to say that what was achieved was 'the work not just of one man but of whole groups of men'.[131] And even in the four years on the Council before he became mayor there is evidence of a seventeen-strong group who consistently (more than 85% of the time) voted with Chamberlain and for his policies.[132] These men were invariably Liberals for, as we have seen in the School Board elections of 1873, Birmingham had become highly politicised through the education battle in 1870, which resulted in a surprise victory for the Church/Conservative party. Chamberlain had issued a call to arms in early 1873 announcing that Liberals must cooperate to secure wherever possible a working majority in every representative body connected to the borough.[133] In the November 1873 election, coinciding with the School Board elections (examined in chapter 3), he was indebted to a team of strong Chamberlain-supporting candidates who fought in the wards and secured a sizeable Liberal majority on the Council; men such as Jesse Collings, George Baker, William Kenrick, Robert Martineau, James Deykin, William Shammon, Richard Chamberlain and William White, the latter winning an especially significant victory for Nonconformist Liberals when he beat the local licensed victuallers champion. They would be stalwarts on the Council and they – along with other Liberals who would join after 1873 – became essential lieutenants to Chamberlain. They formed a tight group of twenty-two Chamberlain allies after 1873, voting almost invariably with their leader, and providing invaluable backing for the municipal revolution now set in train.[134]

We find them on key committees but, like Chamberlain, many were also involved in other branches of the Machine's work. Jesse Collings was a central figure in the National Education League, and would later be a prominent Liberal Unionist following Chamberlain in his break from Gladstone. George Baker (see end of this chapter), already knowledgeable about sanitation from long service on the Council, joined the new Gas and Water committees in 1875, also chairing the important Works sub-committee; beyond that he was a member of the Birmingham Education Society, stood for the School Board, and was a leading light in the fight to open up the governance of the King Edward's Grammar School.[135] We first saw Robert Martineau (also see end of this chapter) at the inception of the National Education League in 1869, and he was to be involved in the Midland Institute and in the promotion of science teaching all his life, but he too found the time to join the Council, to chair the Health committee and the Interception of Sewage sub-committee, and so be at the heart of the core issues of the Chamberlain revolution – water, sanitation and public health.[136] Of first importance was William Harris, whom we met (chapter 1) refining the Birmingham Liberal Association and devising the Caucus's electoral methods in 1868, while also being intimately involved in the shaping and launch of the National Education League. He was elected to the Town Council in 1871, serving until the major work of utility reform was being brought to fruition in 1875. His campaigning experience was invaluable.

Chamberlain's brother-in-law, William Kenrick (further information at the end of this chapter), was just as catholic in his interests, as we saw in the Introduction. Apart from his work for the Birmingham School of Art, as a governor of King Edward's School, and as Chairman of the General committee of Chamberlain's brainchild – the National Liberal Federation – his great municipal work during the Chamberlain era was as a Chairman of the Watch committee from 1874, as a member of the Mayor's new Improvement committee in 1875, and subsequently as Mayor of Birmingham in his turn. In that capacity, he continued the civic revolution. His loyalty never wavered; like Collings he became a Liberal Unionist MP (for Birmingham North), backing Joseph Chamberlain's unique radical brand of Unionism.[137] Another lifelong loyalist and Liberal Unionist was William White, a Quaker and prominent Severn Street teacher, who would be Chamberlain's right-hand man on the slum clearance and rebuilding scheme inaugurated in 1875, chairing the Improvement committee and rivalling his accomplished leader in oratorical colour, before going on to chair the Council's Public Works, Parks and Baths committees.[138] In a noted speech to the Council in October 1875 he awakened members to the deprivation in the centre of Birmingham, as we will see later in the chapter, when he prepared them for the bold plan of clearance and renovation he and Chamberlain had drafted. The point is that in this, a bold and controversial scheme, it was the visible and articulate support of men such as White that helped him carry both the Council and the policy.

Others who joined the Council after 1873 were also to be valuable allies. C.E. Mathews, was a valued associate at the formation of the National Education League, becoming its Parliamentary committee chairman. He was to be an active campaigner for the reform of the King Edward's School governing body, going on to represent the Council there. Yet he still found time to join the Birmingham Town Council in 1875, whence he rapidly became a trusted member of the Water and Estates committees. Like Collings, White and Kenrick, his allegiance to Chamberlain and his brand of Liberalism survived the Home Rule hiatus of 1886, after which he chaired Edgbaston's Liberal Unionist Association.[139]

Equally important was Samuel Edwards, who joined the Council in 1874. He, like many of his contemporaries, was a man of varied and seemingly inexhaustible interests, running Birmingham's most successful house and property agency, being a senior deacon and superintendant of Ebenezer Congregational Chapel, sitting on the Free Libraries committee, helping establish the Police Institute, and joining the School Board in 1888. He found time to be deeply involved in the many affairs of the Council. He sat on the Improvement committee, chaired the Tame and Rea Drainage board, later led the Water committee and for nine years was chairman of the Public Works committee. His tenure was marked by the town's tramway construction, and by the creation of John Bright Street, which opened a direct road from the western suburbs into the heart of the town, and in so doing swept away several narrow streets and close courts.

At the centre of much that was achieved in Chamberlain's municipal revolution was James Deykin. Scion of a successful button and electroplating family who later – unsuccessfully – diversified into property development, Deykin arrived on the Council in 1869 representing first St Peter's ward where his factory (Venetian works) was located. He was a Liberal who, from the start of his councillorship, had a passion for the improvement of the town. This is reflected in his outstanding work on the Watch, Improvement and Water committees, which between them encompassed Birmingham law and order, slum clearance and urban renewal, and the provision of clean water for all. He became chairman of the first two committees; such was his commitment to the town's improvement that he provided a personal guarantee of £5,000 to help fund the purchase of condemned houses in Birmingham's centre. He was also one of three councillors who negotiated with the waterworks company in the municipal take-over masterminded by Chamberlain, and he was the sole councillor on the local drainage board. He was signally loyal in his support for all that the Chamberlain clique assayed in the municipal revolution, so much so that *The Dart* described him as 'the chief whip of the Chamberlain party'.[140]

Because they were active Liberals the strategic positions of such allies on the crucial committees which inaugurated the civic revolution ensured for Chamberlain a swift and loyal execution of his plans. He took a close interest in his team and he evidently had powers of patronage in determining the choice of candidates standing for Council. So, he recognised the threat posed by an independent working-class movement to Liberal control in Birmingham, and in 1875 made its leading light, W.J. Davis an offer: 'If you want to be on the School Board or on the Town Council, come to me.'[141] Again, in 1875 he can be found encouraging a local physician to stand, while his lieutenant Schnadhorst was trying to persuade a wholesale confectioner to contest another ward.[142] Everywhere he thought it his duty to enthuse and sustain his followers, writing to Collings in 1876 that: 'I have attended another ward meeting at St Mary's and have two more in hand. I take the opportunity for a preachment of the duties and work of the Council.'[143]

Many of his party had cut their teeth in the Edgbaston Debating Society and had attended one of the Nonconformist chapels or meeting houses. Almost invariably they shared with each other and with Joseph Chamberlain a passion for education reform, teaching at Sunday schools or campaigning for the National Education League, serving on the School Board, or involvement in restructuring the Anglican monopoly of the King Edward's Foundation. Like Chamberlain they came to recognise that the Town Council provided the vehicle by which social reform could best be channelled to the poor, the ill-housed, the unhealthy in Birmingham. And like him they were sustained by a philosophy articulated by three prominent Liberal sympathisers who could not, as ministers, sit on the Council, namely George Dawson, Henry Crosskey and Robert Dale; they provided Liberal activists with the justification and the noble idealism to underpin their municipal mission.

They may have been barred from standing themselves, but they were all effective Liberal campaigners in the municipal battles of the early 1870s and, as such, important components in the electoral machine which operated the levers of power in Birmingham. For example, the biographers of Henry Crosskey observed that:

> November after November in the municipal contests – indeed all the year through – wherever there was a chance of preaching the municipal gospel, he pleaded with pathetic earnestness and with passion for the new policy. When the contests were on he went to two or three meetings night after night in the obscurest parts of the town and appealed for the 'right' man. His intensity was astonishing. He spoke as if the whole fate of the town depended on the result of the ward elections. Dr Crosskey's speeches did (his working-class audience) good, just as if they were to look up from their narrow courts and see the constellations moving slowly over their little patch of sky.[144]

Here we see Crosskey exemplifying the highly organised Liberal campaigning inherited from William Harris and now perfected by a new electoral Svengali, Francis Schnadhorst, who was busy refining the techniques of canvassing, pamphleteering and soap box politics which would consolidate the party's dominance for years to come in Birmingham. The importance of these ministers to the municipal revolution went beyond involvement in the campaign, for in the case of Dawson and Dale, their sermons and speeches exalted civic service and set out to attract to the Council talented businessmen who would provide impetus and vision to local government. George Dawson led the way and his speech on the opening of Birmingham's fine new Free Reference Library in October 1866 proved to be an enduring statement of the potentialities of civic government:

… a great town exists to discharge towards the people of that town the duties that a great nation exists to discharge towards the people of that nation. A town exists by the Grace of God, and is a solemn organism through which should flow, and in which should be shaped, all the highest, loftiest and truest ends of a man's intellectual and moral nature. We are a Corporation who have undertaken the highest duty that is possible for us. We have made provision for our people – all our people – God's greatest and best gifts unto Man.[145]

At this early stage Dawson was talking largely about municipal provision of the facilities to educate and stimulate intellectually, namely a great Library. But he was – as Charles Kingsley said – 'one of the greatest talkers of his age', and he unquestionably inspired those who attended his addresses at the Church of the Saviour, men like William Harris and Jesse Collings; his aspirations for municipal reform were to be closely echoed by Chamberlain. One can see here where Chamberlain might have picked up the notion of the Council as a veritable Parliament, with its Mayor acting as a Prime Minister.

Robert Dale, an equally robust and vigorous speaker, both at his Carr's Lane chapel and on the political platform, was also hugely influential in summoning up the transfiguring powers of local government, in what would – aptly – be known as the civic gospel. He helped Chamberlain attract the brightest and best to the discipleship. In a sermon in 1867, subsequently printed and circulated, he called on Birmingham's successful and prosperous men to take up their civic responsibilities:

> They ought to be Aldermen and Town Councillors. They ought to give their time as well as their money to whatever improvements are intended to develop the intelligence of the community. They ought to be reformers of local abuses. They ought to see to it that the towns and parishes in which they live are well drained, well lighted, well paved; that there are good schools for every class of the population; that there are harmless public amusements; that all parochial and municipal affairs are conducted honourably and equitably.[146]

He and Dawson were effectively recruiting sergeants for the reform party. And Henry Crosskey, arriving in Birmingham slightly later, rapidly fell under their influence and absorbed the reformative passion of those attending his own Church of the Messiah: 'To Dr Crosskey,' (write Armstrong and MacCarthy), 'the atmosphere he found among his immediate friends was exhilarating, even intoxicating.'[147] Those congregational members included Joseph, Arthur and Richard Chamberlain, William Kenrick and R.F. Martineau. He became as powerful an advocate of the Liberal municipal mission as Dawson and Dale, giving it coherence and a sense of its intrinsic worth.

In his *Memoranda* he wrote that: 'The Liberal policy was a policy of civilisation. It meant the enjoyment by the great mass of people of the blessing of a beautiful and civilised life.' An article he wrote in *Macmillan's Magazine* expanded on this: 'Time and trouble were lavished in Birmingham to persuade the people at large that political interests are the interests of civilisation in the broadest sense. The improvements of the dwellings of the poor; the promotion of temperance; the multiplication of libraries and art galleries; the management of grammar schools as well as elementary schools, were all discussed as questions of Liberal policy.'[148] Henry Crosskey, then, was an integral part of Chamberlain's Public Relations effort, to elevate the cultural aims of the mission, and to explain the rationale behind the politicisation of municipal contests.

Yet for all that the Machine, and its human constituents, were fundamental to the accomplishments of the civic revolution, they cannot eclipse the personal contribution of Joseph Chamberlain. Before he ever became Mayor he had researched Birmingham's private Gas companies and had concluded that a municipal take-over of the means by which Birmingham lit her streets and houses would yield substantial profits. He presented his detailed scheme to the Council in January 1874 within months of taking office. A municipal monopoly would bring an end to wasteful competition between companies often involving pavements being ripped up as rivals laid down new duplicate mains. But the central point was that – with Birmingham cash-strapped – this scheme promised financial salvation, because it would be highly profitable. The substantial yields from gas sales could be invested in essential Council projects, notably to improve sanitation and to provide clean running water for the town's inhabitants. Those profits would also enable rates to be reduced. It seemed almost too good to be true.

The Council – reflecting the strength of his supporters – endorsed the plan overwhelmingly (54 votes to 2) but the ratepayers gave him a sterner examination. When asked by one citizen: 'Would you give that for it?', he replied, 'If the Town Council will take this bargain and farm it out to me, I will pay them £20,000 [149] a year for it, and at the end of fourteen years I shall have a snug little fortune of £150,000 to £200,000.' The project was subsequently agreed. Indeed, the monopoly netted £785,000 in profits by 1884.[150] Just as he argued the case at Council, and among ratepayers, so he took personal charge of the negotiations with the two private Gas companies and was the Council's advocate when the enabling bill was discussed at the Parliamentary Select committee. As we have seen, once enacted he managed the scheme's practical application by creating a Gas committee, peopled with allies, and he made sure he was its chairman, closely scrutinising the early encouraging trends in profits.

Thomas Avery had earlier tried to reform Birmingham's management of water supplies but had been defeated by a Council daunted by the scale of the problem. It seems that Chamberlain was the first to see that the solution lay in a connection between Birmingham's Gas and Water: that incisive action on gas would provide the profits with which to cut the Gordian knot binding water reform, which required substantial investment. Although the private Birmingham Water Works Company produced reasonably acceptable water and a constant supply to the town, the problem was that its charges (inevitably highest in the poorest districts where the cost of repairs and collection were greatest) precluded between 25% and 30% of the population from having clean water – they had to rely on surface wells, often tainted and horribly polluted by percolated sewage.[151] In such districts the price in human life was great. Municipal gas profits would be used to buy out the Water Works, and thence to invest in clean water for all.

Once again, Chamberlain had done his homework before presenting the motion to the Council in December 1874, calling for the compulsory purchase of the water system, failing transfer by agreement. His case was fortuitously strengthened by the spectre of disease in the shape of a scarlet fever epidemic in 1874, which concentrated minds on reform. The speed with which he worked, as well as his capacity for that work, are remarkable, for he was still engaged on the gas issue. So too is his power of advocacy, which inspired his team, and provided direction for the Machine; Garvin writes that: 'His speech carried the Council to a man, and he never made a statement more completely silencing criticism. Not wasting a word, lucid, restrained yet damning.' This is when he expounded his philosophy that all State monopolies should be in the hands of the people.[152]

The unanimity of the Council provided Chamberlain with the confidence to move forward, to win over the ratepayers and then to take the argument to Parliament, there overcoming critical voices in the House of Lords. By the start of 1876, the year in which he surrendered the chain of office, the Gas and the Water works were in municipal hands. After so many years of indecisiveness and a paucity of imagination, a veritable revolution in public health and in the urban environment was being initiated. Assisted by the Public Health Act of 1872, which insisted on the appointment of a medical officer to every large borough, Chamberlain and his team implemented urgent sanitary reform, giving short shrift to the complacent local assumption that 'Birmingham was as healthy as a large town could be'.[153] The instrument for change was the Sanitary committee, radically overhauled in the wake of the Chamberlainite electoral victory in the borough in 1873, with a loyalist, Dr Alfred Barratt taking the chair. It multiplied the number of sanitary inspectors; it closed the town's wells, breeding grounds for disease in Birmingham's poorest areas; and with the Mayor as its leading counsel it carried controversial bye-laws to control the quality of housebuilding.

Within weeks after that famous election victory the Sewage committee was acting boldly to specify the ratio of privies to all new houses. Shortly after, the Public Works committee served notice on householders in specified streets that these must be levelled, paved, flagged and channelled. The Mayor and the Council took on powers later in 1874 from the Local Government Board allowing them to act as the Nuisance Authority; they then resolved to control lodging houses, specify the numbers of occupants, bedsteads, and privies permitted, impose standards and determine the frequency of cleansing, lime-washing and floor-washing.[154] These initiatives, augmented by Louisa Ryland's gift to the town of two significant parks – Cannon Hill and Small Heath – collectively comprised an environmental revolution for Birmingham's citizens. It was a transformation characterised by the conclusiveness and sense of authority of its Mayor, and of his team on their various Council committees, where they took inspiration from his frequent presence and his unremitting focus on their affairs. In a letter to his intimate friend Jesse Collings he well conveys the urgency, incisiveness, ruthlessness and mastery of protocol which characterise his entire municipal enterprise:

> I took the matter in hand myself, explained the position of affairs to the Council and begged them to pass the (Building) Bye-laws without discussion of the details. This they did like trumps as they are, and the whole set was printed and approved before the opposition had time to turn around and while they were arranging for interminable criticism and hostility.[155]

That environmental revolution culminated in the most ambitious policy of all, an Improvement scheme to eradicate the worst slums in the centre of Birmingham and so rebuild a more dignified commercial and retail quarter. Here, as with Gas and Water municipalisation, he was not an originator. Instead he observed the pioneering work of Glasgow and Edinburgh and studied the potentialities offered by Richard Cross's Artisans' and Labourers' Dwellings Act of 1875, legislation on the details of which he had himself been consulted. Chamberlain saw the three-fold possibility for a major sanitary reform in the jerry-built slums of the St Mary's ward, for dignifying the centre of Birmingham with streets and buildings which reflected the town's size and growing reputation, and finally, for encouraging the town's commercial sector, boosting her shopping and service businesses.

The story of his advocacy in the Council, as he sought to win the support of fellow councillors, was promptly published by the Council itself – the *Proceedings on the Adoption by the Council of a Scheme for the Improvement of the Borough (1875)* – so illustrating

Chamberlain's intuitive understanding of the need to communicate with and win over the public. His friend and ally J.T. Bunce would later recapitulate the saga in his *History* in exhaustive detail, so establishing an official version of events. The *Proceedings* record Chamberlain's mastery of process and of the law. He successfully argued for a new Improvement committee of the Council which soon numbered valued loyalists like R.F. Martineau, James Deykin, William Cook (a protégé of White's) and William White among its members. He tutored the Council on the sequence by which permission would be won for the Improvement scheme: the approach to the (new) Local Government Board; then persuading it to set in motion a provisional order for a private Improvement Act enabling the Council to institute compulsory purchase (permitted by Cross's brand-new Act); the next steps of laying out new streets; the terms by which land was to be leased for commercial development; and the conditions of borrowing from the Treasury. Predictably he was the Council's counsel at the Local Government Board's enquiry, eventually winning the day against strong opposition from some Birmingham property holders.

Just as masterful was his grasp of the scheme's detail, street by street. More even than that, his oft-quoted speech to the Council on 12 October 1875 illustrates both his compassion and his persuasive powers of oratory:

> We bring up a population in the dank, dark, dreary, filthy courts and alleys such as are to be found throughout the area which we have selected; we surround them with noxious influences of every kind, and place them under conditions in which the observance of even ordinary decency is impossible; and what is the result? What can we expect from that kind of thing? I think Mr White said the other day that to some extent the position of the people was their own fault, but I am sure Mr White only meant that to be true in a very limited sense. Their fault! Yes, it is legally their fault and when they steal we send them to gaol and when they commit murder we hang them. But if the members of this Council had been placed under similar conditions – if from infancy they had grown up in the same way – does any one of us believe that he should have run no risk of the gaol or the hangman? For my part I have not sufficient confidence in my own inherent goodness to believe that anything can make headway against such frightful conditions as those I have described. The fact is, it is no more the fault of these people that they are vicious and intemperate than it is their fault that they are stunted, deformed, debilitated and diseased. The one is due to the physical atmosphere – the moral atmosphere as necessarily and surely produces the other. Let us remove the conditions and we may hope to see disease and crime removed.[156]

Like George Cadbury, the Quaker businessman and philanthropist, who asked: 'How is it possible for a man to cultivate high ideals when his home is a slum?', Chamberlain's thinking had evolved; simply to reform education without first dealing with the squalid living conditions of many of the town's working class would fail to tackle the root causes of immorality and criminality.[157] Others among his allies had started in the Birmingham Education Society or the National Education League – men like Collings, Crosskey, Harris and Robert Martineau – and had a similar revelation. So, it was not a lone crusade. As we have seen above, William White, the first chairman of the Improvement committee, was an invaluable collaborator. He was a powerful proponent of radical reform and echoed the concern of many of his contemporaries that slum conditions promoted recourse to drink; more than that, his reputation as a Quaker, as a man who had spent his life among Birmingham's poor, appealed to a newly awakened conscience on public health:[158]

> The only prosperous people in that neighbourhood are publicans. There is light and warmth in their dwellings, if not sweetness. They are the only escape of the people from the darkness of their lives. The more misery, the fewer bakers and the more publicans; this is I believe, the experience of every town. All over the districts are courts which are dens of misery. If I were to repeat a hundred times, 'Dirt, damp, dilapidation,' I should inadequately describe the condition of things. Wherever one goes there is the same indescribable dampness and dirt. It seems impossible that there can be dryness, wholesomeness or sweetness in their dwellings. The floors of the houses are damp, some of them are lower than the level of the courts and some suffer from the oozing of filth and nastiness through the walls, emitting horrible stenches; and battle with them as they may, people seem utterly unable to remove the evils. The amount of sickness which is evidenced by the death-rate is enormous. It is quite time that the Council should bestir ourselves to leave no stone unturned by which all or part of such evils may be removed.[159]

White was a great help to Chamberlain because of his reputation for trustworthiness and the simplicity and honesty of his message. Together, Chamberlain and White won the Council around to the Improvement scheme. But advocacy of the scheme's town improvement elements was left to Chamberlain. There was sufficient business experience on the Council that the vision of a Hausmannised Birmingham, fit to rival Paris with its own new boulevards, and prosperous in a modern commercial quarter, found resonance. Chamberlain summarised the commercial concept saying: 'I have always held that Birmingham ought to be the metropolis of the Midland Counties. To it should come all the principal retail trade of those counties. (The scheme) would change what has been a straggling village with little of beauty to delight the eye and very little to interest the mind into what a large town should be.'[160] Councillors were persuaded and responded favourably to promises of increased rateable values and of broad, dignified streets replacing the ramshackle muddle of housing in Aston Road and Bull Street.

Yet, despite the transformation wrought by the clearance of the courts and slums of St Mary's, and the creation of Corporation Street, a grand statement to complement the new Council House, Art Gallery, and Board Schools, this Improvement element of Chamberlain's reform prospectus rapidly drew criticism from some quarters and it was left to his successors – after he had re-focused his attention on Westminster from 1876 – to struggle with the consequences. The scheme was expensive, partly because the compulsory purchase involved not just slum property but some expensive Georgian houses; the result was that the municipal debt grew to £3 million. Shop-sites on the new thoroughfares proved more difficult to let than Chamberlain anticipated; the end of the boom years and the onset of a long depression after 1876 exacerbated the difficulties. It fell to one of the new members of the Machine, J. Powell Williams (who became Chamberlain's most trusted lieutenant right through to their shared membership of a Unionist cabinet at the end of the century) to tackle it. Powell Williams joined the Council in 1877 and the financial expertise he had shown when he helped establish the Post Office Savings scheme saw him rapidly promoted to the chairmanship of the Finance committee. He persuaded the Local Government Board to allow him to reschedule the debt.[161]

Secondly, the extravagant promise of working-class housing provision 'that the committee would probably make for the poor' made by Chamberlain in October 1875 proved false. Only 62 houses had been built by 1885 to replace the 600 or more bulldozed for the Improvement scheme. There was a deep reluctance for the Council to step in and build themselves; instead it thought the service should be provided by private housebuilders. Yet they found land purchase too expensive. It was partly in frustration at municipal inaction, and at inadequate jerry builders, that George Cadbury embarked on his Bournville model village scheme in the mid-1890s.[162] It was a major setback that the grand vision of urban renewal conjured by Chamberlainite Liberals in the mid 1870s proved to be a mirage. Perhaps the departure of Chamberlain for London, and a consequent loss of his momentum, or perhaps too close an adherence to orthodox finance which decreed councils should not borrow to build, explain this failure. Others in the team had unwittingly contributed to the deception. Henry Crosskey in 1877 had talked about 'the sites acquired for proper dwellings for the working classes', while J.T. Bunce, the mouthpiece of the Liberal Machine, as editor of the *Birmingham Post*, had written of 'clearing and remodelling of unhealthy areas, so as to improve the houses of the artisans'.[163]

If the Improvement scheme was imperfect, it nevertheless ensured that Birmingham had a centre with buildings of which it could be proud, fit for a town aspiring in the 1880s to be a city. Disease was reduced by this and other sanitation measures given impetus by Chamberlain and his team. Indeed, much else was achieved besides in the two and a half years that comprised Chamberlain's mayoralty. He famously wrote to Collings that: 'The town will be parked, paved, assized, marketed, gas and watered and improved, all as a result of three years' active work and with the approval of the great bulk of the ratepayers.'[164] That succinct summary reflects the wide scope of the project and the achievement which encompassed new branch libraries (he even found time to sit on the Free Libraries committee under Jesse Collings), new parks, public gardens and recreation grounds, '100 miles of footways' (in his own words) and the creation of Birmingham's own assize courts, to which must be added the thirty or so new Board Schools founded in his coterminous time as Chairman of the Birmingham School Board.

Still, the achievement was not his alone. He relied on lieutenants who from a comparable background had a similar outlook and philosophy. Sound men like Baker and R.F. Martineau could be relied on to steer the Gas committee along Chamberlainite lines. George Baker, again, with Edwards and Mathews were equally reliable in the stewardship of the Water committee. And William White, Deykin, Edwards and Martineau (again) provided invaluable support on the Improvement committee. Although Chamberlain surrendered the position of Mayor in 1876 to become an MP, he was then an alderman and remained on the Council until 1880 to serve on the Gas, Improvement and Health committees, by so doing guarding his legacy and by his very presence deterring any attempt to change policy.

His close collaborators ensured the continuity of the Liberal civic revolution. Leslie Rosenthal has shown how nineteen Chamberlain loyalists stuck together after his translation to Westminster in a group focused around Richard Chamberlain, William Kenrick, Robert Martineau and his brother Thomas (elected to the Council in 1876). This was the family circle, and to it were attached the reliable figures of James Deykin, the Baker brothers – George and Edward – and Richard Cadbury Barrow. 'Even as Chamberlain was withdrawing from Birmingham,' writes Rosenthal, 'his political associates still formed a coherent and well-integrated bloc of voters on the Birmingham town council.'[165]

George Baker succeeded Chamberlain as Mayor in 1876; William Kenrick followed in 1877 and then it was Jesse Collings' turn, to be succeeded in 1879 by Richard Chamberlain (Joseph's loyal brother). William White was Mayor in 1882 and Thomas Martineau served three terms from 1884. And in the Council elections, Liberals had a largely unbroken run of success, at least until the hiatus of 1886 when the party split. So, in 1877 the Conservatives failed to contest any of the 16 wards, and the next year, when they did manage to find candidates for 12 wards, they were roundly beaten. At least in the four contests they managed in 1879, they had a solitary success, but that brief hope was snuffed out in the next year's elections when there was a Liberal whitewash. However, the early 1880s provided the Conservative opposition with a scintilla of hope. Several ward seats were won in the period up to 1885, reflecting the invigorating campaigning of Sir Fred Burnaby and Lord Randolph Churchill in Birmingham's parliamentary constituencies, and the understandable unpopularity in working-class wards like St Mary's where housing had been sacrificed to the grand vision of Improvement. For the Liberal Machine had to fight hardest to hold those inner Birmingham wards most affected by the destruction of working-class housing. Even so, it perpetuated Chamberlain's hold on Birmingham's local government right through to the last years of the decade. Only then, in the three-cornered fights between Chamberlain's Radical Unionists, their uncomfortable allies the Conservative Unionists, and the Gladstonian Liberals, was it clear that his near-total domination of the borough had been ended. Indeed, in 1893 out of 72 seats, only 28 were Radical Unionists, with Conservatives (22) and Gladstonians (22) close behind.[166]

Until 1886 the Machine controlled most aspects of Birmingham's affairs. After all, Chamberlain, Powell Williams, Collings and Schnadhorst influenced the selection of Justices of the Peace, of local Liberal candidates, of appointments to the Board of Guardians, even sub-inspectors of factories and local postmasters. That control was of a piece with the control the Liberal party exercised over the School Board, and in Birmingham's parliamentary contests, with an unbroken run of success from the 1850s to 1886. Only the agonising fratricidal rifts of that year brought a remarkable period of one-party municipal domination to an end.

William Kenrick

William Kenrick was born in 1831 and educated at University College in London, before becoming a partner and commercial manager of Archibald Kenrick and Sons Ltd., one of the country's leading producers of tinned hollowware. He and his brother, John Archibald, followed their father, Archibald, and uncle, Timothy, in affiliating to the Liberal party and – while John Archibald dedicated his public service to West Bromwich, home of the Kenricks' factory, where he chaired the board of guardians and the town's improvement committee – William would become a significant player in Birmingham's political life.

Perhaps this was inevitable, given that he married Mary Chamberlain (Joseph Chamberlain's elder sister), while his sister Harriet married Joseph, and – after Harriet's tragically early death – his cousin Florence became Joseph's second wife. The two families were quite evidently very close, and William became his brother-in-law's life-long friend and ally. His journey into public life followed a similar trajectory, influenced by Dawson's civic gospel and sharing a Unitarian faith which set much store by rational reform and active involvement in the world. He too came to understand the urgent need for education reform after he had become associated with the establishment and management of the Summit Schools in Spon Lane, West Bromwich; he subsequently became a founding member of the National Education League in 1869 and was an energetic chairman of the Branches Committee while sitting on the League's Executive Committee.

Like Chamberlain he had wide-ranging involvement in affairs in Birmingham and beyond. So, even while he was serving on the committee which guided the fortunes of the National Education League he was being elected to the bench (finishing up as 'father of the bench'), and – more party politically – to the Town Council, one of that group of Liberal reformers convinced that Forster's Education Act would empower local councillors to run new school boards. They were to be rudely disabused, but he nevertheless continued to serve on the Council for the Edgbaston ward from 1870 to 1911, an extraordinary period of 41 unbroken years. There he was a loyal adherent of Chamberlain's, chairing the Watch committee (1874–76) and the newly established Gas committee from 1880–83, a sign of the trust Chamberlain felt in him – this was after all a project dear to the ex-Mayor's heart. Kenrick had also become Mayor in his own right in 1877, just a year after Chamberlain's departure for Westminster. Kenrick and Baker, his immediate predecessor, played an important role in ensuring the continuity of the Chamberlain revolution. By the time he retired from the Council in 1911 he had assumed the role of a senior statesman, recognised by the award of the freedom of the city.

Aside from this, his municipal career betrays certain clear personal interests. He remained determined to preside over a revolution in education, being one of those Machine Liberals preoccupied by the injustice of King Edward's School's governance. He became a governor, as a Council nominee on the reformed board, and he led the campaign to open a King Edward's High School for girls. Like many influenced by Dawson, who evangelised the belief that art, culture and learning should be made freely available to all citizens by enlightened municipal governors, he gave practical expression to the aspiration by joining the Free Libraries Committee. He also chaired the Council's Museum and School of Art Committee (being on this committee for 40 years), and was a founder member of the Art Gallery purchase committee from 1880. He was a most generous donor to the new Municipal Art Gallery, contributing one of its prize possessions, Millais's Blind Girl. *He was on the management committee of the Birmingham School of Art (becoming chairman in 1883) and was instrumental in the setting up of the Jewellers' School, being a powerful advocate of education in the crafts. When he died in 1919 the* Birmingham Daily Post *paid tribute to his legacy, opining that: 'He devoted his time and ability, with other enlightened leaders of communal life, to the building up of a Birmingham of which its citizens could be proud.'*

It is a tribute to his stamina and sense of public duty that this litany of municipal service is by no means the whole story of Kenrick's achievements. He followed Chamberlain as the latter wound down the National Education League and sought to develop a grassroots organisation to reflect the policies of local Liberal campaigners. William Kenrick had been prominent in the Birmingham Liberal Association from the late 1860s and was naturally a part of that Chamberlainite initiative to export Birmingham's methods to a bigger national stage, becoming a founder member in 1877 of the National Liberal Federation, there being a key figure as chairman of the general committee. Unlike Chamberlain, Kenrick remained deeply involved in Council affairs well into the next century.

When the great Liberal implosion occurred over Home Rule in 1886, Birmingham was at its epicentre. There never seems to have been any doubt that Kenrick would follow Chamberlain into the Radical Unionists. He had been elected as Liberal MP for North Birmingham in 1885; he voted against Gladstone's Home Rule bill, helping ensure its defeat and then retaining the seat in 1886 as a very different sort of Liberal, one opposing his leader Gladstone. Subsequently he would accept the label Liberal Unionist, holding on to Birmingham North until 1899, and meanwhile establishing a reputation on the Commons standing committee dealing with policing and sanitary regulations, in other words drawing on that rich seam of experience built up when he was on Birmingham's Watch and Gas committees. Later he became a privy councillor.

Kenrick was a vital constituent element of the glue that bound Chamberlain's team together. He was talented, he had broad shoulders and an appetite for hard work; above all his loyalty was absolute, and it was on just such men – the Powell Williams, the Collings, the Mathews – that Chamberlain was to rely. They were doers, and to appropriate a phrase later applied to Lloyd George's circle of wartime associates, they were 'men of push and go'.

Charles Edward Mathews

C.E. Mathews was born in Kidderminster in 1833 and educated there at the King Charles I School. Unlike many of the members of Chamberlain's Machine he was not a businessman but trained as a solicitor. In that role he first became involved with the Birmingham School Board, as its solicitor; he was also Clerk to the Peace, legal adviser to the Aston Tram Company, and a later chairman of Birmingham Law Society. However, he steadily became involved in politics himself, and the Edgbaston Debating Society proved as formative for him as it did for contemporaries like George Dixon, Joseph Chamberlain, William Kenrick and Robert Martineau. When the Birmingham Daily Post, *in its obituary in October 1905, commented on his membership it concluded that: 'These and some others formed the group of progressive spirits who throwing themselves into discussion of public questions with ardent minds and untiring energy, set in motion numerous enterprises for public good.'*

Through the Debating Society he made the contacts that drew him into the fledgling National Education League in 1869; he was immediately elevated to the executive committee and chairmanship of the Parliamentary committee. He was also one of the early speakers sent out from Birmingham to explain the League's arguments to nascent NEL cells in the provinces. Like William Kenrick and George Baker he campaigned vigorously for the reform of the Anglican monopoly which controlled the governance of the King Edward's School foundation; his letters to the Post *under the signature 'Historicus' gave impulse and direction to the reform movement, his main contention centring on the necessity of Town Council involvement in the school's management. After he had won his case he became first a governor, then the Chairman of the Governing Body's School committee.*

From the 1860s he had shown himself a Liberal of advanced views; his apprenticeship in Liberal politics in the highly politicised environment of the National Education League prepared him to follow the same path as a number of his political confrères – by joining the Town Council. In 1875, at the height of the Chamberlain revolution, he became councillor for Edgbaston, succeeding Jesse Collings who had been elected an alderman. Chamberlain took no time in utilising Mathews' talents, ensuring his appointment to the strategically vital new Water committee, and to the Estates committee. Mathews led the way in fighting to convert the dilapidated Park Street burial ground ('a disgrace to the town', wrote the Post*) into a pleasant garden. This desire to improve Birmingham's milieu for the benefit of all its inhabitants placed Mathews firmly in the mainstream of Birmingham reformers influenced by the teaching of George Dawson.*

When he died the Post *wrote that: 'Till his fatal illness he had been in practically all the other movements in which Mr Chamberlain led the way.' So, we find Charles Mathews loyally adhering to Chamberlain when the Home Rule split occurred, subsequently chairing the Edgbaston Liberal Unionist Association and playing a vital role in smoothing relations between the two types of Unionist, Liberal and Conservative. He was instrumental in persuading Liberal Unionists to accede in the nomination of a Conservative (F. Lowe) as replacement for George Dixon as MP after his death. Mathews became a member of the national joint Unionist Committee. He also took a leading part in organising the great civic dinner to celebrate Joseph Chamberlain's departure for South Africa in 1902.*

That Post *article in 1905 had gone on to say that: 'He was not a mere follower – he had those qualities of energy and perception that led him often to strike out on his own.' So he showed the breadth of his interests and the depth of his dedication to the city by involving himself in many other aspects of Birmingham civic life. For many years he was a member of the Midland Institute's governing Council, he was one of two founders of the Birmingham Children's Hospital, he was a member of the Birmingham Library Committee and he was Honorary Secretary of the Shakespeare Memorial Library. Yet his reputation extended well beyond Birmingham for another reason entirely – he was one of Europe's most famous Alpinists. He was one of the founders of the Alpine Club in 1858, and was its president from 1877-1882. He climbed the Matterhorn three times and Mont Blanc twice amongst countless other mountains.*

His obituaries referred to his 'brilliant and strenuous career', for he was 'a man of culture, learning, law, a political fighter, a littérateur *and a great Alpine climber'. It was through recruiting such multi-talented men that Chamberlain manufactured the powerful and successful Liberal Machine in the last third of the nineteenth century.*

George Baker

George Baker was, according to his obituarist in the Birmingham Daily Post *on 15 January 1910, 'one of a knot of men who have changed the composition of the Council. He has helped weed out the undesirable members and to send in their stead gentlemen with some qualifications and abilities for government.' There could not be a clearer statement of Dawson and Dale's vision of a municipal revolution in which successful businessmen joined the Council to import entrepreneurial skills and to elevate the tone of a body too long dominated by time-servers and second-class brains. Alderman George Baker, who served for fifty years, was perceived as very much one of the Liberal new brooms which swept clean the Council chambers in Chamberlain's coup.*

His background replicates that of so many influential Birmingham men in the nineteenth century. He was a Nonconformist, a Quaker, born in 1825, though he was brought up in Yorkshire, attending Ackworth school (like John Bright). He then came to Birmingham where like William White, and George and Richard Cadbury he started teaching at Severn Street Day School. So, as with many of Chamberlain's allies in the Machine, he became familiar with the shortcomings of educational provision for the working classes. Like many other Machine Liberals he joined the Birmingham Education Society and he sympathised with the project of free universal education for all espoused by the National Education League. He stood on that programme as a candidate (unsuccessfully) for the Birmingham School Board. Along with J.S. Wright, C.E. Mathews and William Kenrick he felt keenly that the King Edward's School endowments should be shared more equitably for the wider benefit of Birmingham's children and so was active in promoting reform of the Foundation. He was one of the first councillors to be elected to represent the Council on the Board.

He early joined the Liberal party, and also involved himself in a range of humanitarian and voluntary projects. He went to Finland in 1857 to help organise the distribution of funds raised in Birmingham to alleviate the worst effects of the Finnish famine. In 1860 he was elected to the Board of Guardians – along with John Skirrow Wright – and became its chairman in 1867. There he reorganised the vaccination department and added wards for women at the workhouse. By then (1865) he had been elected to the Town Council for St George's ward, soon allying with Thomas Avery to campaign for reform of Birmingham's antediluvian systems for sewage disposal. He was, therefore, undergoing a municipal apprenticeship well before Chamberlain had commenced his local political career.

Baker was to become something of an expert on sanitation. When Chamberlain initiated the necessary amalgamation of sewage authorities in Birmingham and its hinterland in 1875, a process culminating in the creation of the Tame and Rea Drainage Board, George Baker became its chairman. He had immediately recognised the rationale behind Chamberlain's plans for municipalisation of water and became an ardent supporter; naturally he became a founder member of the new Water committee, in the same month as he also became a member of the Gas committee. No other councillor served on both committees at the same time. Quite evidently Chamberlain recognised both Baker's loyalty and his executive abilities. Indeed, the trust he placed in him is demonstrated by the fact that Baker was elevated to the chairmanship of the Works sub-committee, and that he was later charged with executing the Chamberlain vision of municipal renewal, when appointed chairman of the Improvement committee. Chamberlain would have had a considerable say in who was to succeed him when he abruptly moved to the Commons in 1876; in any case Baker's election as mayor was unanimous.

In that role he presided at the great public meeting when William Gladstone in 1877 came to Birmingham to speak at the inauguration of Chamberlain's new organisation, the National Liberal Federation, an enterprise with which Baker had sympathy.

He shared with William Kenrick an interest in broadening the cultural horizons of Birmingham's citizens. For many years he sat on the Museums and School of Art committee. He can be credited with persuading the National Gallery to permit loans of art works to the provinces, being the convener in 1877 of a conference of municipal authorities aiming to persuade London to share its treasures.

George Baker had a career of almost unparalleled public service spanning over fifty years and in that time he witnessed the reform of the town's sanitation, the implementation of a civic revolution in the 1870s, Birmingham's elevation to city-status and he died just as preparations were being made to multiply its power and its reach by the creation of Greater Birmingham (in 1911). The Birmingham Daily Post *summarised his importance when it wrote: 'He was one of the reformers of the municipal administration in Birmingham and took an active part in the promotion of developments which contributed to the material and social advancement of the community.'*

Sir Thomas and Robert Martineau

Thomas (1828-1893) and Robert Francis Martineau (1831-1909) were sons of Robert Martineau, who was both a prominent metal work manufacturer and local politician, being Mayor of Birmingham in 1846. The Martineaus were of Huguenot stock, their antecedents fleeing France after the Edict of Nantes in 1685. Robert senior's younger sister was Harriet Martineau, the renowned political author and sociologist. Their religious nonconformity found expression in their Unitarianism; like the Chamberlains and the Kenricks, father and sons were worshippers at the Church of the Messiah. Thomas and Robert were educated at the Birmingham and Edgbaston proprietary school established by their father in protest at the Anglicanism of the local Grammar School; both, as with so many members of the Chamberlain circle, belonged to the Birmingham and Edgbaston Debating Society where they refined their rhetorical skills, and both were attracted like their co-religionists to the Liberal Party.

Robert joined his father's business as a travelling salesman. He first signalled his strong sense of public duty, and his considerable ability, in his role as secretary of the Lancashire (cotton) Relief Fund, set up to assist workers suffering from the disruption of cotton supplies during the American Civil War. So successful was this organisation that it achieved a surplus, applied to the founding of a sanatorium in Birmingham. Others noticed and he was asked to join the executive of the National Education League in 1869 as Chairman of the Branches committee. Like many multi-taskers in the Machine he moved seamlessly from education organisation into the Town Council in 1874, representing St Bart's ward. He became a central figure in executing the municipal revolution, chairing the Health and Interception of Sewage committees. In service which stretched unbroken from 1874 to 1900 he took a particular interest in the Free Libraries committee, and in education; he was on the Council's Education committee and became chairman of the Technical School committee. It had been he who masterminded the transfer of science teaching in the city from the Birmingham and Midland Institute (of which he was a leading light) to the City Council; such was his fascination for technical education that he spent years travelling on the continent observing best practice. His subsequent advice shaped Birmingham's science teaching; it in turn became a model which influenced national thinking. His interest in education found further expression when Birmingham University was founded in 1899; he duly became a life governor.

This may seem surprising. The University was Joseph Chamberlain's pet project, and Robert Martineau had fallen out with him over Home Rule in 1886. Robert supported Gladstone and remained a member of the Liberal Party. Furthermore, he made clear his opposition to the Boer War – and therefore to Chamberlain's foreign policy – from 1899. His disapproval of a proposal to confer the freedom of the city on the general, Lord Roberts, then at the height of his reputation, 'brought a storm about his ears', according to his obituary in the Birmingham Daily Post *in 1909.*

Thomas Martineau's path diverged from his brother's. From 1844 he was articled to Arthur Ryland, a solicitor, whom he joined in partnership in 1851. The Martineau name remains significant in Birmingham legal circles to the present day, with Shakespeare Martineau being one of the city's largest law firms. Only when well-established, with a strong reputation locally, did Thomas enter local government, some years after his younger brother. He had already learnt something of Liberal politics, acting as a volunteer election agent, and his involvement in the Chamberlain Machine was made the more inevitable by his marriage in 1860 to Emily Kenrick, sister of Florence Chamberlain. Once elected to the Council (for Edgbaston ward) he began a notable municipal career, his legal experience making him invaluable, especially in piloting the Birmingham Consolidation Bill through Parliament. He also promoted the scheme by which Birmingham was awarded assize status; the building of the new law courts in Birmingham was the triumphant culmination of his campaign. He was Mayor (holding the office for three consecutive terms) in March 1887, when Queen Victoria came to the city to lay the foundation stone for the law courts; he was rewarded with a knighthood in recognition of his endeavours, and the French Renaissance-style buildings enhanced Birmingham's centre in just the grand manner that Chamberlain had envisaged in his great Improvement scheme. He also capped off Birmingham's water reforms, initiated twenty years earlier, when in 1892 he piloted the Birmingham Water Bill, securing Welsh water for the city, through Parliament before his untimely death.

Like his brother he was prominent in the Birmingham and Midland Institute, where he was a member of the governing council. Unlike Robert, he thought Home Rule an abomination, following Joseph Chamberlain into the Liberal Unionist party and thereafter being an important figure in Chamberlain's National Liberal Union based in Birmingham. He and Robert exemplify the way the internecine Liberal battle of Gladstone versus Chamberlain was even reflected within hitherto close-knit families and affected the harmony of the Machine itself.

CREATING A NATIONAL CAUCUS

By 1877 Chamberlain and his team's domination of Birmingham was complete with the Council, the School Board, the Board of Guardians and most local committees colonised by trusted Liberal supporters. But Chamberlain's ambitions had evolved. Now the lure of national politics drew him to Westminster and to plot the takeover of the Liberal party. He and his allies, Harris and Schnadhorst, devised the National Liberal Federation (NLF), to develop a democratic network of local Liberal associations modelled, of course, on Birmingham and based there. Benjamin Disraeli christened it the Caucus and some of its methods proved every bit as controversial as its American counterpart.[168]

The *Yorkshire Post* articulated the feelings of many critics: 'For ways that are dark and tricks that are vain, no political organisation in England can match the Birmingham Caucus.'[169] Just as scathing was the Liberal MP, A.J. Mundella who – as discussed earlier – believed that 'Joseph Chamberlain was scheming to create a phalanx of marionettes with the wires pulled by himself from Birmingham'.[170] Yet for all that, Chamberlain's opponents recognised the effectiveness of Birmingham's construct. As mentioned in chapter 1, Lord Beaconsfield (Benjamin Disraeli) told the Queen after defeat in the 1880 general election that his own party had had nothing to match Liberal firepower: 'The Liberals worked,' he said enviously, 'on that American system called Caucus, originated by that great Radical Mr. Chamberlain.' Asa Briggs, Birmingham's historian, endorsed that judgement many years later: 'Birmingham stood for the most powerful political machine in the kingdom.'[171]

We have already seen (chapter 1) how the Birmingham Liberal Association was reshaped, around the time of the Second Reform Act, by William Harris and others, making it both more democratic and better attuned to the new demands of permanent electioneering. It was closely aligned with the National Education League, a pressure group, centred on Birmingham, staffed by Liberal loyalists. The evident success of Birmingham methods, and an existential crisis in the League partially explain the timing and the shape of this new Federation project. The Liberals' defeat in the 1874 General Election prompted Chamberlain and his close associates to conclude that the sort of single-issue politics they and other Radicals had espoused – education reform, disestablishment and abolitionism – had failed to develop a wide enough base or to appeal to working-class voters. They realised that programme politics, rather on the lines of Chamberlain's own successful mayoral programme, would broaden the party's appeal.[172]

In keeping with this realisation that pressure-group politics failed to engage large enough numbers, Chamberlain and Harris, as we saw in chapter 2, decided to wind up the National Education League. The League's legacy had been invaluable in the sense that it provided Chamberlain and his inner circle with a wealth of detailed information on constituency politics, and with Radical contacts and the beginnings of a national following. Here for Harris was the germ of a new idea. As Chamberlain said in a speech at Darlington: 'The whole credit for having initiated and carried this new machinery belongs to my friend Mr Harris.'[173]

What Harris proposed was a novel national Radical organisation incorporating the National Education League, the National Radical Union, the Liberation Society, the Land Reform Association and based on local Liberal Associations just like his own in Birmingham, which would be its centre. There was a resonance in this with Birmingham's past; Chamberlain himself was well aware of the history of the Birmingham Political Union and there were times when he would consciously echo Thomas Attwood forty years earlier, who had called for his union 'to collect and organise the peaceful expression of public opinion so as to bring it to act on the legislature'. The NLF was to be the second act in a developing story of Birmingham Imperialism.

Furthermore, the foundations on which to erect a federation of local Liberal associations were already being laid around the country. Independently, reconstruction at the local level was underway in Manchester, Leeds and Sheffield in the aftermath to the shocking defeat incurred in 1874. And in many cases they borrowed from Birmingham, whose immunity from the Liberals' wider electoral disaster suggested that it must be doing something right. Indeed, from 1874 Francis Schnadhorst spent much of his time both travelling and writing to expound the Birmingham system to other urban constituencies; he was the Machine's export salesman.[174] Thus, Manchester soon had its 800, Leeds its 600; and in the case of the latter, Sir Wemyss Reid, the editor of the *Leeds Mercury*, observed caustically that the Leeds Liberal Association was infected by a new breed of Liberal, of 'extreme opinions', often supporting 'the truest and most honest Liberal of the day, Joseph Chamberlain', and part of 'a great revolution (which) had been suddenly and silently wrought (whereby) control of the Liberal Party had in great measure passed out of the hands of its old leaders into those of the men who managed the new 'machine'.'[175] In truth the Leeds Liberal Association, in emulating the all-encompassing influence of its Birmingham counterpart, had among its objects: 'To superintend the registration of Parliamentary, Municipal and Poor Law electors. To promote in the Borough the return of Liberal representatives to Parliament, the Town Council, the School Board, the Board of Guardians and the Board of Overseers.'[176]

So, the process of federation in 1877 was eased by an underlying predisposition to accept Birmingham's lead.

What did Birmingham's Liberal generals – and especially Chamberlain himself – hope that the Federation would achieve at its first meeting (see below) in May 1877? Their aims were Radical and democratic and betray deep frustration at the current state of the Liberal party. Its lack of discipline, and of clear goals and policies, offended Birmingham men who had thrived on planning, clarity and control. Underlying their analysis was a near visceral loathing of the Whigs – who they saw dominating the Liberal party – and their old-school methods, shaped by wealth, social standing and a prevailing condescension.

Chamberlain, in *A New Political Organisation*, an influential article explaining the ideas behind this National Liberal Federation, argued that 'the new organisation will result in greater definiteness being given to the aims and objects of the party'. It would be an institutional umbrella sheltering all Liberal Associations; indeed, it was to proselytise the good news of association by encouraging the creation of new local organisations which would send delegates to meetings of the new Federation. Such parochial associations, like the central Federation, would be well disciplined; they had their model, for 'the Birmingham Liberal Association is the type to which all organisations approach'.[177] Henry Crosskey extolled its virtues: 'The discipline of the electoral body was perfect; the forces at the disposal of the Birmingham Liberal Association were not hordes of wayward freelances, they were armies of disciplined men, well accustomed to stand side by side and move in unbroken battalions.'[178] The purpose behind the discipline on which Harris, Schnadhorst and Chamberlain insisted was to effect the will of the majority in the party; as Chamberlain said when he welcomed delegates to the Federation's inauguration: 'We may see a meeting of what will be really a Liberal parliament outside the Imperial Legislature and – unlike it – elected by universal suffrage, and with some regard to a fair distribution of power.'[179] A year later when reviewing the work of the 'Caucus', Chamberlain wrote with some self-satisfaction that: 'Its only merit has been that it has allowed the party to develop its strength, it has served to popularise policy, and has enlisted tens of thousands of our most active citizens in its defence.'[180]

This 'Liberal parliament' would discuss policy and determine an order of priorities. As William Harris said at that same inaugural meeting, the Federation 'by collecting together the majority of the people in great centres of political activity should be able to speak on whatever questions arose with full authority of the national voice'. The power of that majority voice logically meant that Liberal MPs should heed it; and from the outset the overt intention of the Federation was to mandate MPs to follow its agreed policy. This would create many difficulties later, as we will see. Also implicit in this democratic shift was that assault on the Whigs who – as already indicated – Birmingham Radicals had targeted in their cross-hairs. Chamberlain deduced that they would 'all view with natural apprehension a scheme by which the 'mob' are for the first time invited and enabled to make their influence felt by means of constitutional machinery'.[181] Predictably he did not invite the Whigs to the Federation's foundation meeting; and Lord Hartington, their leader, refused an invitation to attend the annual conference in 1879. In the eyes of the Birmingham faction these Whigs had ensured that the Liberal party was elitist, for policy was determined, and candidates too often chosen, by a self-selected and self-perpetuating leadership.[182] It is, then, deeply ironical that Chamberlain after 1886 would find himself sharing with Lord Hartington the leadership of the Liberal Unionists, many of whom were Whig defectors from the Liberal party.

Behind this criticism, and the elevation of the voice of the people, was a ruthless power grab. Chamberlain believed that Liberal opinion in the country was far more radical than that of the party leadership and its MPs. Indeed, it was Chamberlain's disappointment on arrival at Westminster as a new MP in 1876 which may explain his later behaviour; he tried to get a Radical party together in the Commons but soon concluded – in a letter to his friend Jesse Collings – that: 'I don't think my new party will come to much. Cowen is unsound and others apart from Dilke have no force.'[183] This was just a few months before the launch of the Federation and it could well be that Chamberlain resolved that a powerful extra-Parliamentary Radical party was preferable to a small, unsound, Commons nexus.

It was not just A.J. Mundella who saw the entire operation as being about the projection of Joseph Chamberlain onto the national stage. Mundella portrayed him as a puppet-master and Chamberlain's own biographer inadvertently confirmed that impression when writing of Schnadhorst 'running up to London' to get his orders from Chamberlain: 'What he wished was what they (his team) did, though very seldom indeed was his prompting audible to the pit.'[184] Apart from the fact that he and that team might be affecting decision-making in the other local associations too, Chamberlain was in an obvious position to benefit from this Federation. There was more than a suspicion that he had used the springboard of the NLF to vault into the Cabinet in 1880, when Gladstone had rewarded him for services rendered by the NLF in the election. Thereafter as a member of the Parliamentary Liberal party and of the Liberal government, he and his Cabinet colleagues needed the support of public opinion. Furthermore, he was the government's leading Radical, whose arguments for a reform programme were greatly augmented by his popularity with the party's grass roots. Garvin wrote that 'outside Parliament the influence of the Radical leader spread as the new system of Liberal Federation extended; Chamberlain was its recognised spokesman'.

If it was a personal and a Radical party power grab, the Federation was just as much about enhancing the power of Birmingham. Chamberlain was clear about this at the outset. When he wrote to John Morley of his plans in February 1877 he said: 'We are going to issue the League dissolution circular announcing at the same time the formation of a federation of Liberal Associations with its headquarters in Birmingham, and the League officers as chief cooks.'[185] This operation was to be entrusted only to the loyal few in the town he knew intimately; he certainly didn't want it centred on London where Whips and Whigs proliferated. He was clear, too, in writing to Jesse Collings: 'I think it is a great mistake to ask Manchester and Leeds to join Birmingham in starting the Federation (for) if these two associations are joined with us they will seriously hamper our action.'[186] As a result, all the officers of the NLF bar one were dependable Machine allies from the National Education League and from the BLA, and they occupied offices in Paradise Street, central Birmingham. The first President was Joseph Chamberlain (Jesse Collings in 1880), the Treasurer was J.S. Wright, the Chairman of the Executive Committee was William Harris, the Honorary Secretary was at first Jesse Collings, then J. Powell Williams, and the Secretary, Francis Schnadhorst. Garvin looked back to the English Civil War for a parallel: 'Chamberlain's new model, like Cromwell's, started from his own troop and grew into a regiment and an army.'[187] But not all were as frankly admiring. *The Yorkshire Post* spoke for many in the North when an editorial attacked:

> … an organisation existing solely for the propagation of Mr Chamberlain. In the inner-most working of the Caucus is Mr Kenrick, Mr Schnadhorst (to whom attaches considerable notoriety by his officiating as organising secretary), Mr Harris – who is of so modest and retiring a temperament that he is never seen or heard, although he is the chief of the wire-pullers – Mr Collings (popularly known as Mr Chamberlain's jackal) and Mr Powell Williams. He and Mr Collings fulfil the useful function of browbeaters in chief to the Caucus, for they perform oratorically and metaphorically the same kind of operation the less sophisticated hired rough, Mr Larry Mark, performs with his fists.[188]
> When any Caucus movement is planned or business transacted, the first step is for the select few composing this inner ring to meet together in a private parlour at an hotel or in the back office of the Birmingham Liberal Association and there everything is very snugly and comfortably arranged.[189]

Here critically anatomised is the Caucus, its leading figures - the same men we have met in different guises in Birmingham already – as well as its methods. What adversary and advocate agreed on was the extent of the town's impact. 'The Birmingham directorate planted associations, it sowed broadcast,' wrote Garvin, and imitation of Birmingham made the Machine system general, with ward committees and a general council often exceeding hundreds. Once established on the Birmingham model, the power of that original inspiration grew steadily: 'By force of habit the cooperation of local Associations with Birmingham became automatic, for a mere telegram from the bigwigs of the Caucus was enough to set those Associations in motion through the country.'[190] That subservience was fostered by Schnadhorst, in particular, who was 'indefatigable, travelling wide to spread the Birmingham plan; (he was) quiet, persuasive, tireless. His touch was on all the threads'.[191] Of all the members of Chamberlain's Machine, Schnadhorst was most important in developing Birmingham's national sway which extended to over 100 local associations by 1880.

Birmingham's political eminence was such that it attracted a host of national figures to come to the town, if for widely different reasons. In the case of former Prime Minister William Gladstone, he came because Chamberlain wooed and pursued him to speak at the first conference of the NLF on 31 May 1877. For Chamberlain, it was a real coup to secure this 'pontifical consecration', because even if Gladstone had surrendered the Liberal party's leadership in the wake of the great defeat of 1874, he remained its prophet and visionary and he could prove a unifying figurehead for Radicals.[192] For Gladstone himself this was an opportunity to generate support for his new mission cause, the assault on Beaconsfieldism and its tolerance of Turkish misgovernment in the Balkans.[193] Up to 30,000 people pressed inside a Bingley Hall whose glass roof was dismantled to permit a better airflow; Gladstone's own diary recorded 'a most intelligent and duly appreciative audience'.[194]

Apart from inveighing against the Turks, he blessed the National Liberal Federation initiative, stating: 'It is in my opinion to the honour of Birmingham that she has held up the banner of a higher and holier principle.'[195] He continued to think well of it for, he wrote: 'A man is not bound by the Birmingham plan to subscribe to any list of political articles.... At Birmingham, you know they are tolerably advanced, but they don't attempt to exclude the most moderate.'[196] He understood that the town's influence was all about organisational mechanics, not about imposing its own pet policies; the programme would emerge from discussion with the grass roots.

Even if Hartington, nominal Liberal Party leader in 1879, stayed away (prompting a disgusted Chamberlain to ask: 'Can the leader afford to ignore altogether so large a section of the party?'), William Harcourt, a principal Whig, did come to Birmingham. John Morley described it as a 'coming down to the lion's den'.[197] He brought his son to be educated in the methods of Chamberlain and his Caucus – 'I think it good for youth to learn early the working of political life' – and what Harcourt himself observed 'gave me hope and a confidence in the unity of the party (strengthening) my conviction of the solid prospects of cooperation between the two wings of the party'.[198]

Birmingham became a magnet for the Conservative party as well. Continuing Liberal success in the town was intensely provoking and prompted considerable soul-searching among party members. We have seen that Beaconsfield attributed the Liberal victory of 1880 to the impact of the Caucus. One consequence in Birmingham itself was that local Conservatives secured the renowned swashbuckler Sir Fred Burnaby, soldier and Imperialist adventurer, to contest general elections there in both 1880 and 1885, during which time he built a substantial local following, running Liberal incumbents close.

Lord Randolph Churchill, shining hope of the younger generation of Conservatives, was also drawn to Birmingham as a Parliamentary candidate in the 1885 General Election. What better way of inflicting terminal damage to the Federation and the Radical tendency could there be than by defeating Chamberlain and Bright in their seemingly impregnable heartlands? Part of him was repelled by the fact that 'the whole of the governing power of Birmingham is in the hands of the Caucus…which owns the gasworks, owns the water supply, they control the lunatic asylum (and) the grammar school… as well as the drainage farm', and that 'every one of their employees knows that he holds his office, his position, his employment, upon the distinct understanding that in all political and municipal matters he must blindly submit himself and upon the slightest show of independence he will lose his employment'.[199] He may have been talking about the Birmingham Caucus but what he said was applicable to the processes employed by its many association imitators in the Federation.

Yet another part of him was frankly admiring and he was quite prepared to champion the remodelling of his own party on Birmingham and NLF lines, by which accordingly a National Union of Conservative and Constitutional Associations (NUCCA) was created, a body formed on the basis of popular representation. At NUCCA's Annual Conference in the calculatedly symbolic venue of Birmingham in 1883, Churchill echoed the spirit of Chamberlain when he made war on the party's hierarchy saying: 'I wish to see the control and guidance of the Tory party transferred from a self-elected body to an annually elected body and the financial resources of our party transferred from an irresponsible body to a responsible body.' He went on to aver: 'No party management can be effective and healthy unless the great labouring classes are directly represented on the Executive of the party.'[200] Here is talk of a coup by the elected representatives of the associations, of democracy with an overt focus on the working classes; there could be no more sincere form of flattery than Churchill's imitation of the aims and methods of Chamberlain's Birmingham-centred NLF.

That same year Lord Salisbury, the Conservative leader and a future Prime Minister, also ventured into the lion's den. He came to Birmingham to attack the Caucus, and its scheming demagogue, who aimed to make the House of Commons its pliant tool. Whilst he loathed the new politics which threatened to relocate the centre of politics from Westminster to the country at large – as much in his own party as in his Liberal opponents – his visit to Birmingham was a back-handed compliment to its power and influence.

This notoriety suggests that the scheme, as Harris, Schnadhorst, Chamberlain and Wright – among others – conceived it, worked out just as they had intended. To what extent was this true? From the beginning, there was that focus on cultivating public opinion. We find Harris and Chamberlain planning to educate and influence the public. In a letter written in late 1878 Chamberlain argued that: 'We ought to do something in the way of publishing by issuing – from time to time – pamphlets on subjects of national importance. This would be a useful part of our work.'[201] Equally, public opinion was to be educed. Again, in correspondence with Harris, Chamberlain writes of the urgent need to forestall the Beaconsfield government's request for money to support its foreign policy regarding Russia and Turkey. 'Bear in mind,' writes Chamberlain, 'that if this demand is made the whole machinery of the Federation would immediately be put into operation to elicit a further expression of public opinion.'[202] Garnering the opinion of grassroots Liberals was the essence of the NLF from its inception.

William Harris had been very clear in the inaugural Conference in 1877: 'The people themselves (not the leaders) ought to decide what the agitation should be, and when it should begin.' Yet for all his rhetoric of the coming democracy as expressed through the NLF, Chamberlain was pulled in a different direction. As we have just seen in his letter to Harris, his instinct was to educate, shape and ultimately to lead the public. So, within months of its establishment the NLF was circularising literature to promote Chamberlain's pet programme of Free Church, Free Land and Free Labour. It fuelled the first suspicions that the NLF would not so much reflect the opinions of ordinary Liberals, as be a vehicle for the propagation of Birmingham, and specifically Chamberlainite, policies. Furthermore, Chamberlain rapidly concluded that the NLF's role was to support the leadership whenever it led with conviction; and that the leadership could not simply follow instructions from its Liberal grass roots, for it had to consider the views of a wider electorate and it had to win elections.

The early years of the NLF were not therefore spent listening to the concerns of the associations but in whipping support for Gladstone's mission cause directed against Beaconsfield's foreign policy. The NLF's annual report in January 1879 admitted that the 'disturbed state of public feeling (on Beaconsfieldism)'... 'diverted attention from questions of domestic legislation'. Chamberlain himself expanded on this, saying that 'personal claims' and 'crotchets (pet enthusiasms) of all descriptions,' as well as 'deep-seated convictions and long-cherished hopes of important reform' must give place to the supreme cause of getting rid of the Beaconsfield government.[203] This self-denial continued up to the General Election of 1880 where the NLF's focus was entirely on anti-Beaconsfieldism, to the exclusion of faddish enthusiasms. It meant that the Liberal leaders came into office without any programme at all; the NLF had failed in its primary purpose of discussing, then prioritising, policy. And when Chamberlain tried to make good the deficit by proposing 'two exhaustive omnibus Bills' dealing with 'the Land and with the Franchise'. Gladstone evaded any commitment. The NLF was expected to continue unquestioningly to back the priorities identified by Prime Minister Gladstone, in the wake of a stunning election victory in 1880.[204]

If several of the NLF's champions were disappointed by events between 1877 and 1880, that election victory provided consolation. Schnadhorst claimed in an NLF pamphlet that 'in nearly all constituencies where it has been established the Liberal candidates were elected'.[205] Chamberlain elaborated in a letter to *The Times*, claiming that of 67 Parliamentary boroughs modelled on Birmingham's pattern of popular representation, '60 of these Liberal seats were gained or retained'.

> This remarkable success is a proof that the new organisation has succeeded in uniting all sections of the party...It has deepened and extended the interest felt in the contest; it has fastened a sense of personal responsibility on the electors; and it has secured the active support, for the most part voluntary and unpaid, of thousands and tens of thousands of voters, who have been willing to work hard for the candidates in whose selection they have for the first time had a voice... The gentlemen who have commended themselves to these popular and somewhat democratic committees have been, on the whole, more decided in their Liberalism than was usually the case with the nominees of the small cliques of local politicians whom the new organisation has superseded.[206]

This distils the essential arguments Chamberlain and his Birmingham team employed to justify the existence of the NLF. It was intended to energise Liberal members, to encourage participation, and to free the party from the thrall of a suffocating Old Guard in the constituencies. However, Schnadhorst and Chamberlain exaggerated the NLF's impact on the election. True, it had helped to eliminate superfluous Liberal candidates who in past elections had divided the Liberal vote and it undoubtedly helped by uniting Liberals behind an agreed slate of candidates. But the pair wilfully ignored the contribution made by Gladstone himself, whose Midlothian campaign had generated huge enthusiasm amongst Radicals and Liberals, especially in the North. It also disregarded the impact of the Irish vote which in 1880 was highly organised and delivered *en bloc* to the Liberals.[207]

If the NLF's efforts impressed its opponents like Beaconsfield, it did not bring about any change in attitude from the Liberal leadership. Liberal members pressing for the Ministry to adopt their sectional enthusiasms (for example, licensing reform or repeal of the Contagious Diseases Act) were to be disappointed; Gladstone believed pursuit of such sectional interests had proved divisive in his last Ministry (1868-1874). He wanted Liberals, through the NLF, to support issues he, the leader, had identified. In this case, he had concluded that the explanation for this latest Ministry's lack of constructive reform since 1880 was not his own reluctance to commit to policies emanating from the grass roots but that the machinery of government was being blocked or obstructed. All Liberals – but most especially Chamberlain's extremely useful Machine – were enjoined by Gladstone to help 'unblock Parliament'.[208] Schnadhorst, speaking at Brighton in 1882 rallied the Federation:

> When Mr Gladstone and the government met the House of Commons and said it was impossible for them to conduct the business with the present antiquated rules… there was only one course open to every loyal member of the Liberal party, to sacrifice his personal convictions, in order to support Mr Gladstone.[209]

Only once that had been effected would Chamberlain and the Caucus make headway in promoting another policy to which all grassroots Liberals could adhere – the extension of the franchise to county householders. Throughout 1883 the National Liberal Federation demanded a democratic franchise for the whole country and with its support Chamberlain prevailed in Cabinet and won a commitment to legislate from the Prime Minister, despite a vigorous rearguard action fought by the Whig Hartington, who averred in a speech at Accrington that 'moderate citizens could not swallow such a Reform Bill as had been sketched by the Radical Caucus'.[210] The Third Reform Act of 1884-5 was – as even its opponents conceded – a triumph for the persistence of Chamberlain's NLF and its leadership.

Until that success, however, the NLF had been shackled to Gladstone's cause of institutional reform in the Commons to counter Irish obstruction. It used all its guile and influence. In Ostrogorski's words:

As soon as the Ministry met with resistance or with a display of hostile feeling in either House, the managers of the central Caucus let loose the Associations, urged them to hold meetings, to send monster petitions to Parliament, to vote resolutions of protest or indignation, to remonstrate with their members or even to give them direct orders. 'We ask you,' ran the Birmingham circulars sometimes, 'to put yourselves at once in communication with your representatives in the House of Commons, strongly urging them to be in their places on …next and to vote for…' By force of habit the co-operation of the local Associations with Birmingham became, so to speak, automatic…they voted all the same, convened public meetings, inveighed against members who were not loyal to Mr Gladstone.[211]

The recommended strategies listed above quite evidently owe everything to the techniques successfully employed by the National Education League, and refined by its Birmingham leaders. A central part of this was the pressure brought to bear on MPs. We see this in another example in 1884 when Schnadhorst drafted a letter to the Liberal Associations in support of the President of the Board of Trade, Joseph Chamberlain, who had staked much political capital on his Merchant Shipping Bill, which aimed to tackle the dangers of overloaded and unseaworthy vessels.

The ship owners are organising a serious opposition to the Bill. The evils which the Bill is intended to remedy are so grave that it will be very lamentable if it should be defeated in the interests of a single class. The only way to prevent this is to induce as many Liberal members as possible to support its reference to a Grand Committee. Will you help in the matter by inducing your Association to pass a Resolution in favour of reference of the Bill to a Grand Committee and by communication with your own or other members of Parliament with whom you are acquainted? [212]

This is how the Birmingham-based machine operated. It was centred on the key personnel in the Paradise Street Headquarters and as Ostrogorski put it: 'The whole process of agitation which was methodically applied throughout all the country, all the resolutions, circulars etc. emanated from three or four persons in the offices of the Federation.' Later he added: 'The Secretary's office – and Mr Schnadhorst was the Federation personified – is the driving-wheel of the Federation (as is the) Publications department.'[213] As we can see then, the NLF leadership (Schnadhorst especially, in cahoots with Chamberlain) directed the agitation – it publicised the chosen issues, it chivvied the local Associations, it demanded loyalty to its favourite causes. It could be brutally direct in its criticisms of recalcitrant members. One NLF circular in 1881 described how:

During the present session of Parliament it appeared there were some who were not heartily loyal to their leaders. (This) has threatened the government with very serious embarrassments. Liberal members recently supported an amendment hostile to the Irish Bill of the Government. The Federation called on the Associations to take measures…[214]

Predictably, the tactic of putting pressure on Liberal members led to accusations that the NLF sought to neuter MPs and turn them into mere delegates. The battles at Bradford and Newcastle, where the sitting MPs, W.E. Forster and J. Cowen, offended their constituency parties, became *causes célèbres* and initiated a wider debate on the behaviour, and the ulterior motives, of the Caucus. A letter in *The Spectator* in 1878 asked: 'Is the judgement of a party committee the best test a constituency can apply to an Old Member's fitness?' Many felt MPs should vote on their consciences and use their own judgement, not simply vote as the Caucus directed.[215] Nonconformists in the Bradford caucus objected to Forster as author of that controversial Education Act of 1870 and Newcastle's Liberal leadership opposed Joseph Cowen because he could not bring himself to support Gladstone's Irish coercion policy and indeed because he clung to his independence. Forster survived; Cowen was driven to retire from public life.

The recurrent question from 1877 onwards was – '*cui bono?*' To what extent were local Associations merely acting at the behest, and for the benefit, of Birmingham and of Joseph Chamberlain? For the Birmingham Machine operating the NLF determined what was deserving of publicity and of support. It could seem a narrow, powerful and manipulative clique. Even Garvin was prepared to concede that: 'Sometimes, perhaps often, wire-pulling did manufacture appearances of popular feeling not in fact corresponding to the true balance of public opinion.'[216] He was only articulating what was common currency in some quarters.

Manchester Liberals, for example, increasingly objected to the way the Federation's guiding lights determined the content of circulars, with little consultation of the hundred or so Associations. Their patience was exhausted by the Federation's circular of 11 February 1882 calling on Liberal Associations to rally behind the plan to change the procedure of the House of Commons to counter Irish filibustering. There had been no attempt by the officers of the Federation to confer with the Associations. It was the high-handedness which offended, not the policy. The *Manchester Guardian* voiced the resentment of a provincial rival to Birmingham. It charged the NLF's General Committee with:

being made up of an overwhelming proportion of representatives from the immediate neighbourhood of Birmingham; they affect to focus opinion and to pull the strings for the whole country... And when it assumes an executive function we venture to say that it entirely oversteps its proper use...encouraged or indeed originated as it may be by Mr Chamberlain.[217]

Some Manchester Liberals resented Chamberlain because he was 'violent and domineering' in his manner.

It was violence of a very different sort in 1884 which besmirched the reputation of the Birmingham Caucus and – by association – the National Liberal Federation with which it was inextricably entwined. In October Birmingham Conservatives organised a rally in support of the House of Lords, which had just rejected the Third Reform (Franchise) Bill, with the aim of getting Gladstone's government to introduce a complementary measure of seat redistribution at the same time. Lord Randolph Churchill and Sir Stafford Northcote were invited to address party members within the park at Aston Manor. Many Birmingham Radicals were affronted by what they perceived as an incursion onto their turf. Large numbers of the c.120,000 tickets issued were purchased by Liberals and Trade Union officials. Conservative organisers also alleged that many tickets were being forged, though 'no one in authority on the Liberal side lent any countenance to such proceedings'. according to Churchill. On the day of the meeting a Liberal counter-demonstration was called, with hand-bills summoning 'the Men of Birmingham and the Midlands to assemble outside the Park. Let all who can get admittance attend the Tory meetings, wear the Gladstone badge and show you are not ashamed of your colours.' Three large processions, some 15,000 strong, converged on waste ground hard by Aston Manor's Park walls and a thoughtfully deployed waggon was used as a platform for ladders to facilitate the scaling of the walls. Planks of wood were then employed as battering rams to breach the wall, allowing thousands of excited Liberal supporters to pour through to the Park.

The Conservatives' open-air meetings in the Park were broken up by rioters; then, once the Great Hall in the Manor itself had been stormed, stones, potatoes and chairs were flung at the Members of Parliament attempting to speak on the platform. Northcote and Churchill were overwhelmed by the ferocity of the assault and driven from the Hall. The platform of Aston's skating-rink collapsed while a free fight raged across it. The celebratory Tory firework display was ruined when the set-piece – a likeness of Sir Stafford Northcote – was ignited upside down, a crowning humiliation for the Conservative interlopers on Liberal home territory.[218]

If the day itself belonged to Birmingham Liberals, the riposte afterwards was choreographed very carefully by Lord Randolph Churchill, who in speech after speech across the country – and most notably in a debate on the affair in the House of Commons

– fastened the responsibility for the disorder and intimidation on Joseph Chamberlain and his Caucus. Indeed, in the House on 30 October 1884 he declared that Chamberlain knew beforehand of the Liberal counter-demonstration and that a riot was planned; he did nothing to prevent it. For Chamberlain, a government minister, it was a dangerous moment and the mood in the House became distinctly unfriendly. He was saved only by the triumphant production of a series of affidavits sworn by local roughs, to the effect that they had been engaged by the Conservative Association to turn Liberals out from the meeting – they admitted to employing violence in so doing.[219]

Chamberlain may have been innocent of foreknowledge, but it was clear soon enough that others in the bowels of the Machine were complicit in shady and disreputable behaviour. Francis Schnadhorst seemed most responsible and was accused of conniving at the manufacture of false tickets. Worse, wrote Garvin, it then emerged that the affidavits had been 'furnished by Schnadhorst (and) were exposed as for the most part the false witness of unsavoury persons; the mystery surrounding them became the subject of summons and counter-summons in the Birmingham Assizes between December 1884 and March 1885'.[220] The whole affair did damage to Chamberlain, to his relations with Schnadhorst – with whom a certain chill grew up – and to the entire Caucus project.

Others were prepared to overlook the seamier side of the Caucus. In 1885, the NLF took a further step to official recognition in the Liberal Party, when through Schnadhorst's initiative, it developed closer cooperation with the chief whip and the Liberal Central Association (LCA) with an immediate positive impact on that year's General Election. The value to the Liberal leadership of the Birmingham Machine's extra-parliamentary organisation was now acknowledged. For what it had done was to transform politics. Where a decade earlier the Liberal party had been represented by bigwigs with local sway who were unaccountable, Chamberlain's NLF had opened up party and policy to democratic influence. That message had reached Ipswich whose *Free Press* commented:

> If the work is carried on (here) as it is in Birmingham, in Glasgow, Leeds and Leicester, the happy result will be that Liberal politics will be wrenched from the grasp of official wirepullers who creep around the backstairs of the party, and be relegated to those alone who have the right to control them, the Liberal electors of the whole country.[221]

Furthermore, the Birmingham Caucus had nationally propagated methods refined in municipal and School Board elections. Associations around the country had emulated its diligent focus on electoral registers, with party officials checking proofs of fact, pursuing cases in law suits, concentrating on the pettifogging details of every household in every street. They learnt that the canvass was critical in identifying and cultivating the floating voter, for house-to-house door-stepping helped differentiate between friends, enemies, the doubtfuls and the waverers.[222] In a letter to Schnadhorst Chamberlain championed methods he helped refine back in the late 1860s:

> I believe that the very success of the Liberals everywhere depends very much upon the thoroughness of their previous canvass and upon the opportunities they have had for educating and interesting the electors.[223]

Birmingham exemplified the importance of public meetings and of lectures. Equally the NLF demonstrated the value of printed material; Schnadhorst's Publications department bombarded its Associations with letters and circulars persuading and hectoring. As we have seen in previous chapters, in Robert Dale, Henry Crosskey, John Skirrow Wright, George Dawson and Joseph Chamberlain himself, Birmingham had blazed a trail in the way of persuasive oratory.

From all this too the Conservative opposition had learnt; the Caucus had transformed all, not just Liberal, politics. At Lord Randolph Churchill's bidding his party had been democratised, the National Union of Conservative Associations had been created, some of the Radical prescriptions espoused by Chamberlain and his allies had been adopted, and Birmingham electoral techniques had been enthusiastically embraced. The Conservatives had gone so far in learning from their rivals as to steal a march by founding the Primrose League in 1883. This body with a membership of *c.*1 million by 1890 provided an army of volunteer canvassers, an invaluable and inimitable electoral asset.

For all the undoubted positive qualities enumerated above, the Aston Manor affair represents a darker side to the story of Birmingham's Caucus and its national manifestation, the NLF. For, to early criticisms of Chamberlainite dictatorship and of assaults on the independence of Liberal MPs, was now added the uncomfortable suspicion that the Caucus was prepared to use riot and thuggery to get its way. The events of the next twenty years only reinforced that impression. It was Birmingham Unionist supporters of Chamberlain who nearly killed David Lloyd George at the Town Hall in 1901 when he came to speak against Joe's South African war. They harried Winston Churchill in 1904 when he dared to make a pro-Free Trade speech in a city committed to Tariff Reform. The election campaign of 1906 was punctuated by boorish disruption of anti-Chamberlain meetings. It seemed that the Birmingham Machine was to become habituated to the use of strong-arm tactics.

Within a few years, the close relationship between the Birmingham Liberal

Association and its progeny – the National Liberal Federation – had been destroyed by Gladstone's commitment to Home Rule in 1886 and by Chamberlain's adamantine resistance to it. What ensued is the subject of the next chapter. Here it is enough to relate that while Birmingham's Liberals backed Chamberlain, when he made an impassioned appeal to the ruling 2,000 in April 1886, many did so reluctantly. In the messy separation which followed, attitudes hardened; some of the Caucus's leaders stayed loyal to Chamberlain, and to the c.70 Liberal MPs who championed Unionism for fear that Home Rule foreshadowed the break-up of Britain and the Empire. Some abandoned him. This painful and bitter Liberal divorce was to be a major set-back to the unity, and the seemingly inexorable progress, of Birmingham's Machine.

When most of the NLF executive at a London meeting in May 1886 voted for Gladstone, the overwhelming bulk of the General Committee, Birmingham men all, resigned: William Harris (the Chairman), J.T. Bunce, Richard Chamberlain, Henry Crosskey, William Kenrick and J. Powell Williams. Schnadhorst did not, staying fiercely loyal to the Prime Minister. Within months the National Liberal Federation had moved to Parliament Street in London, next door to the Liberal Central Association, allowing Schnadhorst to be secretary to both bodies at once and to gain a singular control of the Liberal party's national organisation. Now, with a metropolitan base, the NLF no longer articulated the provincial voice.[224] Self-evidently it ceased in 1886 to be a projection of the Chamberlain Machine and the Birmingham Caucus. Its leaders now sought a new vehicle for their national ambitions.

Francis Schnadhorst

Chamberlain thought Schnadhorst the model of loyal efficiency for more than a decade. Their views on how politics should be organised coincided completely, and they appear co-conspirators at times as they expanded the influence of the National Liberal Federation. Yet, their relationship was strictly professional; they did not become close friends who shared intimacies. And when their paths diverged in 1886 they quickly became sworn enemies; Chamberlain did not easily forgive opposition from former lieutenants and allies, as John Morley would also find to his cost.

Schnadhorst was born in Birmingham on 24 August 1840 and educated at King Edward's School. The son of a draper and hosier, he succeeded to the family business on his father's death. Early on he became interested in public affairs, being connected to the Birmingham Mutual Society, the Central Literary Association and then the Central Nonconformist Committee. By birth and education, he was an ardent Liberal although, unlike many other members of the Machine, he was not drawn to municipal action by encountering the civic gospel or by rubbing shoulders with fellow worshippers in Birmingham's chapels. His first party political involvement was as vice-chairman of the local ward committee, when supporting George Dixon in his campaign in July 1867 to succeed William Scholefield as one of Birmingham's MPs.

It was as secretary of the Central Nonconformist Committee from 1870 – a role for which he had been identified by Robert Dale and Henry Crosskey – that he first proved his worth as an organiser. He fought the Nonconformist battle over the Endowed Schools Act before the House of Commons Select Commission, and proved equally articulate both in person and on paper. His reputation was such that he was asked to be secretary of the Birmingham Liberal Association, where he proved he had absorbed all the lessons of how to mastermind a campaign taught by the acknowledged master of caucus politics, William Harris. Schnadhorst proved his mettle in the November 1873 elections, both municipal – this was the occasion of Chamberlain's election as Mayor – and School Board. In the latter he ensured, by close management of the Liberal vote, that there was no repeat of the embarrassments of 1870; this time there was a handsome Liberal victory. Schnadhorst had himself been one of the Liberal contingent in the Town Council, representing St Mary's ward but his personal defeat at this election prompted his withdrawal from front-line involvement for good. In 1885 he was given first refusal on one of two new Birmingham seats created by the Third Reform Act; again, in 1891 he was courted by Newcastle. Still he declined to enter Parliament. He preferred to wield power from behind the arras.

His formidable organising skills were showcased in the 1874 General Election when, despite a strong national swing to Disraeli's Conservatives, Birmingham's Liberal candidates once again swept the board. That success awakened interest in Birmingham's Caucus among Liberals across the country and Schnadhorst became a peripatetic salesman, encouraging the establishment of new Liberal Associations founded on democratic principles. Inevitably he became a central figure in the National Liberal Federation – he was appointed its first Secretary in 1877. He worked ceaselessly to establish popular control in borough Liberal parties, motivated by a dislike of the older methods of party management which relied on wealth and influence. His Paradise Street HQ dispatched circulars and publicity material to generate support for Liberal leaders from Associations affiliated to the NLF. Schnadhorst and Chamberlain both argued in the columns of the national Press that Gladstone's stunning Liberal victory in the 1880 General Election was essentially due to the radical reforms introduced by the NLF.

Yet Schnadhorst knew that while the Party had done well in the boroughs it had failed to break through in the counties, where Conservative landowners dominated and Whig control of the Liberal party persisted. He worked hard to ensure that Whig magnates did not compromise with their Conservative neighbours and simply allow them a clear run in the county constituencies, as had frequently happened. He initiated a programme which targeted villages, and he and Chamberlain publicised plans for a new Reform Bill, which would extend the vote to county householders – the agricultural labourers. He worked so hard in these years that it affected his health, and despite a therapeutic break in Australia in 1882–3 the heavier and heavier work of the Federation forced him in 1884 to hand over the secretaryship of the Birmingham Liberal Association.

He continued to lobby for Parliamentary reform and indeed had considerable influence on the debate on redistribution of seats, his long-standing support for single-member constituencies being rewarded in the Reform Act of 1885. His anger at the obstruction of the Reform Bill by the House of Lords in the autumn of 1884 led him into some disreputable behaviour at Aston Manor, Birmingham in October 1884. It appears he was party to the issue of forged tickets issued to allow Birmingham Liberals to disrupt a large Conservative rally in the town; and that he was involved in false affidavits by local thugs purporting to prove that Conservatives had hired them to mete out retribution to Liberal trespassers. The taint of foul play certainly clung to Schnadhorst for a while after this. When Lord Randolph Churchill contested John Bright's seat in Birmingham in 1885 he alluded on the platform to 'the dark and evil deeds of Mr Schnadhorst'.

Gladstone's commitment to Home Rule for Ireland acted like an exploding grenade on the hitherto largely harmonious and well-ordered relationships in the NLF and Birmingham Caucus. Joseph Chamberlain opposed a Home Rule Parliament for Ireland as signalling the break-up of the United Kingdom and of the Empire; he also feared for Ulster. He presented his arguments to a meeting of the Birmingham Liberal Association's '2000' in April 1886 and only his compelling advocacy and the strategically significant intervention of Robert Dale and

J.T. Bunce allowed him to prevail over Gladstone's supporters – led by Francis Schnadhorst. This was the occasion of a deep and lasting split between Chamberlain and Schnadhorst. It also explains why Schnadhorst abandoned Birmingham which – after various vicissitudes between 1886 and 1889 – became an increasingly impregnable fortress for Chamberlain and Unionism. Instead Schnadhorst took the NLF to London, shorn of virtually all the Birmingham team who had staffed the organisation. It based itself next to the Liberal Central Association, the official body of national Liberalism. Accordingly, the mouthpiece of grass-roots Liberalism achieved the imprimatur of the whips and party leaders. Schnadhorst was secretary to both establishments.

His years in these posts were marked by a struggle to raise money for the Liberal party which, with the loss of the Whigs to the Unionists in 1886, had suffered a severely reduced income. His secret arrangement with Cecil Rhodes by which he accepted £5000 from the controversial Empire-builder led to embarrassment when it was revealed and to accusations that the foreign policy of a future Liberal government was being compromised.

Schnadhorst's central position in the party gave him considerable influence over the choice of Liberal candidates. His own espousal of the candidature of the leading trade unionist, Henry Broadhurst, at Cirencester may have foundered but it was indicative of his determination to expand the number of Labour candidates for Liberal seats in these years. The number of Labour candidates did increase while Schnadhorst was secretary of the LCA (21 in 1892), though his encouragement to Liberal Associations to extend a warm welcome to newly enfranchised working men had not been universally well received. That General Election of 1892 was to be the last in which he played a part; the Liberals did win, although with a majority of only 40, and the party relied on the Irish vote to carry legislation. By now he was suffering regular bouts of serious illness. He retired from the secretaryships of the NLF and the LCA, in 1893 and 1894 respectively. Although he complained to Broadhurst that 'there is not the slightest intention of recognising my work in any way', he had in fact been rewarded serially: £1,000 in 1877 by a grateful Chamberlain on behalf of Birmingham Liberals; £10,000 in 1887 by a Liberal party to which he had remained loyal in the split of 1886; and again another £5,000 in 1892. Despite that rather unattractive streak of self-pity, this Liberal generosity is evidence of the high esteem in which the party held his rare political gifts. The Times *obituary concluded: 'The secret of that success lay in his knowledge of men. A ten minutes' interview would suffice for him to arrive at a fairly accurate estimate of a newcomer's capabilities and weaknesses.'*

His end was truly bathetic. He died in January 1900, not in his home city of Birmingham, but at the Priory, a private lunatic asylum in Roehampton. Besides debilitating deafness, he had endured an illness whose convulsions afflicted him for six long years.

John Thackray Bunce

J.T. Bunce was one of the most important members of the Birmingham Machine, its acknowledged historian and publicist. From the inception of the Caucus in the 1860s to the establishment of Birmingham Unionism in 1886 he was omnipresent, and his considerable influence in the Press ensured that he was valued and cultivated by Chamberlain and other Birmingham Liberal leaders.

Born in Faringdon (now Oxfordshire) in 1828, the son of a watchmaker, he moved with his family when nine years old to Birmingham, as his father had set himself up as a watchmaker and silversmith in Digbeth. Educated at the Gem Street school – one of the branch schools established by the King Edward's Foundation – he never progressed to the Grammar School itself, instead embarking on a seven-year printing apprenticeship on the Midland Counties Herald. *Whilst there he wrote a letter for the paper arguing that Birmingham needed an art gallery and museum. That letter impressed the editorial team and he was given a job as a reporter on the newspaper. It was the start of a journalistic career which built him a national reputation; further, the letter's subject matter marked him out as a progressive, ahead of George Dawson and the advocates of the civic gospel who would bring about a Birmingham Enlightenment, in his vision of a better educated, more cultured citizen.*

Although he moved on to report for a Tory newspaper, Aris's Birmingham Gazette, *in 1852, his personal inclinations were increasingly Liberal, the result of listening to one of John Bright's Town Hall addresses. This conversion coincided with the offer of the editorship of the* Birmingham Daily Post *in 1862, a position he held until 1898, in which time he became acknowledged as 'the leading journalist of the Midlands'. It helped that there was such a close identity of interests between himself and the proprietor, John Jaffray, who was an ardent Liberal and fellow Machine member, the first treasurer of the Birmingham Liberal Association, active in the National Liberal Federation, a member of the Free Library committee and a trustee of the Picture Gallery Fund. Bunce's own sympathies – Liberal, educational and cultural –therefore found an echo in his employer.*

As editor of the Birmingham Daily Post *and the* Birmingham Weekly Post *he wrote the papers' leaders and oversaw their news departments. The papers' political inclinations reflected his own and those of his proprietor. The* Post *provided robust support for the civic gospel, the Birmingham Education Society, the National Education League, the National Liberal Federation and eventually Unionism.*

Bunce's own role in the mid-century transformation of Birmingham expressed itself in his interest in the edification of its citizens. He was a committee member of the Old Library; he served on the committee that planned the central library from its establishment in 1860 and was one of the founders of the Shakespeare Library. In these roles he was living out a deep faith in the power of the written word to improve the lot of common man.

Membership of the Edgbaston Debating Society opened doors to an influential network of ambitious and high-minded Liberal young men, and he encountered the Chamberlains, Kenricks, Martineaus and C.E. Mathews among others. By 1869 he was already a key and trusted member of Chamberlain's circle when he became the Chairman of the Publishing Committee on the Executive Committee of the new National Education League. In his dual roles with the NEL and the Post *Bunce ensured that reports of significant League events were fully covered in the pages of his weekly. At the same time, he was a committee member of the Birmingham Liberal Association from 1869, in those crucial years when it established the party's grip on Birmingham's levers of power.*

In 1877, like Collings, Harris and others, he passed seamlessly from the recently extinguished corpse of the NEL to the nascent National Liberal Federation; he ensured the Post's *editorials gave strong support to the Liberal policies the NLF championed. That backing was rewarded both with his own appointment to a borough magistracy and – in time – with a knighthood for his proprietor, Sir John Jaffray. Chamberlain evidently valued him for more than endorsement of his newspaper. His correspondence with Bunce is punctuated with requests to re-phrase or polish 'with your proverbial skill', League and then Federation literature; there are references too to Bunce's advocacy of 'the Birmingham theory of municipal government'.*

J.T. Bunce's loyalty to Chamberlain was never better illustrated than by his actions in the spring of 1886. He and Robert Dale secured a meeting for Chamberlain with Birmingham's Liberal General Committee, the '2000,' in the wake of his resignation from Cabinet over Home Rule. Bunce did so in the teeth of an increasingly hostile Francis Schnadhorst, who remained both constant to Gladstone and determined to spike Chamberlain's guns. Dale and J.T. Bunce also ensured that a vote was taken to secure the support of the majority for their rebellious MP. Still, Bunce was greatly unsettled by the events of 1886-1888 as Liberals decided whether to support Gladstone, or embrace Unionism, and descended into internecine in-fighting. His Birmingham Post *reflected his own position – that he hoped to effect reconciliation between the two warring factions, for many Birmingham Liberal Association meetings had descended into recrimination and disorder. Bunce stood down from all his positions in the Liberal party. By 1888, with growing clarity in Birmingham politics, Bunce had thrown in his lot with Chamberlain's Unionist party and the* Post *articulated his position of support for the new Birmingham Liberal Unionist Association, and the Radical/Imperial policies that Chamberlain's West Midlands brand of Unionism promoted.*

J.T. Bunce was equally important as an historian, his two-volume History of the Corporation of Birmingham *(1878-1885) establishing a persuasive and enduring narrative of the nobility of the municipal mission, which he christened the 'civic gospel'. He shared with William Kenrick, a close ally in the Machine, an abiding passion for the Fine Arts, and like him was a pioneer in the establishment of the Birmingham School of Art, arguing for a municipal school in the columns of the* Post *in 1879 and, with the help of funds from local businessman Richard Tangye, winning the argument. The Birmingham School of Art (opened in 1885) was the first such school to be run municipally. He remained involved as a member of the management sub-committee of the Museum and School of Art.*

He died at his home in Edgbaston in June 1899, just as his long-standing friend and ally, the Colonial Secretary Joseph Chamberlain, embarked on his controversial Imperial escapade at the expense of the Boers in South Africa.

BUILDING ANEW AFTER THE CRASH OF 1886

O nly an incorrigible optimist with an iron constitution could have survived the sequence of political disasters which afflicted Joseph Chamberlain in 1886. Reviled by many Liberals and Irish as 'the man who killed Home Rule', and as the Brutus who had knifed their leader, Chamberlain faced a troublingly uncertain future in national politics. Old friends and allies abandoned him, and even his NLF sided with Gladstone against him. Birmingham too for a while failed to provide unquestioned, rock-solid support after the Home Rule debacle. Yet, within a few short years, signs of a new power base were visible, the outlines of what would become the most impregnable electoral fortress in British political history, Chamberlain's Duchy. It was a citadel of Unionism which stayed loyal to the memory of its first leader long after his death. This chapter traces the demise of Chamberlain's first Caucus, and the creation after 1886 of the complex apparatus which would replace it.

A showdown between the ageing Prime Minister, William Gladstone, and Birmingham's Radical champion, seemed inevitable by early 1886. Chamberlain was frustrated by Gladstone's lukewarm reception for both his Unauthorised Programme of social reforms in 1885 and his ideas for a municipal-style devolution of powers to Ireland. He also believed the Grand Old Man should make way for the next generation, for which he was the standard-bearer. Gladstone for his part resented Chamberlain's ambitions, and his tendency to ignore traditions of Cabinet collective responsibility when making Radical pronouncements. But the proximate cause of their complete rift was Gladstone's proposal of Irish Home Rule. Increasingly he believed fifty years of Irish violence and intractability could only be solved by a dramatic change of policy, that of conceding to Ireland its own Parliament. He saw what was called 'Home Rule for Ireland' as a great mission cause, which would enlist and unite all classes in pursuit of a higher goal. He was determined to reveal this volte-face in his own time, for he was well aware how deeply unpopular this would be to many Englishmen. Once the election of 1885 had secured him a majority (with Irish National support) the new Prime Minister set about appointing a Cabinet and preparing the ground. He had included Chamberlain in his Cabinet – in the lowly position of President of the Local Government Board – but within weeks the disclosure of his Home Rule plans in Cabinet had precipitated Chamberlain's dramatic resignation.[225]

For Chamberlain, the issues were multifaceted. Home Rule threatened to initiate the dissolution of the United Kingdom and ultimately the Empire. Hence his policy was that of Unionism. He worried that an Irish Parliament would persecute protestant Ulster.

This Home Rule proposal of Gladstone's implied a degree of separation such that Irish MPs would be excluded from Westminster, resurrecting the old battle cry 'No taxation without representation'. He objected to Gladstone's choice of this specific mission cause; to Chamberlain it was simply one giant distraction from the social issues – education, land, local government – urgently needing attention in mainland Britain. Yet when Chamberlain resigned in frustration and disappointment in April 1886 it caused consternation even among his friends in his heartland of Birmingham. Schnadhorst, in that spring of 1886, rapidly changed from sympathising with Chamberlain's mistreatment at the hands of the Prime Minister: 'You cannot be treated unfairly or unjustly without those working with you feeling keen resentment,' to one deploring any falling-out: 'I should regard your severance from Mr Gladstone as a great calamity.' He later wrote: 'If it were not for the personal loyalty to yourself an overwhelming majority of Liberals would support the government. Cannot the breach be healed? Every party and personal consideration points to the desirability if possible of seeking some way of securing unity of the party to support the principle of the bill.' [226]

This was a harbinger of a wider split in the Birmingham Caucus. As alluded to in chapter 5, through the auspices of Bunce and Dr Dale, Chamberlain secured a meeting of Birmingham's ruling 2000 (on 21 April 1886) immediately after he had voted against the second reading of Gladstone's Home Rule Bill. At this Birmingham meeting he studiously avoided attacking both Gladstone directly and Home Rule as a principle, but he demanded amendments to what he argued was a flawed Bill. He tapped a deep reservoir of loyalty to win overwhelming support that night. Still, he failed to win round Schnadhorst, who he already detected to be cooling; soon enough he was to defect with the NLF, lock, stock and barrel to London. This was a near mortal wound for the Birmingham Caucus. It was later compounded by the desertion of William Harris, the Caucus's architect and a master builder of electoral edifices; a number of other supporters joined them from the Birmingham Liberal Association.

Even the loyalty of those closest to him in the Machine, like Powell Williams, was tested. In April 1886 the latter was enthusiastically writing: 'I believe your course will more and more commend itself to all those whose minds are not governed by fetishism or led away by spitefulness; for my part I am convinced you have done the right thing.' Within a fortnight, he had lost his nerve, for he told Chamberlain: 'The people are stark mad about the G.O.M (Grand Old Man) and if they got the idea that we were working against Home Rule it would be impossible to hold them.' Thereafter he counselled caution – abstain from the Bill, don't oppose it; don't be seen with Hartington at public meetings, for he was a bête noir for many Radicals. His aim was to temper the wrath of those Liberals bent on retribution against Chamberlain. The latter ignored these suggestions. Still, it was reassuring in the final vote in June to have Powell Williams' unconditional support: 'I intend to follow you into the lobby, partly because I value your friendship in a very special degree and partly because, having supported you in the manly course you have taken, I will not be guilty of the meanness of standing aloof from you in this critical moment.'[227]

It was a 'critical moment' indeed and around Powell Williams and a few others who did not 'stand aloof' from him Chamberlain was to construct a new organisation to replace the Caucus. However, we must be careful to avoid attributing the leadership of the rebellion entirely to Chamberlain. He was not absolutely alone. Nationally, Lord Hartington and his Whigs had helped swell the numbers of Liberal dissidents, for they recoiled from making concessions to what they deemed to be Irish criminals, and they feared the progressive dissolution of the British Empire. Hartington formed his own Liberal Unionist Committee (later, renamed the Liberal Unionist Association, which was the national body for Liberal Unionism) in May 1886, which Chamberlain later joined. Hartington's followers and those looking to Chamberlain, comprised the 93 Liberal MPs who voted against Gladstone's Home Rule Bill in June 1886; the defeat precipitated Gladstone's resignation and a dissolution.[228]

Lord Salisbury, the Conservative leader, in gratitude for their role in stopping Gladstone so abruptly, vowed not to oppose those Liberals who had rebelled and so demonstrated their attachment to the Union, a gesture reciprocated by the Liberal Unionists led by Hartington. This meant that Chamberlain's Birmingham redoubt was largely free from open Conservative opposition in the ensuing General Election of summer 1886. With Liberals in Birmingham fractured and fractious, and the Gladstonians either disorganised or unwilling to oppose in the hope of future party reunification, 6 out of 7 of the Birmingham seats returned Chamberlainite Liberals with the seventh being a Conservative, Henry Matthews. Altogether, nationally, 77 Liberal Unionists were returned. Of these some 17 or so were supporters of Chamberlain.

Chamberlain held himself apart. For from the very start – in a perplexingly complex situation – he found himself faced by opposition on several fronts. He had alienated himself from the Gladstonians by his articulate opposition to the Home Rule Bill. He had for years despised the reactionary influence of the Whigs on the Liberal party; their baleful influence had prompted the creation of the NLF (see chapter 5). Now Hartington was comfortably settling in to an alliance with the reviled Tories, represented by the aristocratic class who Chamberlain had but a year earlier derided, saying 'they toil not neither do they spin'. To preserve his Radical credentials it was important that

Chamberlain not be seen to have sold out to the old class enemy, even if their shared response to the threat to the Union threw them together.

Thus it was that while Hartington was founding the Liberal Unionist Committee (LUC), Chamberlain was determined to preserve an independent organisation, and announced the creation of the National Radical Union, his new equivalent to the old National Liberal Federation. He outlined his thoughts to his brother, Arthur, in early June 1886. Family and intimates were to be the core of his new Machine:

> I am not at all indisposed to forming a separate committee from the LUC with a headquarters in Birmingham. Will you take it over with a few friends? Would you take over the chairmanship with half a dozen men to help you? Its aim will be to secure the extension of local government to all parts of the UK under the supreme authority of the Imperial Parliament.
>
> President – JC; Chairman of the Executive Committee – Jesse Collings; Treasurer – Arthur Chamberlain. Dale, Dixon, Powell Williams, W. Kenrick and J.A. Kenrick might be asked.
>
> We want someone clever with his hands to draw up circulars. We might imitate the League and have a Chairman of the Publishing Committee – Jennings? Harris could run an Electoral Committee…
>
> The best name will be 'National Radical Union'. We should get out a private circular asking people to join as Vice Presidents. I will subscribe £1,000 to be called up as needed. W.S. Caine and W. Kenrick will be VPs. We should ask every one of the 46 radical MPs who were in the division last night to be VPs. I have prepared an address to the electors.[229]

This battery of instructions reveals Chamberlain's sense of urgency, his desire to develop his own operation, his understanding of the mechanics of how to organise a new Political Machine and finally his reliance on a small group of intimates. He was even dubious about the loyalty of Dale and of Bunce, who distanced themselves from Chamberlain's stand. Chamberlain concluded the correspondence with his brother with the injunction to 'ask Bunce, though he is no good'. This was an unfair and spontaneous aside; fortunately for Chamberlain and his cause Bunce, the proprietor John Jaffray and the *Birmingham Daily Post* abundantly proved their loyalty in the years to come.

Although the National Radical Union (NRU) was small – when it first met in the Midland Institute in Birmingham in June 1886 'the room was but partially filled' – it punched above its weight because of the exposure Chamberlain, its leader, brought it. Yet critics mocked it as a party of 'his brothers, his brothers-in-law, his Whips and his henchmen'.[230] A few years later, in 1889, a more confident Chamberlain would wryly refer to this in jest, saying to laughter: 'We have had a conference of over 1000 delegates, and our opponents said that "Mr Chamberlain had his family party".[231]

The National Radical Union was to provide the constructive reform programme which Gladstonian Liberals by their obsession with Home Rule had ignored. In some ways the crash of 1886 must have felt like a liberation for Chamberlain for he could now shape a party with policies much more to his liking than that of Gladstone's Liberals in the early 1880s. West Birmingham's Liberals avowed: 'We are not only Unionist but we are Radical Unionist and though we welcome the Conservatives when they come up to standard, we do not go for Toryism.' Birmingham's brand of Unionism would be distinctive, and would add a new socially reformative dimension to the Unionist alliance but, from the start, 'the NRU acted as a separate though friendly organisation'.[232] Even Salisbury recognised its electoral value in 1886, which explains his policy of not challenging Liberal Unionist seats. He could see that Chamberlain would appeal to large numbers of working-class voters in town and country.

The National Radical Union had its own branches (as, for example, at Bradford), its own canvassing, publicity and lectures for working men, and its emphasis differed from the Hartingtonian Liberal Unionist Association which focused on preserving the Union, while the NRU reflected Chamberlain's interest in local government reform and espoused industrial, housing and land reforms. At times, it seemed that Chamberlain was intent on building a rival national organisation to the larger Hartington's Liberal Unionist Association. Hartington himself certainly thought so: 'I know that one or two places where he (Chamberlain) went last year he suggested to our local branches that they should affiliate themselves to his National Radical Union.'[233]

In the first year after the Home Rule debacle Chamberlain's party was a sickly child, and its progenitor a troubled figure fighting for political survival. To navigate between the shoals of Conservatives, Hartington supporters and Gladstonians, and chart his own course, he relied for a while on a friendship with the Chancellor of the Exchequer, Lord Randolph Churchill, who had many of the same reforming instincts and who was a 'soothing influence' in Birmingham in helping reconcile Conservatives to laying down arms against the old Liberal enemy on Salisbury's orders.[234] They talked wistfully of creating a new centre party with a radical flavour. Churchill overreached himself in his dealings with his party leader, Lord Salisbury, and felt compelled to resign at Christmas in 1886; Chamberlain lost a valued ally in the government. For a while his isolation forced him to seek reunification with Gladstone at the Round Table Conference in early 1887 but Gladstone's intransigence scuppered any progress. His isolation was increased by his dislike for the use of coercion in Ireland, a policy supported by Tories and almost all Liberal Unionists.

All the while there were steady defections as nationally Liberal Unionists drifted back to the Gladstonian camp. And in Birmingham itself, the Birmingham Liberal Association was divided, with the Gladstonians – who had created a Birmingham Home Rule Association to advertise their sound credentials on the issue of the day – increasingly in the ascendant, and with Radical Unionists fighting for survival. Only in late 1887 did Chamberlain's fortunes change, and they did so because he accepted an offer from Salisbury to head a Fisheries Commission to resolve a dispute between the United States and Canada. A successful outcome 'brought enormous benefits' by raising his stock with Salisbury and Balfour, the Conservative leaders, it gave him an international reputation, it allowed him to expound on ideas of Imperial integration, and it brought him domestic happiness in the youthful form of his third wife, Mary Endicott, whom he met in America.[235]

On his return in early 1888 he was re-invigorated. This was reflected in the way he adapted and re-shaped his political organisation. For two years, he had tried to work through the old Caucus, the Birmingham Liberal Association, but Gladstonians in it, 'with Schnadhorst pulling the strings', were now actively contesting municipal elections and indeed 'Radical Unionists had been reduced to minorities in almost all the wards of the town and Gladstonians were preparing to make a clean sweep of the divisional associations'.[236]

5 April 1888 was when the tide turned in Birmingham. A meeting there of the National Radical Union, attended by 250 people, saw the launch of another Machine model, the Birmingham Liberal Unionist Association (BLUA), to work alongside Chamberlain's national organisation, the NRU. Its mechanics are familiar to the student of the Caucus and there are echoes of the language used in the creation of the National Liberal Federation eleven years earlier (see chapter 5). It was avowedly 'popular', and 'anxious to enlist as large a proportion as possible of those who agreed with us, in the work of the party'. It had a recognisable pyramidical structure. There would be '... an annual meeting in every ward of the borough and in areas beyond the municipal borough which form parts of the Party representation. Ward committees would be elected. Representatives would attend divisional councils, and these once elected formed the Grand Committee. A Central Management Committee would then be formed of officers of the associations.' By September 1889 Chamberlain, inevitably the Birmingham Liberal Unionist Association President, was boasting of 5,486 ward members with a Grand Committee of between 2,000 and 2,500. He went on to tell party loyalists that: 'I will not be satisfied until each ward committee numbers 1000 so that we shall be able to maintain the distinctive feature of this great city which, out of

all the great cities of England, has alone returned a solid reputation in favour of the Union.'[237] He was delighted with the way the BLUA developed. He wrote to Mary Endicott: 'My new organisation is going like wild fire; I will give my opponents a taste of my quality and teach them not to tread on my tail again.'[238]

Even as he planned its structure, Chamberlain sought to win the support of the 'Old Firm' of Caucus regulars at the top of his new party. He wrote to Bunce in April 1888 to urge him to commit after two years of havering:

> I sincerely hope you will not accept your nomination to the Liberal Association. It has become a Home Rule Association. (On the other hand) there is every probability that the new Association (the BLUA) will become of supreme importance and will secure the majority of working Liberals. I should like you to be on the Management Committee. I sincerely hope that Dale and Crosskey will throw in their lot with us at this critical time.[239]

Bunce was minded to re-heat his old warm relationship with Chamberlain because increasingly he felt a sympathy for his Imperial instincts, vowing to support him 'through thick and thin in all Imperial matters'.[240] In once again building a team of trusted friends, Chamberlain also secured Powell Williams as Chairman of the new Executive Committee, C.A. Vince (formerly his constituency chairman within the Birmingham Liberal Association), and C.E. Mathews. Vince, the BLUA secretary, became a valued pair of eyes and a source of local wisdom; his letters relate Duchy matters, negotiations managed and political allies squared. Occasionally he had to communicate unpalatable truths as when he reported on conversations he had overheard in Leamington in the midst of the row between Conservative and Liberal Unionists there in 1895, when Chamberlain was referred to disrespectfully by the Conservative chief agent Middleton.

Chamberlain worked hard to enthuse and inspire grassroots members and reports of his ward meetings with them reveal their relentless concentration on electoral success. For example, he attended the joint All Saints, St Paul's and Rotton Park Ward meetings in October 1889. There he learnt that of 1,000 All Saints members, some 400 were active workers, and was assured: 'It would be easy to flood the ward with Liberal Unionist canvassers in 24 hours and to get preliminary returns on the canvass within 3 days.' He gathered that in a first canvass of St Paul's ward, of 1,648 voters willing to declare their allegiance, 981 avowed themselves Liberal Unionists.[241] It was through such attention to the granular detail in the wards that Chamberlain and his BLUA lieutenants, like C.A. Vince and Powell Williams, wrested the initiative back from the Gladstonians.

The creative energy which summoned up the new Birmingham Liberal Unionist Association in 1888 was equally apparent in other developments. Firstly, there was the formation in October the same year of a Birmingham Women's Liberal Unionist Association (WLUA) in Corporation Street, a branch of the national WLUA founded the previous May in Kensington. Birmingham became 'the leading place' for WLUAs, under the vice-presidency of Mrs Herbert Chamberlain (Joseph's brother, Herbert's, wife) and Mrs George Dixon. By 1892 there were 2,000 members in the city. Chamberlain recognised the Birmingham WLUA's 'importance as one of the great branches of our political organisation'. He may have been reactionary in arguing 'it is not a good thing for women to be mixed up in the rough and tumble of our political agitation', but he came to appreciate women's efforts in tracing and registering voters in the 1892 election.[242] By the 1906 General Election campaign they were making an impact on more than registration in Birmingham. The *Birmingham Mail* noted: 'It is being whispered that the lady worker has contributed no mean part to the sweeping successes of the Unionist candidates. Up to three hundred ladies have been setting out in fair and foul weather to canvass the constituencies.'[243]

That creativity was also evident in a further manifestation, the Rural Labourers League, founded in Birmingham in May 1888. Jesse Collings, Chamberlain's close friend and ally and a long-standing champion of agricultural workers, had been cruelly ousted from his National Allotments and Smallholdings Association by a Gladstonian coup. Chamberlain saw an opportunity to extend the appeal of his Radical Union into the countryside, and to force Conservative Unionists in government to legislate for rural labourers. The League would also be a new opportunity for Collings. Its methods would be those of other arms of the Chamberlain Machine: publicity, through the *Rural World* weekly newspaper, recruiting through an army of 3,000 'local village volunteers', and through twenty-five travelling agents. The National Liberal Unionist organisation under Lord Wolmer subsidised it in hopes of winning rural votes but after 1892 interest, influence and support tailed off.[244]

Nor was Chamberlain's feverish reorganisation exhausted yet. Powell Williams explained that it had become 'apparent that the term "radical" had its disadvantages when the object in view was to make an appeal to the Liberal Party generally'.[245] So, the National Radical Union was re-christened the National Liberal Union (NLU) in October 1888. It accentuated its point of difference from the main Liberal Unionist Association headed by Hartington, by being about more than simple preservation of the Union, instead promoting other reforms, such as local government in England, Wales, Scotland and Ireland. Salisbury's government obliged by passing the 1888 Local Government Act as a token of Chamberlain's new-found influence with the Conservative leadership.

At the first annual meeting of the NLU Chamberlain spoke about Birmingham's place in a national Liberal Unionist operation. 'Birmingham has been for a generation the citadel of Liberalism of a very advanced kind. We stand by constructive Liberalism which we learnt from Mr Bright.' He could then be more relaxed about a deepening relationship with the Conservatives which 'has borne the test of experience and the strain of battle and …(Has) brought forth such fruits as the Local Government Bill, the Allotments Bill and the financial policies of Goschen (the Chancellor of the Exchequer, a Liberal Unionist in a Conservative government)'.[246] The recent local elections had seen 'Liberal and Radical Unionists voting Conservative and vice versa'.[247] On the platform were those loyal Birmingham figures, experienced survivors of the vicissitudes of twenty years of political battle – George Dixon, Sir Thomas Martineau, Alderman Kenrick, and a newcomer, freshly initiated in the workings of Chamberlain's Machine, Austen Chamberlain. These men provided continuity with the early days of Joseph Chamberlain's political organisation.

The reader might detect, in those words of Chamberlain, a new bounce and confidence. This was the result of an exceptional Liberal Unionist by-election victory in Central Birmingham in April 1889 which repays detailed examination because it reveals both the unique local attraction of Chamberlain's radical prospectus and the workings of his electoral Machine. The vacancy occurred on the death of John Bright, a Radical hero and long-time ally of Chamberlain, whose prestige was such that his timely opposition to the Home Rule Bill in 1886 saved Chamberlain from defeat and possible political extinction. His Central Birmingham seat was unquestionably Liberal Unionist but the Conservatives believed they were due some reward for their forbearance in allowing Liberal Unionist incumbents a clear run at the 1886 General Election, and in many subsequent municipal contests.

To further complicate matters it seems that Chamberlain had indicated that he would support the claims of his old friend and Birmingham opponent, Lord Randolph Churchill. Chamberlain had written to his son Austen in late 1888: 'I agree that if Randolph wants to stand we must back him and it might be the best solution for us.'[248] Others on the Conservative side had heard the same message. Now he reversed abruptly, possibly fearful of letting into Birmingham a 'potential rival for popular idolatry'. possibly because it was clear Randolph was thought a liability by Conservative high command, and probably because Liberal Unionists nationally had suffered a string of by-election reverses, and to lose a further seat, albeit to the Conservatives, was more than he could tolerate; it might initiate an irreversible abandonment of Liberal Unionism.[249] He persuaded Salisbury and Balfour to lean on Churchill to withdraw. It meant many local

Conservatives were offended; some might be put off from voting Unionist in this by-election. Powell Williams even counselled Chamberlain to stay away from the campaign for fear of provoking a Conservative reaction.

In addition, as we have seen, Birmingham's Gladstonians in late 1888 were in the ascendancy. Chamberlain and his party Machine went into a battle in which the stakes were very high with little surety of success, on behalf of an untried candidate, John's son Albert Bright. The latter's main recommendation was that his family name reverberated with significance for all Liberals. Chamberlain's Machine left little to chance. Powell Williams' and Austen Chamberlain's daily letters in mid-April 1889, from the Central Committee Rooms on Corporation Street to their leader, reveal the meticulous care with which campaigning was prosecuted. Registrations were scrutinised on a register eight months old; the numbers of dead and disqualified since then were carefully counted. Their ward canvasses were scrupulously recorded, Austen giving his father figures day by day of those voters for, those against, the neutrals, the doubtful, the removals and the dead. He concluded: 'All I see leads me to believe the Liberal Unionists are much stronger than is generally supposed.'[250] Powell Williams was even more excited: 'The canvass goes on well and frightens me because it is too good.'[251]

The next day Austen reported that:

> We have tested our canvass in this ward with the best results. I sent Green of the Rural Labourers League to Irving Street and Great Colmore Street, to voters who had promised to vote for us. The names were taken at random. Green said in each case: 'I have come to ask you to vote for Beale' (the Gladstonian opponent). In Irving Street he saw 7 people and all told him they were for Bright and refused to vote for Beale. In Gt. Colmore Street he saw 11 people. All said they were for Bright.[252]

As well as indulging in a little sleight of hand, the campaign monitored its Press coverage closely. Austen went on to tell his father: 'Bright spoke very well, the meeting was most enthusiastic, and far more so than the *Post* report shows. Powell Williams told Bunce this; Bunce has already blown up his reporters telling them they were not fair.' The local Press, and most particularly Bunce (once again a trusted team member), was now very much onside. We see Powell Williams' experience and combativeness when the Gladstonians tried their own trickery. He reported to Chamberlain that:

> They had tried to persuade Tories to stay at home – 'how could they support a candidate like Bright brought in to the seat by 'a breach of faith?' I immediately prepared a counter-blast. We had 10 men on all night directing envelopes and it went out by post delivered this morning to every man who had promised us. I

wrote a letter to the Press entitled 'Another dirty Gladstonian trick'. Satchell Hopkins (the Conservative Chairman) got red posters on walls signed by him telling voters not to be misled. As for their posters, I shall be knocked up at my home when their posters appear and our riposte will be sent to the printer immediately.

That we shall win well I have no manner of doubt. The canvass is extraordinarily good.[253]

His confidence was not misplaced. That collective experience of electioneering, accrued over twenty years by Chamberlain and his team, enabled Albert Bright to win a signal victory, by a majority of 2:1. This was of great and lasting significance. As Hurst puts it in his seminal essay on the subject: 'For the first time the Birmingham Liberal Unionist Association got to grips with the electorate and was surprised by the strength it found.'[254] Chamberlain had proved he could appeal, with a radical, reforming programme, to working-men in large numbers. Apart from evidence of working-class support for Liberal Unionists in Cornwall, Birmingham's Liberal Unionist working-class appeal was unique.[255]

There is another point here. Chamberlain had headed the Liberal Party operation in Birmingham up to 1886. By that date, working-class support was slipping away to the Conservatives over issues like higher rates and a shortage of working-class housing; the Conservatives were gradually winning an increasing share of the municipal vote (41.5% in 1885). Suddenly, after 1886 Chamberlain – as a Liberal Unionist – had contrived to shed his close association with the Liberal regime he had headed and shaped, to recruit to his banner those who had shifted to a Conservative allegiance.[256]

This by-election success in bucking a national trend of reverses – and a desire to immure Chamberlain, to stop him ranging across the country and recruiting to his new NLU – persuaded Hartington, the national leader of the Liberal Unionists, to visit Birmingham after the by-election triumph in 1889 and to ordain that Chamberlain and his friends should be confined to a 'Grand Duchy' in the West Midlands.[257] The Duchy, so called because it seemed like a medieval princely apanage, comprised more than thirty seats in the three counties Worcestershire, Warwickshire and Staffordshire – abutting Birmingham and would become Chamberlain's unique electoral fortress for many years.

The Conservative leadership also took note of Central Birmingham. An arrangement with Chamberlain could help the Conservatives to access support from sources their reactionary background hitherto denied them. Relations between Conservatives and Birmingham Liberal Unionists warmed to the point that in 1891 the Conservatives'

Above: William Kenrick, archetypal Machine member –
brother-in-law, councillor, mayor, educator, founder member
of the NLF and Liberal Unionist MP.

Left: A formidable political organiser, Francis
Schnadhorst was Joseph Chamberlain's most valuable ally,
until they split irrevocably over Home Rule in the 1880s.

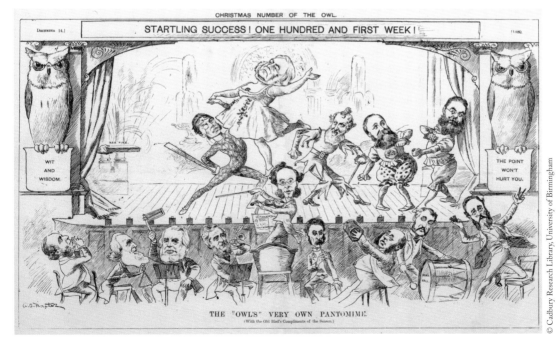

Schnadhorst conducts the antics of ascendant Liberal politicians, including Chamberlain (left),
John Bright replete in tutu, and Robert Dale (far right).

Above: The Council House, 1892. Chamberlain and his allies aspired to improve Birmingham physically as well as organisationally, and they succeeded.

Left: George Baker. Loyal Chamberlain supporter, succeeding him as mayor. He spent fifty years on the council, was chair of the Drainage committee and member of Gas and Water committees.

Above: Editor JT Bunce (left) and proprietor J Jaffray were vital allies for Chamberlain, providing robust support for his schemes in *The Birmingham Daily Post*.

Left: Newspaper seller in Victoria Square in December 1901. Not all newspapers were so supportive of the Machine, many printing cartoons satirising Chamberlain and his allies.

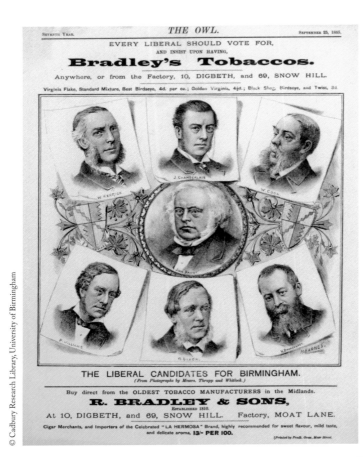

Left: The seven Liberal candidates who swept the board in the 1885 General Election against strong Tory opposition led by Lord Randolph Churchill.

Below: *The Dart* satirises another Liberal triumph. Robert Dale is drawn in a chariot by a lion wearing a blindfold inscribed 'Vote as you are told'. Schnadhorst, chief Machine manipulator, bears the fasces, and Chamberlain is the spear-carrier in the foreground.

Joseph Powell Williams. Close friend of Robert Dale, Williams was a dedicated reformer whose furious hard work for the cause may have contributed to his early death.

Family formed a vital part of the Machine. Arthur Chamberlain was a successful Birmingham businessman whom elder brother Joseph drew upon for political support.

Birmingham defied national trends in 1906 and returned a clean sweep of Chamberlainite tariff reformers.

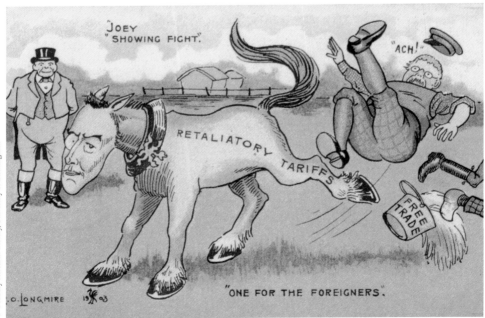

In a Tariff Reform postcard, John Bull looks on approvingly as an equine Chamberlain kicks out at foreign importers.

Joseph Chamberlain embraced the new discipline of economics with enthusiasm, recruiting William Ashley (above) and William Hewins (below), both academics, to the cause of Tariff Reform to bring weight and expertise to the debate.

The Dart celebrates Chamberlain's split with Schnadhorst, and the end of the latter's influence on city politics, 1886.

Chamberlain, Kenrick and Martineau family tree

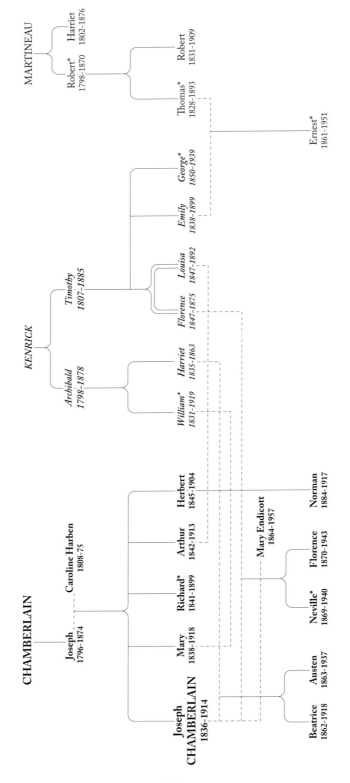

Chamberlain, Kenrick and Martineau family tree. Only individuals relevant to the text are included.
* denotes Mayor of Birmingham.

National Union held its annual conference in Birmingham and Chamberlain and Salisbury shared a platform.

There was a further benign consequence. That Central Birmingham result shifted the momentum in Birmingham irrevocably. It was the beginning of a series of Gladstonian humiliations; Chamberlain used Albert Bright's victory as the spur to consolidate the BLUA's grip on Birmingham.

When the next great electoral test came around, the 1892 General Election, Chamberlain was fighting both regionally and nationally. Primarily, he led the charge against the Gladstonians in his Duchy, every one of whose seats was being contested. He prioritised the defence of these, speaking in all Duchy constituencies, and venturing out only once to address to address a meeting in Manchester. He was entirely successful – the 6 Liberal Unionist Birmingham seats, and the 4 surrounding seats of Handsworth, Aston, East Worcestershire and Lichfield were secured and majorities increased.[258] Beyond these, he spoke in the Conservative Unionist constituencies of the three counties, in so doing improving relations between the two parties. These speaking efforts, directed especially at the working-class voter by emphasising social issues such as old age pensions, workers' compensation for industrial accidents, courts of arbitration in labour disputes and a miners' eight-hour day, ensured victory in 30 out of 39 seats. 'You have done gloriously, simply gloriously in the Midlands,' wrote an ecstatic Lord Wolmer, national chief of the Liberal Unionist Association.[259] Success in these constituencies was sufficient to deprive Gladstone of a popular mandate for Home Rule.

Although elsewhere Hartington's national organisation (the Liberal Unionist Assiciation, to which Chamberlain belonged) had quite failed to establish proper structures, Chamberlain wanted to ensure that at least in his own domain a different level of order and organisation would prevail. This explains why he made a further refinement to his Political Machine, transforming the NLU months after the 1892 Election into a new organisation, the Midlands Liberal Unionist Association, inevitably based in Birmingham. Its commissariat was led by the BLUA's able and energetic secretary, C.A. Vince, doubling up to ensure efficiency and consistency. Chamberlain, its President, outlined its purpose: 'To improve and strengthen the organisation of the party in the three counties of Staffordshire, Warwickshire and Worcestershire and to form in every constituency an Association on a thoroughly popular basis, and to include in each polling district a properly organised committee which every Liberal Unionist voter would be invited to join.'[260] Again we see the democratic ideals which motivated him in 1877, when he originally conceived the National Liberal Federation. What is clear is that he had by now limited his mission; where first the NRU, then later the NLU, had made much of its national ambitions, and had indeed projected its ideas as far as the Welsh Marches and Bradford, now the new Midlands Liberal Unionist Association (perhaps responding to the urgings of Hartington) confined itself to a distinct geographical area, the 39 seats comprising the Duchy and its contiguous constituencies.

Chamberlain went on to describe the MLUA's methodology with the easy familiarity of one who had patented these electoral devices:

> Agents were instructed to visit every house, distribute literature and invite signatures to a declaration of membership to the Association, and have been despatched throughout the constituencies. They report results each week. Those who have joined are summoned to meetings and officers elected. All but 8 out of 39 constituencies have been canvassed. 13.75% of the electorate in Birmingham are members of the LUA, and 10.3% elsewhere in the area. Women's Liberal Unionist Associations are being established, the agents are cultivating friendly relations with the Conservatives, and numerous small meetings and demonstrations have taken place. Finally, the number of active workers at elections has been very largely increased.[261]

One can sense Chamberlain's energy, sheer competence and sharp focus in this address and it certainly had an impact. A ringing endorsement came from Sir Charles Wolseley at Lichfield who testified 'to the great assistance which the organisation at Lichfield has on occasion received from the officers of the Midland Association, especially its able secretary Mr Vince'.[262]

Chamberlain and his team defended their rights in and around the Duchy tigerishly. This is evident in two famous incidents. In 1892 a vacant seat occurred in East Worcestershire, in whose northern boundary lay Highbury, Chamberlain's 'home'. Chamberlain claimed it for the Liberal Unionists even though it had been held by Conservatives. He wanted his son Austen to be nominated. Local Conservatives, led by their Association chairman, Victor Milward, demanded that Austen openly disavow disestablishment of the Anglican Church, a Nonconformist and Liberal Unionist axiom. Chamberlain was indignant that strings should thus be attached to the nomination. Balfour stepped in and persuaded the local party to withdraw its conditions; Milward climbed down and Chamberlain's hold on a portion of the Duchy was reaffirmed.

In a second, widely publicised and more contentious clash in Leamington in 1895, Chamberlain was once again swift to stand on what he perceived to be his rights and those of the Liberal Unionist Duchy. The retirement of Speaker Peel – a Liberal Unionist after 1886 who had thereafter, as Speaker, not contested his seat – prompted Chamberlain to claim the seat for his party and for Peel's son, George Peel. Local

Conservatives had their own candidate selected already. They refused to abide by instructions issued by Balfour, keen to bolster his Unionist ally Chamberlain, to back Peel. Chamberlain was excoriated in the Conservative press for his imperious manner in claiming Leamington. Eventually a compromise candidate, Alfred Lyttleton, was accepted by all sides, though the spat wounded Chamberlain, who realised the limits of his support among ordinary Conservatives. For a study of the Birmingham Machine it is important to note that Chamberlain fought as hard as he did in order to defend the integrity of his fortress from the attacks of Tories hell-bent on breaching his ramparts. He would have been aware that senior Conservatives such as Middleton were speculating about the durability of the 1886 electoral pact which had allowed the Liberal Unionists a clear run in many constituencies. Chamberlain could not view such a threat to his power base with equanimity.[263]

He was of course more than just a prince in his bailiwick but also a national leader of the Liberal Unionist Association. With Hartington's succession as Duke of Devonshire in 1891 Chamberlain inherited the leadership of the national party in the Commons. When he took stock of the situation country-wide it became apparent just how exceptional was Birmingham and the Duchy. Nationally, the Liberal Unionists slipped in 1892 to 47 seats; apart from the West Midlands, they lost ground in all areas. The party had from its inception been reliant on pockets of local strength, built around powerful local figures or traditions. Chamberlain was determined in the aftermath to that election to tackle what to him was its glaring weakness.'What is necessary in order that our side might win at the election? He told his audience at the Liberal Unionist Club in March 1892: 'What is necessary that our side might win at the election? Of course, organisation.'[264]

He and his team turned their attentions to exporting their Birmingham know-how to the Liberal Unionist Association itself. That disappointing General Election result underscored the need for a fresh approach. The six years from 1886 had seen the Party run as if it were an 'aristocratic club': it had relied too heavily on its Conservative allies and their electoral apparatus, and finally, in Chamberlain's view, the Liberal Unionist message nationally had been too negative, emphasising the iniquities of Home Rule and popery at the expense of constructive social reform.[265] Chamberlain animated the whole operation; he was open to the potential of new technologies and new resources in a way that Hartington manifestly was not. As a result, the Liberal Unionist party seized the opportunities created by new colour printing technologies, developing attractive campaign literature tailored particularly to appeal to working-class voters and investing in colour posters which were innovatory. Research on the subject has concluded that the

Liberal Unionists were in the forefront of exploiting the use of visual, musical and print propaganda.[266] Chamberlain was not, of course, a lone pioneer; John Boraston, the incumbent LUA Secretary seems to have become more active and to have led the way in disseminating new publicity materials after 1892.

Birmingham Machine methods also followed Chamberlain into Liberal Unionist headquarters, with the arrival of Powell Williams, originally organiser of the National Liberal Union in the Midlands; officially he became the Chairman of the national Liberal Unionist Association but he 'occupied the position of manager', taking over from Lord Wolmer. After the party's greatly improved showing in the 1895 election his value was such that it was agreed 'all points of importance' were to be referred 'for Williams' decision'; Boraston was to consult Williams 'who will give him an hour two or three times a week'.[267] Williams brought deep experience developed when serving on Birmingham Town Council, as Secretary of the Birmingham Liberal Association, and as Honorary Secretary of the National Liberal Federation. He became versed in electoral campaigning techniques when securing victories for John Bright, Philip Muntz and Joseph Chamberlain in the 1880 General Election, and then again when ensuring a strong Liberal showing in the 1882 School Board elections. He was also an experienced MP himself, representing South Birmingham from 1886. He did much to establish efficient local organisation in seats contested by Liberal Unionists, 'helping find candidates, interviewing, selecting, and approving agents for each district in the country'.[268] By 1895 canvassing was being focused on winnable seats. Letters emanated from the central organisation to LUA local secretaries advising on how to combat Liberal publicity, and how to ensure favourable voters were registered. Some of these initiatives echoed the structures being developed in the Midlands Liberal Unionist Association. Williams must, along with Boraston, take some credit for the revival of Liberal Unionist fortunes in 1895.

So, too, should Chamberlain himself. Gladstone had won the General Election of 1892 and returned to power. He introduced a Second Home Rule Bill which was defeated largely because of Chamberlain's relentless advocacy of the Unionist case. That defeat prompted Gladstone to resign in 1894, and the Liberal government meandered to an inglorious and demoralised dissolution. In the subsequent election in 1895 there were tensions between Conservative and Liberal Unionists, for many Conservatives disliked the sacrifices made to accommodate Chamberlain and his party, and resented the belligerence with which he fought his corner. We have seen the consequences at Leamington (above). Conservatives were unimpressed by his methods; George Curzon published an article in April 1895 to this effect. 'It is to wire-pulling that he has devoted his narrow and powerful intelligence and he has done so to such purpose that he has in his hands more constituencies than a rich patron in the bad old days ever held in his pocket.' Chamberlain cannot have enjoyed comparisons with a prominent eighteenth-century Whig like the Duke of Newcastle!

Chamberlain's speeches were widely reported; the reforming prospectus he presented attracted working-class support in Scotland and the North as well as in his own West Midland fastness. In the West Midlands his success had a long-lasting depressive effect on the independent labour movement.[269] Although Conservative Unionists made a powerful appeal to a working-class electorate, for instance, characterising Liberals as kill-joys intent on depriving working men of their beer and football, they might well have benefited from Chamberlain's promotion of social policies, even if for many they were unpalatable.

The 1895 Election resulted in sweeping Unionist gains, with Liberal Unionists winning 71 seats (47 in 1892). In the aftermath, a number of Liberal Unionists joined Salisbury's administration: Chamberlain became Colonial Secretary, Powell Williams became Financial Secretary to the War Office, Jesse Collings was appointed under-secretary to the Home department, and Austen Chamberlain went to the Admiralty under another Liberal Unionist, G.J. Goschen. Salisbury who was very nervous of Chamberlain's loud articulation of social policy, could be content that Chamberlain would have his hands full with overseas matters. Elements of the Birmingham Machine were now firmly integrated into central government. But it might also be said that by joining the Unionist Cabinet Chamberlain had recognised he was not strong enough to keep fighting battles such as that at Leamington.[270] Now, perhaps because Chamberlain's new focus was inevitably imperial; or because Powell Williams also had new interests; or because Home Rule seemed no longer a realistic possibility – for whatever reasons, Liberal Unionism nationally lost some of its distinctiveness and drive.

Powell Williams gave up his managerial role in the LUA and does not appear to have been replaced. Chamberlain in 1896, uncharacteristically, appears to have become almost relaxed both at the prospect of fusion of the two Unionist parties, and at the surrender of the almost suffocating control of Liberal Unionist associations he exercised in his pomp. By degrees he was becoming closer to his Conservative allies in Cabinet; he only attended the Birmingham Liberal Unionist Association annual meetings in 1897 and 1898, and appeared at no other Liberal Unionist assemblies. It was the strong local reaction to the prospect of amalgamation which gave him pause, prompting a reversal of the policy of allowing local Unionist parties to merge in 1898. He said then: 'Wherever there is already a fair number of Liberal Unionists, the organisation of the party should be maintained in full efficiency.'[271]

Thereafter, several events conspired to undermine Liberal Unionist unity. The Boer War (1899-1902), envisioned and prosecuted by Joseph Chamberlain, drove away those Nonconformist Liberal Unionist supporters still attached to a moral foreign policy.[272] It made little difference to the result of the Khaki Election, called in the middle of the War in 1900. Sixty-four Liberal Unionist MPs were elected in a Unionist landslide (402 seats to the Liberals' 184), a good result tempered perhaps by the fact that 27 were returned unopposed. By now that unique selling point of Chamberlain's Radical Unionism, its social reform, had evaporated; he barely mentioned social issues, his time and attention taken up by vehement assaults on his critics for giving succour to the Boers. Still more damaging to Liberal Unionism was the Balfour government's Education Act in 1902, which alienated Nonconformists when it abolished their beloved School Boards and put denominational schools on the rates. The Liberal Unionist leader, the Duke of Devonshire, was a co-architect of the policy. The historian of Liberal Unionism, Ian Cawood, has concluded that 'much of the disappearance of Liberal Unionism is traceable to the Education Act of 1902'.[273] Chamberlain had recognised the danger straight away but had felt constrained by membership of the Cabinet and by a loyalty to the new Prime Minister, Arthur Balfour, his long-time friend and ally. He was to chide Devonshire in 1903: 'The greatest blow struck at Liberal Unionist influence has been – as I warned it would be – the introduction of the Education Act for which you were in a special degree responsible – which has driven from our ranks many of our most energetic Nonconformist members.'[274] Damage from this was to be compounded by Chamberlain's dramatic announcement of his conversion to Protection in 1903, and by his aggressive purging of Free Traders, including Devonshire himself, from the national Liberal Unionist Association. This is the subject of the next chapter.

Even if the national influence of Birmingham's Machine was diminishing from 1895 onwards, with Powell Williams and Chamberlain distracted by office and attracted to the idea of fusion, Liberal Unionism in the Duchy thrived. In the Khaki Election, the Liberal opposition could summon up only one candidate in Birmingham itself (in Birmingham East). Indeed, in the wider Duchy, 20 of the 39 seats were uncontested; 33 Unionists were returned to Westminster. An efficient Unionist organisation, facing a demoralised adversary, forced onto the defensive by a jingoistic frenzy, had a relatively straightforward task. The Duchy had proved once again to be a stronghold of Chamberlainite Unionism.

The elements of Chamberlain's successful operation were still much in evidence after 1900 in Birmingham, even when the national tide of Unionism was ebbing. This was clear in the strong reaction to the local Liberal Association's invitation to David Lloyd

George, an articulate Liberal pro-Boer, to speak in the Town Hall (see chapter 5). Liberal Unionists continued to summon up loyalists from a compliant Press, local party commissariat and ordinary Unionist foot soldiers, demonstrating how the components in this Birmingham Machine had been well maintained and were in good working order. So, the *Post* led Unionist opinion, averring: 'It is thoroughly discreditable that any handful of pro-Boer politicians should bring into the city and give a platform at the Town Hall to a firebrand like Mr Lloyd George, a violent speaker.' When things went wrong on the day of the visit, the paper continued to hold the Liberals responsible: 'The demonstrations on the street were in our opinion, the inevitable result of the provocation wantonly excited by those who persisted in holding this meeting.'[275]

Party officials would appear to have been behind various nefarious deeds such as the circulation of 'spurious tickets' to the Liberal meeting at the Town Hall, the forging of a telegram to the Press giving Lloyd George's whereabouts in the city, and finally the employment of sandwich-board men on public promenades throughout the day carrying bills, 'calling on the crowd to assemble at the Town Hall to defend the King, the Government and Mr Chamberlain, and to denounce Brum Boers'.[276] This action seems both deliberately provocative and dangerously irresponsible.

Liberal Unionist Party supporters made up a good proportion of a crowd of 50,000 which thronged Victoria Square beside the Town Hall on the evening of the meeting. Demonstrators outside the Hall bombarded it with bricks and stones, and it was alleged that revolvers were fired by members of the crowd. Some Unionist protesters had also broken into the meeting itself, barracking speakers and drowning out their speeches with a volley of calls for 'Mr Chamberlain', 'the boys at the front', 'the soldiers of the Queen', etc., creating such pandemonium that when Lloyd George appeared on stage, revellers outside took it as a cue to smash windows and to storm the doors of the Hall. Lloyd George escaped, dressed as a policeman, in an undignified scramble for the stage doors. Police were injured, several rioters (among whom were young working-men – a joiner, machinist, railway shunter and sundry youths) were apprehended and fined, and one unfortunate member of the public died. The echoes of Aston Manor reverberated. Once again Chamberlain's Birmingham operation had revealed its darker side, and its tolerance of direct action to secure its hold on the Duchy.

In Birmingham and much of the Duchy there demonstrably persisted a deep personal attachment to Chamberlain, and to the party organisation, even if the gloss had been knocked off his reputation by disappointments associated with his Boer War strategies. He sedulously cultivated this local support, exploiting a loophole in the Corrupt and Illegal Practices Act of 1883 which had dramatically limited candidates' expenses, so curtailing treating and bribery. He found that regular garden parties at Highbury for BLUA sympathisers (often in their thousands) and strategically targeted donations to local bazaars and shows – what was called 'nursing the constituency' – were both electorally efficacious and avoided proscription.[277]

On the eve of the next and last incarnation of the Machine which occurred in 1903 (see chapter 7) an indication of the extraordinary and singular position Chamberlain held can be discerned in the junketing in November 1902 that accompanied his departure for South Africa in the wake of Britain's long-awaited victory in the Boer War. *The Times* may have exaggerated but its account of a lavish banquet; torch-lined routes from the Town Hall to the city boundaries; and huge processions accompanying their Hector's carriage, led it to conclude that the demonstration 'was one of the most remarkable tributes ever offered to a statesman by the spontaneous admiration of free citizens'.[278] Those celebrations were visible and eloquent evidence of his – and his Machine's – continuing hold over the allegiance of thousands in the West Midlands.

Joseph Powell Williams

Joseph Powell Williams was one of Chamberlain's most devoted friends and allies, one of those who loyally negotiated the hiatus of 1886, when Home Rule divided friend from friend in Liberal politics, holding hard to the Chamberlain coat-tails.

He was born in 1840 in Worcester, before moving to Birmingham to be schooled at the Hagley Road Proprietary School. Life thereafter was a good deal more adventurous, for he went to America as the business representative of a number of Birmingham firms. Whilst there he witnessed the Civil War. On his return to Britain he worked in London in the General Post Office under Sir Rowland Hill; he assisted in setting up the Post Office savings scheme before being promoted to the Surveyor's department where he became a close friend of the novelist Anthony Trollope. His experience as a sales representative, and his financial training in the Post Office provided him with skills which would be invaluable in his later life of public and party service.

He returned to Birmingham in 1873 when he joined the Liberal group and, in the words of his obituary in the Birmingham Daily Post *in February 1904, he 'helped materially to strengthen the Liberal Association, which under his guidance and that of others became perhaps the perfect political organisation in the country'. Like William Harris and Francis Schnadhorst his talent for structuring and operating a political machine seems to have been at least partly innate. Powell Williams became Honorary Secretary of the Birmingham Liberal Association where he would have served a formative apprenticeship in Caucus techniques originally refined by William Harris. Like most of the Birmingham Liberal Association's prominent figures, he beat a path to the Town Council, the means by which a municipal revolution was being effected in the 1870s. He entered in 1877 as a councillor for the St Thomas's ward, continuing to represent it for thirteen years. It seems that he immediately gave proof of his financial acumen for within three years he was Chairman of the Finance Committee. Not for the last time his most important work was to tidy up after the man who would be his political master, in this instance tackling Birmingham's outstanding debt, built up in Chamberlain's mayoralty. He persuaded the Local Government Board to allow him to convert the debt. He was also the instigator of an important extension of the use of Corporation stock, obtaining from the Local Government Board permission to make advances for capital expenditure incurred by Birmingham School Board, the Board of Guardians and the Drainage Board, all committees effectively run by the Liberal Machine. In other words, his financial creativity significantly augmented the expansionary schemes of Birmingham's municipal bodies.*

The inspiration for many years of civic service appears to have been derived from his friendship with Dr Robert Dale; Powell Williams attended his Carr's Lane Chapel and imbibed there the ideas of civic duty which underpinned the commitment of so many of this generation of Birmingham Liberal politicians.

Powell Williams earned a reputation early on for being ferociously hard-working, a proximate cause of his untimely death. While he was still a councillor and Chairman of the Finance Committee, Chamberlain recruited him to be Honorary Secretary of the National Liberal Federation in which capacity he was author of pamphlets on county government and the Ballot Act. At the same time he continued to labour on behalf of the Birmingham Liberal Association, working hard in the General Election of 1880 to secure the victories of Phillip Muntz, John Bright and Joseph Chamberlain and masterminding the safe return of nine Liberals to the Birmingham School Board in 1882, so guaranteeing continued Liberal control. His electoral know-how was invaluable in 1884-5 when Birmingham expanded its representation from three to seven seats; he ensured that Liberal interests prevailed at the Boundary Commission enquiry in Birmingham prompted by the Third Reform (Redistribution) Act. He subsequently stood as Liberal candidate for Birmingham South and was part of that 1885 General Election clean sweep which first prompted the slogan 'We Are Seven'.

He was unwaveringly loyal when Chamberlain opposed Gladstone over Home Rule in 1886, writing to him: 'For my part I am convinced you have done the right thing.' Although he feared the strong attraction Gladstone exerted, he nevertheless supported Chamberlain through the lobby when it came to voting on the Home Rule Bill – 'I will not be guilty of the meanness of standing aloof from you in the critical moment.' Thereafter he was a key figure in establishing first a Birmingham, then an efficient national, Liberal Unionist Association. He became Chairman of the Executive Committee of the new Birmingham Liberal Unionist Association. As much as his political boss, Chamberlain, he tenaciously defended their party's corner in the perennial battle to prevent Conservatives encroaching on Liberal Unionist territory. He wrote to Chamberlain in 1889: 'I feel strongly…if the number of Liberal Unionists in Parliament is decreased and that of the Conservative Unionists is increased, there will be a gradual but certain defection of Liberal Unionists to the Gladstone camp.'

He led from the front in campaigning for his party, for example, engaging in daily canvasses of voters throughout the crucial, and in the event triumphant, Central Birmingham by-election campaign in April 1889. He was an integral part of the leadership of the NRU and its later incarnation the Midlands Liberal Unionist Association. He was a visible supporter of the recently founded Birmingham Women's Liberal Unionist Association in 1889.

When Chamberlain acceded to the leadership of the Liberal Unionists in the Commons at the end of 1891 it was to Powell Williams that he turned to bring order to an ill-disciplined organisation. Powell Williams became the manager of the LUA and he was central to all decisions on constituency representation, and on electoral campaigning. His exercise of the diplomatic arts ensured he stayed on good terms with both of the Liberal Unionist leaders, Hartington and Chamberlain, and he was a useful intermediary between them for, temperamentally poles apart, they sometimes disagreed about policy and consequent action. The new professionalism of the organisation was reflected by a net gain of over 20 seats in the 1895 General Election. In Birmingham South he won a thumping majority of 3573, part of another Unionist whitewash in the city.

The aftermath of the Election saw Chamberlain negotiate the appointment of four Liberal Unionists to Salisbury's administration; Powell Williams became Financial Secretary to the War Office. He was also made a Privy Councillor.

He supported Chamberlain's policy towards South Africa from 1899 onwards but he became implicated – along with the Chamberlain family, especially Arthur Chamberlain – in the scandal over government contracts placed with firms in which some Unionist politicians had an interest and from which they stood to benefit financially. The Chamberlain family's involvement in Hoskins which supplied ship's berths to the Navy, and with Kynochs – the primary source of cordite for army shells – prompted Lloyd George's relentless pursuit of the family in the Commons. Caught up in the fall-out, Powell Williams was alleged to have shown undue favouritism to Kynochs in the tendering process.

When Chamberlain came out as a tariff reformer and a protectionist in 1903 Powell Williams followed his lead, not simply out of a touching personal regard, evident in that seminal moment in 1886, but also as a reflection of the long-standing Fair Trade (protectionist) sympathies of many Birmingham manufacturers. His inestimable value as a trustworthy ally who Chamberlain knew would be sound and sensible, saw Powell Williams appointed Chairman of the Imperial Tariff Committee; he was on the Council of the Tariff Reform League; and he also became a key member of the executive of Chamberlain's own Birmingham-based Tariff Reform Committee, joining a hardy band of loyalists: Charles Vince, Neville Chamberlain, and members of the Kenrick and Nettlefold families. The Machine had metamorphosed again, but the operators remained recognisable.

Also familiar was the sheer weight of responsibility placed on Powell Williams' shoulders: he was a Birmingham MP; as we have seen he was closely involved in the Tariff Reform wars which raged after 1903, in the prosecution of which Chamberlain was a demanding general; and he also found himself in the eye of the storm at Liberal Unionist Association headquarters, as Chamberlain from late 1903 manoeuvred to expel Free Traders, even perhaps the Duke of Devonshire himself. The days before his apoplectic seizure on the floor of the House of Commons in February 1904 were full of Liberal Unionist committee business. Contemporaries attributed *his death to the excessive strain caused by an especially turbulent period in politics. Certainly, Chamberlain himself recognised that he had driven him and the rest of his small team too hard: profoundly shaken by his personal and professional loss, he confessed: 'It is my fault, I have worked him to death.'*

When it came to the deserved obsequies, as befitted a significant public figure, Jesse Collings chose a local perspective. 'His regard for and pride in Birmingham was very deep and the service he has rendered the city is very great indeed,' he wrote in the Post. *Powell Williams has no entry in the Dictionary of National Biography so it is perhaps right to see him primarily as an enduring and irreplaceable component in Chamberlain's extraordinary Birmingham Political Machine, and as a man who in protean ways utilised his considerable gifts in acting out the ideals of the civic gospel.*

Arthur Chamberlain

A steel core of family loyalty – 'his brothers and his brothers-in-law' in the judgement of the Birmingham Daily Gazette – ran through nearly every incarnation of the Birmingham Political Machine. Kenricks and Chamberlains were seemingly ubiquitous in the committees of the NFL, the Town Council, the Midland Institute, the Birmingham Liberal Association and its successors.

The brothers were Richard and Arthur Chamberlain, and while Richard was a valued councillor during Joseph Chamberlain's municipal revolution in the early 1870s and later MP for Islington West (so moving away from Birmingham), Arthur was the more significant politically in Birmingham and indeed, at a critical time in his famous brother's career, he was one of the very few reliable allies on whom he could rely.

Arthur and Joseph had much in common in the early years. Born six years after his more famous sibling in 1842, Arthur followed his brother to University College School and then to Birmingham, into the Church of the Messiah and the Kenrick family, marrying Louise, the identical twin of Florence (Joseph's wife). Then he joined the wood-screw business of Nettlefold and Chamberlain, although Nettlefold's resentment at the arrangement led by 1863 to Arthur's transfer into another of his father's business interests, Smith and Chamberlain, the brass founders. Again, like his brother, he showed a rare commercial talent. He not only made a success of the brass foundry, but went on to build up firms specialising in electric light, in electric meters, in tubes and most famously in taking over the ailing Kynochs, the cartridge manufacturer in Witton and Stirchley, Birmingham. He became chairman of Kynochs in 1889, streamlining and rationalising production to reduce costs before investing in new rolling mills; in time, he diversified into the munitions industry, particularly focusing on explosives. He tripled the work force to 6,000 and opened factories around the UK.

Other investments included the Birmingham Investment Trust, Weldless Tube, and Hoskins and Son, the makers of ships' berths in which firm his nephew, Neville Chamberlain, earned his reputation as a shrewd and industrious businessman.

Where his brother Joseph sold Nettlefolds in 1874 to pursue a political career (though his outlook remained that of an Entrepreneur in Politics, in the title of Peter Marsh's biography), Arthur would remain primarily a businessman. So much so that much of his energy was expended as a leader of the Birmingham Chamber of Commerce and serving the Association of UK Chambers of Commerce and the Empire in the 1900s.

Like his famous elder brother he responded to Dawson and Dale's urgings – that rich and able businessmen should serve the community in that mission cause, the social and intellectual improvement of the industrial working classes. Along with brother Richard Chamberlain (a co-director of Smith and Chamberlain) he was on the Council when Mayor Joseph Chamberlain devised the strategy of taking over the gas companies; their support added weight to the approbation of Joseph Chamberlain's municipal peers.

Arthur Chamberlain was for many years both confidant and unquestioning political stalwart for his elder brother. When Joseph Chamberlain's second wife died in 1875 it was Arthur (along with Jesse Collings and William Kenrick) who enabled the grieving widower to find consolation and distraction (on a Scottish fishing trip). Eleven years later Joseph was fighting for his political life after leading the attack on the Home Rule Bill. It was Arthur, a Birmingham Liberal Association member, whom he trusted to manage the fall-out in the seven Birmingham constituencies in the summer of 1886. Joseph used Arthur as his sounding-board and his major-domo as he planned the National Radical Union, the Birmingham organisation to rival the National Liberal Unionist Association. It is clear from the tenor of Joseph's letters that he trusted Arthur to have the contacts and the influence to build up and expand this small local family-based party enterprise. That it did establish itself and – in its later incarnations, the National Liberal Union and the Midlands Liberal Unionist Association – was due not a little to Arthur's patient negotiation skills.

Where Joseph had effectively transmuted into a London politician – with the West Midlands providing him with a solid base on which he could rely and to which he could return – Arthur remained very much a Birmingham figure. He was a JP in 1884 and was chairman of the Licensing Committee in the city from 1893 to 1903, holding a more trenchant position than his brother on the responsibility of local authorities to control working-class drunkenness. He was an early supporter of his brother's initiative of founding the University of Birmingham; predictably, his real passion was for the establishment of the faculty of commerce, for which he drafted a practical business syllabus for a three-year course. Despite all this valiant local endeavour, he was drawn reluctantly into national politics, when he found himself in the eye of a storm generated by Lloyd George over War Office contracts awarded to munitions firms in the Boer War. The charge was that the War Office cultivated and coached certain firms – of which Kynochs was one – before tendering for munitions contracts. Arthur's proximity to the Colonial Secretary who was prosecuting the War, and Joseph's proximity and that of his sons Austen and Neville to his brother, made for a long-running, and damaging, scandal.

Yet that was probably the last time when the brothers found themselves on the same side on a political issue. They were to fall out on two matters. Perhaps the less important was that over the licensing of public houses. Arthur Chamberlain and his allies on the bench used their regulatory powers to compel brewers to surrender many of their public house licences; Joseph, now allied to brewers and in general more relaxed about alcohol than in his Nonconformist youth, found the action altogether too draconian. More serious was the disagreement between the brothers over tariffs. Arthur Chamberlain – unusually for a Birmingham metal manufacturer – was a long-standing Free Trader.

Joseph's seminal speech in May 1903 advocating tariffs and Imperial preference prompted Arthur openly to attack his brother at the Birmingham Chamber of Commerce in July, a speech which – by being reported in The Times *– set the seal on their estrangement. This must have been difficult given that the brothers were neighbours in South West Birmingham, Joseph at Highbury and Arthur over the fence at Moor Green, and the two families continued to socialise with each other. Neville Chamberlain has described the ensuing tensions: 'The two brothers were like rival terriers, their hair began to bristle directly they saw one another, and one provocation or sarcastic remark would follow another until there was an explosion.'*

Tariff Reform, like Home Rule twenty years before, certainly damaged several components in the Chamberlain Machine; John Sutton Nettlefold, Arthur Chamberlain's son-in-law (and Joseph Chamberlain's nephew) felt so strongly that he resigned from the MLUA and the BLUA and came increasingly to side with local Liberals; effectively he led the Free Trade movement in Birmingham against his uncle.

Arthur, like Joseph, spent his declining years wheelchair-bound and predeceased him in 1913. His importance in this narrative is that he exemplifies that strain of reliable and loyal family members in Chamberlain's network of allies and supporters – at key moments, just as with Austen and Neville, Arthur was an invaluable cog in a very effective political association.

THE MACHINE'S FINAL INCARNATION – TARIFF REFORM

There is no better illustration of Churchill's contention that Chamberlain was 'the one who made the weather' than the hurricane he generated by his speech in Birmingham on 15 May 1903, when he signalled his abandonment of Free Trade orthodoxy.[279] The damage wrought was extensive; indeed, it re-shaped the political landscape, sundering Unionists and driving Liberals together, overturning one government and invigorating its successor. Chamberlain himself resigned from the Cabinet to take his argument to the country in September 1903; he would never hold office again.

Personal conviction and intense competitivity then compelled him to overhaul his Political Machine, the better to engage in the bitter and divisive struggle over tariffs that he had initiated: he was driven to wrest control of the National Liberal Unionist Association, and to create a number of wholly new operations to fight Free Trade's many defenders. These consisted of the Tariff Reform League (TRL), the Birmingham Tariff Reform Committee, the Trade Union Tariff Reform Association (TUTRA) and the Tariff Reform Commission (TRC). Taken together they comprise the mature expression of all Chamberlain and his allies had learnt from more than thirty years of organisation and campaigning. The speed with which they were established; their national reach; the professionalism with which they were run; the quality of big-name supporters they recruited; the scale of the financial support on which they drew; the employment of the very latest means of mass communication – in every way Chamberlain showed in this, his last act as a national politician, complete mastery of a gamut of political skills and techniques.

Chamberlain's biographer, Julian Amery, claimed: 'No speech in British history has ever caused such a sensation or led to such momentous consequences.'[280] His father, (Chamberlain's ally and contemporary) Leo Amery, compared it for its drama and its heretical ramifications with Martin Luther's 95 *Theses*, nailed onto the church doors in Wittenberg in 1517.[281] For in this speech Chamberlain challenged the country to remake Imperial policy, to glue the Empire together through reciprocal tariffs, and – by implication – to impose tariffs on foreign, non-Imperial imports. He may not have appreciated the extent and tenacity of support for Free Trade he aroused. It was associated with Britain's prosperity after the agonies of the 'Hungry Forties' (the depression of the 1840s), with openness and – even – moral goodness for it served the consumer and it fostered international peace. Tariffs were seen as serving only the producer and the middle-man, in consequence raising prices and hurting the housewife and the worker struggling to feed his family.[282] Because the 'momentous consequences' of which Amery spoke comprised three successive election defeats for the Unionists who had espoused Chamberlain's tariff policy, historians have ever since sought to rationalise this dramatic conversion.

The most convincing explanation for his abandonment of Free Trade, to which he had cleaved as a self-evident truth through the first twenty-five years of his career, was the one he himself gave: that he had become increasingly seized by a belief in the integrity of the British Empire since the days when he had attacked Home Rule for its implicit threat to its unity. His years as Colonial Secretary served to strengthen his vision of a 'Greater Britain', with countries of the Empire closely bound together through preferential arrangements, which secured a huge potential market and resource base.[283]

Meetings with Sir Wilfred Laurier, the Canadian Prime Minister, with whom Chamberlain discussed preferential treatment for Canadian corn at the turn of the century, aroused his interest. For Imperial preference would address the fear that had grown on him as the Boer War neared its end, and as the common belligerent purpose engendered between Britain and her dominions dissipated; his fear was that Britain's Empire was merely 'a loose bundle of sticks, bound together by a thin tie of sentiment and sympathy... so slender that a rough blow might shatter it'.[284] Chamberlain was infected by a pervading gloom about Britain's future, with the USA and Germany in 1900 overtaking it in the world share of manufacturing production.[285] He became convinced that only large integrated trading areas like recently unified Germany, and the United States, could compete in the future, and so a more tightly bound British Empire appealed to him.

In 1902, he thought he spied his chance. Such were the costs of the Boer War that the Unionist Chancellor of the Exchequer, Sir Michael Hicks Beach, was forced to introduce a small duty on imported wheat or corn. This was a portentous decision; it was a first breach in Free Trade's adamantine defences. As important for Chamberlain was that he was able to persuade the Cabinet to use it to give preferential treatment to Canadian corn, a first step, he hoped, to a wider Imperial reciprocal trading arrangement.[286] He sailed to South Africa in autumn 1902 elated by the new Imperial vision which he saw materialising. So, his disappointment was all the greater on his return the next spring when he found that in his absence the new Chancellor, C.T. Ritchie, had persuaded the Cabinet to abandon both the corn tax and thus the Imperial preference on which he had set his heart.[287] For many observers, this reverse explains Chamberlain's dramatic announcement in Birmingham in May 1903.

He was frustrated in his ambitions for Imperial unity; he was also wounded by the defeat in Cabinet at the hands of Ritchie. But beyond that other factors were at work. Birmingham manufacturers – and many artisan employees – had for 25 years supported the Fair Trade movement which called for the imposition of duties on foreign manufactures and on food imported to Britain. Although Chamberlain as a Liberal had loyally defended Free Trade he was aware of the attraction of Protection – all seven Conservative candidates (led by Lord Randolph Churchill) in the 1885 election had espoused Fair Trade and run Liberals close. By the late 1890s he had been converted by evidence both of foreign manufacturers dumping cheap goods to undercut Birmingham firms; and of the travails of those same Birmingham firms suffering from high tariff barriers when they tried to export their (primarily) metal goods abroad. Chamberlain would reinforce his hold over Birmingham and over much of the Duchy by embracing a policy designed to protect their industries. The actions of the Birmingham Chamber of Commerce demonstrate this for it rushed to endorse Chamberlain's implicitly Protectionist message in 1903 'by an overwhelming majority', welcoming 'the imposition of customs duties on products and manufactures of foreign countries'.[288]

It has also been argued that Chamberlain adopted tariffs to generate funds for social legislation, such as Old Age Pensions (on which subject he had been very quiet since the Boer War started), so avoiding giving offence to Conservatives by having to impose progressive taxation.[289] Other historians agree that political calculation lies behind Chamberlain's move. He was aware that Balfour's Education Act in 1902 had offended many Nonconformists in Liberal Unionist ranks; tariffs would be a distraction, they would allow him to generate new momentum for the Unionist alliance and manufacture a new appeal to the working classes.[290] Here was a chance for Chamberlain – rather than Balfour – to make the running and to seize back the initiative in Cabinet. He detected passivity in Balfour's administration, while he himself embodied drive, energy, action, qualities which he hoped would re-establish him after his defeats over education, corn levies and Imperial preference.[291] In his partiality to great inspiring causes there is more than a trace of Gladstone in Chamberlain.

For a varied patchwork of different reasons, then, Chamberlain took an historically significant gamble in May 1903. He did so – with calculated symbolism – in Birmingham, his political fastness, and a city where he knew the protectionist implications of his message would reverberate and resonate. Birmingham had repeatedly shown that it was more enthusiastic for Imperialism than any other British city. Where elsewhere jingoistic fervour cooled with growing disillusionment at a protracted and expensive Boer War, Birmingham rioted in pro-War enthusiasm to evict its foremost critic, David Lloyd George (see chapter 6). Citizens still celebrated Empire in their thousands when they junketed in the autumn of 1902 to mark Chamberlain's departure for South Africa. Empire Day was marked more enthusiastically by the working classes in the city than in most others right up to the start of the First World War.[292] And in its wake, as he planned how to proselytise the tariff message, it was Birmingham methods which would be adopted by his new single-issue pressure groups, Birmingham which would be the physical base for at least half the operations, and Birmingham personnel who would colonise the executive positions in most organisations he established. The Machine swung into action only a few weeks after his 15 May speech and after his equally portentous performance at the Despatch Box of the House of Commons at the end of the month, when he conceded that taxes on foreign food were the inevitable corollary of preference for colonial imports.[293]

Entirely predictably, Chamberlain at the outset sought to establish a completely loyal tariff machinery in Birmingham. He confessed as much to his stalwart, Jesse Collings, himself a swift adherent to the new fiscal policy, in a letter of July 1903:

> I cannot depend entirely on the Tariff Reform League (see below) and I must have my own organisation, entirely under control, which will deal with points that others might omit. That is the reason for the Birmingham Tariff Committee and I do not think it is a bad thing that it should be recognised as more, or less, connected with me.[294]

This Tariff Committee was but a different manifestation of the Birmingham Liberal Unionist Association. The two organisations shared the guiding hand of C.A. Vince, who was responsible for publications. The BLUA and Tariff Committee shared the same premises in Edmund Street, even though there was a separate tariff telephone and telegraphic address ('Consistency'). Other now familiar faces were Edward Nettlefold, the Treasurer, and committee members Jesse Collings, Powell Williams, Neville Chamberlain, and Byng Kenrick. It was indeed a family affair – a son, Neville (with brother Austen closely engaged with another arm of the Machine, the Tariff Reform League) and Kenrick and Nettlefold relations. As Amery concludes: 'The control of the new body was thus firmly in the hands of the Chamberlain clan.'[295] One word of caution is necessary, however. Although all Birmingham's Unionist MPs and the great majority of the BLUA followed Chamberlain's new line, some members did not, notably Arthur Chamberlain and John Sutton Nettlefold, hitherto 'clan' allies. Relationships became increasingly acrimonious. Still, they were always in a small minority in a city which swung decisively to Protection after 1903. What is apparent is how much the Machine was trailing in the determined wake of its increasingly imperious progenitor; it was less of a free-standing operation than it had been, and now much more at Chamberlain's beck and call.

Charles Vince, steeped in campaigning know-how accrued from over fifteen years running the BLUA and MLUA, seized the initiative straight away, taking advantage of a concession Chamberlain had wrung from Balfour and the Cabinet after he had launched his tariff programme. This was to the effect that, whilst for the sake of party unity they had all agreed to avoid controversial statements on the tariff issue, Chamberlain had persuaded them to exempt pamphlets. 'They had no conception of the scale on which he meant to act,' wrote Amery.[296] Vince also exploited the network which linked local Liberal Unionist Associations, acting on the optimistic presumption that the whole organisation had already signed up to Chamberlain's tariff heresy. The (hostile) *Westminster Gazette* took issue in July 1903 with the way Vince was using the local Birmingham 'machinery' to capture the Unionist party 'in the interests of what Mr Vince calls 'our' side of the case', and it quoted extensively from Vince's letter to local LUAs emanating from the Tariff Committee of Birmingham:

> I would be obliged if you could let me know how Mr Chamberlain's fiscal policy has been received by Unionists in your district, and whether he has met favourable or unfavourable criticism. And what special arguments have been used with most effect against the policy, so that special leaflets be prepared giving our side of the case. And please give me the names and addresses of gentlemen in your District who are public speakers and supporters of the Chamberlain policy.[297]

It was this sort of activity, by which Birmingham was seeking to suborn the whole national Liberal Unionist party, that riled Free Trade Liberal Unionist MPs like Winston Churchill, soon to abandon it for the Liberals. He wrote to his party leader, the Duke of Devonshire, to protest that:

> I receive complaints from my constituency chairman and from other Free Traders on the Committee that the Birmingham Tariff Committee has been in touch not only with the central party organisation in Oldham, and the recognised leaders and officials of the Association, but also with separate ward committees and that literature has been pressed on them and they have been invited to distribute it...
> I think we have some reason to complain that a Minister should countenance the tampering with subordinate members of the party organisation.[298]

The *Daily Mail* subsequently ran a feature on the feverish organisational activity in Birmingham. It averred: 'The busiest and most effective leaflet agency in Britain, at this moment, is the Tariff Committee of the BLUA.' Vince had corrected the reporter; it was no longer the 'Birmingham Tariff Committee' but the 'Imperial Tariff Committee' though, the *Mail* added: 'Whatever its name, it is a phenomenal body.' The reporter had asked about its constitution. 'No,' replied Vince, 'it is not elected, but made up of certain gentlemen associated with the Liberal Unionist organisation who wish to help.' It was a small committee and Vince claimed: 'I take all the responsibility for what is done here.

I issue the pamphlets, the circulars and leaflets, and the committee takes the names of persons willing to distribute literature and sends it out. Every reference in newspapers brings us letters. We have sent out to Unionist and Conservative agents and most have favourably replied.' Here then Vince admits that he was openly recruiting for Chamberlain's Tariff Reform crusade and employing Liberal Unionist agents on the assumption that – naturally – they were available to propagate the Birmingham message. Here, too, is evidence of that tight autocratic control which characterised the Machine's methodology.[299]

The *Mail* article also gave details of the publications. Vince claimed that there was at that time demand for 3 million leaflets; he estimated the forthcoming output at 10 million copies. At the time of writing there were 15 different titles, either completed or in the pipeline, such as 'Your Wages in Danger', 'A Lesson from America', 'Tariffs and Food'. In the confused situation country-wide under which the Liberal Unionist Association laboured – with some Liberal Unionists following Chamberlain and some like the leader, the Duke of Devonshire, adhering to Free Trade – a compromise aimed at preserving neutrality was agreed, whereby the national LUA Executive Committee created a joint editorial board to reflect the polarised positions of its leadership; it published a list of available pamphlets on the fiscal question, some labelled (A) Pro-tariff and some (B) Against tariffs. Category (A) pamphlets outnumbered (B), were sharper and better directed to addressing the salient issues, and they were virtually all written by Vince. Birmingham's Tariff Committee was therefore shaping and energising the tariff campaign nationally. The tensions on the LUA were only ended in 1904 when, with consummate ruthlessness, Chamberlain engineered a coup, forced Devonshire out by securing the Presidency for himself, and purged the Association of Free Trade supporters. The Birmingham Machine's take-over of a national party was now complete.

The Birmingham Tariff Committee's influence would be further consolidated by the success of the *Short Handbook for speakers and students of the policy of Preferential Tariffs*, written by Vince and sent to agents in the summer of 1903. Some 5,000 copies were printed in the first run. Within a month of the *Mail* article, *The Times* was reporting that 8 to 9 million leaflets had been circularised by the Imperial Tariff Committee. A separate publications department run by William Jenkins (Vince's close associate) had been established in Congreve Street and engaged 70 to 80 workers to pack leaflets, invoice and despatch them and to keep up with correspondence.[300] It was also planning before the winter to produce lantern slides which would illustrate graphically the most important of the statistical tables supporting the tariff case. The Birmingham-based Committee would prove adept at visual publicity over the next few years, exploiting technological innovations such as new lithographic techniques and full-page picture postcards.[301] When it came to the 1906 General Election its poster campaign caught the attention of the *Birmingham Daily Mail* which noted how the principal central hoardings from Edmund Street to Great Charles Street were covered with 3,500 square feet of Tariff Reform posters.[302] Cartoons were displayed on 'every unguarded square of wall space'.[303] The *Birmingham Daily Mail* observed the prominence in January 1906 of picture postcards emanating from the Imperial Tariff Committee (ITC) which depicted John Bull (the personification of Britain) rejecting a package labelled (Liberal) Home Rule.

Yet it is also important to record that the Imperial Tariff Committee and its alter ego the Birmingham Liberal Unionist Association were equally accomplished in the exercise of habitual Machine electoral tactics. So, when its 1906 Election canvass returns showed Sir Benjamin Stone's candidature to be imperilled in East Birmingham, as the *Post* put it: 'A cry of distress went up and every Unionist party worker, that could be spared, rallied to East Birmingham, and it was a brand snatched from the burning.'[304] Stone's victory was secured; Chamberlainite Unionism therefore continued to dominate absolutely in Birmingham. The electoral Machine had proved its worth. It did so in other ways too, sustaining its intimidating reputation for active political protest, and therefore demonstrating the truth of Jon Lawrence's contention that 'the use of physical force remained a central and widely tolerated element in popular politics'.[305] BLUA and Tariff Reform supporters harried Free Trade opponents, Winston Churchill and Lord Hugh Cecil, in Birmingham in late 1903 and did great damage to their cause; rallied to outnumber and intimidate Free Fooders at a meeting called by J.S. Nettlefold to attack tariffs, in the middle of the Election campaign of 1906; and silenced Lloyd George when he came to speak in the same week in neighbouring Leamington. Lloyd George said his meeting had been disturbed by 'free imports from Birmingham!'.[306]

Birmingham's Imperial Tariff Committee had other functions apart from publicity. It served an important function for Chamberlain in gathering information. For example, early in the campaign, in July 1903, Vince wrote to 102 Chamber of Commerce branches all over the country to elicit answers to questions which would then shape Chamberlain's pro-Tariff arguments. He wanted to know whether Canadian preferential tariffs had benefited any of their trades; whether they expected future benefits from planned preferential arrangements; whether they had suffered from 'dumping' of cheap foreign goods in UK markets and from state-subsidised foreign competition; and importantly whether they had been adversely affected by hostile tariffs.[307]

Another role assigned to the Committee was to be a recruiting agent for the Tariff crusade. Vince was asked to found new Tariff Reform clubs throughout the Midlands and North Wales. Much of this area was familiar to him, comprising the Duchy he had worked so hard to organise for Chamberlain through the MLUA in the 1890s. Chamberlain apparently believed that these industrial regions were more likely to respond favourably to an agitation directed from Birmingham than from London.[308] Quite evidently then, despite the existence of a national Tariff Reform machinery, Chamberlain needed, and relied on, the Birmingham-based Imperial Tariff Reform Committee which he knew would secure a Midlands citadel completely under his hegemony. He was immeasurably helped that – aside from support from most national newspapers, notably *The Times, Daily Telegraph* and *Daily Express* – he also had unwavering local Press backing from the *Gazette*, the *Mail*, the *Midland Express* and the only disappointment was the failure to win the endorsement of the *Post* which remained critical until the editor – A.H. Pountney – was replaced by J. V. Morton in 1905, ensuring that the organ was firmly aligned with Tariff Reform by the time the General Election was called in 1906. Just as in the heyday of Bunce and Jaffray, the *Post* once again articulated the vision of Chamberlain and his team.[309]

So far, we have concentrated on the Birmingham and Imperial Tariff Committees. Their subjection to Chamberlain's direction was overt. Yet from the outset of his new Tariff Reform campaign he recognised that a national non-party pressure-group was essential to appeal to Liberal voters as much as to Unionists. While he would act as stage-manager in the wings, he let others among the ranks of Unionist MPs, financiers, businessmen, journalists and academics, and led by the Duke of Sutherland, organise inaugural meetings which culminated on 21 July 1903 in the establishment of the Tariff Reform League. Based in Victoria Street, Westminster, not in Birmingham, Sutherland was to be its President, C.A. Pearson owner of the *Daily Express* and of the *Standard* was to be its Chairman, a lawyer, Ratcliffe Cousins, its secretary and Unionist MPs including A. Griffith-Boscawen and Evelyn Cecil on its Executive Committee.[310] The League was to be committed to 'advocate the employment of a tariff, to develop and consolidate the resources of the Empire and to defend the industry of the United Kingdom'. Its leaders and members shared with Chamberlain a fear that the white colonies were growing away from the Mother Country and that the growth of Germany and Austria posed an existential threat to Britain's trading future. 'What would make it so formidable was the combination of Imperial patriotism and of crusading zeal,' writes Andrew Thompson.[311]

This 'formidable' message and impressive energy found expression in one of the most comprehensive extra-parliamentary organisations since the Anti-Corn Law League in the 1840s. Although the destruction of many of the Tariff Reform League's records makes it difficult to be precise, it seems that by 1910 there were over 600 branches, with the largest – Bristol – boasting over 4,000 members. They were grouped in nineteen regional federations, which oversaw canvassing at election time, the organisation of lectures and distribution of literature. Their activities were generously funded. Members' subscriptions, and donations from wealthy benefactors, swelled coffers – in 1907 alone over £23,000 was raised, a considerable sum, enabling the League to make a significant mark on national politics. The League's ability to spend freely in election campaigns upset its opponents; as a pressure group, rather than as a political party, it was able to evade the Corrupt and Illegal Practices Act's strict limits on candidates' expenses.[312] Of all living politicians Chamberlain would have been most aware of how to exploit this loophole.

The central point for a study of Chamberlain's electoral Machine is this: for all that the Tariff Reform League was intended to be studiously non-party political, it had his and Birmingham's finger-prints all over it. He had greater experience of how to organise a national pressure-group than anyone alive, having been in on the establishment of the NEL at the beginning in 1869. He knew more than most about employing agents, about generating literature, about founding a speakers' network – such activities, which were central to the League's modus operandi, were all second nature to him. Significantly, he was appointed Vice-President at its inauguration. He spoke at its first annual meeting in July 1904, concentrating the minds of his followers on what was at stake in this crusade: 'It is given to this generation to solve the great problem of a United Empire – if we do not solve it, disaster is certain.' He communicated with its branches, for example congratulating the Leicester Tariff Reform League on its educational work in 1905; he intervened in the national organisation, manoeuvring Pearson out of the chairmanship because the latter's evident interest was in protection, rather than in Chamberlain's personal enthusiasm, Imperial Preference.[313] He ensured the more congenial Imperial enthusiast Matthew White Ridley succeeded him.

In many regards, therefore, as one authority on the League has observed: 'The Tariff Reform League became Chamberlain's new caucus.'[314] Then, as Chamberlain flagged, so his son Austen became his reliable fiscal mouthpiece, safeguarding family interests, as he grew increasingly prominent in Tariff Reform League counsels. Indeed, he just occasionally showed flashes of his father's crowd-pulling power for in 1906 the League's Kent branch ran trains from the countryside to Canterbury, enabling over 6,000 people to hear Austen Chamberlain speak on tariffs. Perhaps most importantly, Joseph Chamberlain blurred the divide between the League and his own organisation in Birmingham. Charles Vince was the agent by which this was achieved.

His Birmingham (later, Imperial) Tariff Committee handbook, which we previously saw launched in 1903, became the indispensable reference tool for League speakers. By

1908, 38,000 copies had been distributed. Just as effective were the *Monthly Notes on Tariff Reform* he launched and he co-edited with A.E. Hunt. Predictably, it was published in Birmingham, by the Imperial Tariff Committee. Its first issue in July 1904 defined its purpose as being 'designed for the use of speakers and debaters', as well as being intended to be a means of communication between tariff reformers in different parts of the country.'[315] That very first edition lays bare the fratricidal divisions Chamberlain's new policy had opened up, for while these *Notes* purported to be factual, they took the opportunity to deride 'the five or six Liberal Unionists, like A. Elliott, whose shrill protest had no more effect than the squeak of a mouse in the wainscot'. Subsequent editions contained reports on a range of industries such as woollen, hosiery, carpet and lace-making, in an effort to demonstrate how they suffered from uncontrolled imports and from invidious foreign tariffs. The *Notes* extensively quoted Chamberlain's speeches, and dinned in his favourite message that working-class employment would immeasurably benefit from tariffs to protect home industry. Yet despite efforts to be balanced in the coverage of industries spanning industrial Britain, West Midlands industry predominated. For example, the chairman of a large Birmingham employer, Joseph Lucas, was cited at length on the dumping of inferior German cycle lamps on the home market, which deleteriously affected sales and by extension his capacity to increase employment in his Birmingham factory.[316]

Vince's *Notes* sold 120,000 copies in 1908. Their national circulation ensured wide dissemination of what was essentially a Birmingham message. In fact, the League's ability to produce such propaganda was unparalleled and was greater even than the two main political parties in the 1910 General Election. It excelled in its utilisation of all branches of contemporary media. By 1909 it could print and circulate 53 million leaflets and pamphlets, and 166,000 posters, many emanating – thanks to a symbiotic relationship – from the Imperial Tariff Committee presses and warehouses in Birmingham. In this, and in the calling of public meetings, there is – unsurprisingly – much that is reminiscent of Joseph Chamberlain's methodology, from the National Education League in 1869 onwards. Back then he was a master of the political pamphlet, of the rousing meeting, of using the Press. And he had always shown an awareness of the possibilities of technological innovation. Vince and others working with the Tariff Reform League were at the forefront in utilising new technologies.

The League broke new ground with its use of the electrophone in January 1904, to enable multiple audiences to hear Chamberlain's great Guildhall speech almost as it was made.[317] It was at the cutting edge in using film-making with, for example, *John Bull's Hearth* (1903), in which John Bull and a colonial representative expel foreigners and replace free with fair trade; and in *International Exchange* (1905), where John Bull is freed from an ugly Free Trade witch.[318] These was among the very first examples of political propaganda films anywhere. The League invented Dump shops and touring Dumping vans, to illustrate the extent to which foreign goods had penetrated British markets.[319] And even if it was not as quick as its rival, the Free Trade Union, to exploit lantern slide shows – Winston Churchill had championed these from mid-1903 – the League did catch up.

Although Chamberlain himself was not responsible for every one of these innovations, the fact is that the campaigning tone nationally was set by him. Indeed, one could go so far as to argue that the entire 1906 General Election (which went so badly, for many reasons, for the Unionists) was fought around the Tariff issue and around the divisive personality of Joseph Chamberlain. Certainly, as far as the conduct of politics is concerned, he and his Birmingham base shaped the Tariff battle. The Liberal chief whip, Herbert Gladstone, said as much when he wrote in early 1904 that 'Chamberlain shows us how to do it'; he was alluding to the industrial quantities of literature pouring off Birmingham's presses and to the unprecedented blitz of agents (18) employed in one Shropshire by-election at Ludlow in late 1903. 'He uses heaps of men who are not paid,' went on Gladstone, pointing up a long-standing characteristic of voluntarism in politics in the Duchy and in the Birmingham Machine.[320]

Chamberlain's crusading zeal enthused and galvanised; but his belligerence and uncompromising attitude infected the Tariff Reform League in a much more negative way. We find its secretary, Ratcliffe Cousins, writing in a letter to *The Times* in January 1904 that: 'The League is determined to oppose the return of all free-fooders, whether Unionist or Radical, and we shall use the whole of our organisation for that object.'[321] Evidently, he was as good as his word; a year later the Unionist Free Trader Lord Robert Cecil listed 25 seats where attacks by Tariff reformers had taken place, 'commonly initiated by the Tariff Reform League, and having the personal support of Joseph Chamberlain'.[322]

His disputatious nature is reflected in the way that – in truth – the Tariff Reform League, which he had ushered into the spotlight to be the national expression of his policy, was responsible for the implosion and dissolution of the Unionist Party, his own Liberal Unionist arm included. It should also be recorded that – master of slogan and political symbol though he was – he was directly responsible for the most egregious error in terms of the fractious debate over Free Trade. In November 1903, he summoned up the contrasting images of the Free Trade and the Tariff Reform loaves, with a practical demonstration on Bingley Hall stage, to try and show that even with food taxes the size of the working man's staple loaf would be barely affected compared to the loaf made with untaxed imported grain. Comparative sizes of loaves, playing on public fears for the bread on their tables, proved a public relations gift to his opponents, one that kept on giving through the Election of 1906 and one that the League could not effectively counter.

In addition to his Birmingham operation, and to the Tariff Reform League, Chamberlain developed an entirely new concept to improve the smooth running of his Machine. It was partly a consequence of the haste and impetuosity with which he had announced his conversion to Imperial Preference in May 1903. He quickly realised that he was not master of his brief. Questions about the details of a tariff structure – how it would apply to a host of different industries, as well as to British farmers – prompted him to shift his argument and sometimes left him floundering. He was quickly also forced to recognise that simplistic notions of single uniform tariffs were unachievable given the extent of vested interests.[323] He felt he could not rely on Board of Trade statistics. The lack of forward planning is seen in the way his mind evidently changed about the end-purpose of this great crusade against Free Trade: at first the emphasis of his tariff programme was on raising funds for social reform, and then it was to protect British industry and agriculture from foreign depredations. Later it became a mission to solve rising unemployment in the working classes. At every turn, it became more apparent that he needed statistical ammunition to make his case convincingly.

For a man like Chamberlain, whose style of argument and of speech-making had relied since the great battles over education on employing salvoes of facts and figures, there was a transparent need in his commissariat for a 'think tank', in biographer Julian Amery's words.[324] So he devised the Tariff Reform Commission of Inquiry, aided and encouraged by Leo Maxse, the editor of the *National Review* (a leading Imperialist journal), by Arthur Pearson, chairman of the Tariff Reform League, and by William Hewins, the Director of the London School of Economics. Hewins had offered early on to write a series of articles on fiscal reform for *The Times* and within months had thrown up an academic career to devote himself wholly to Chamberlain's cause. It is a sign of the march of time that back in the late 1860s Chamberlain would not have dreamt of employing economists in his political teams for their academic discipline then barely existed; now this relatively new discipline was essential to him as he embarked on a campaign which relied on the marshalling of persuasive statistical data.

The announcement of this Commission in *The Times* in December 1903 smacked of a government initiating a Royal Commission, and the emphasis throughout was on independent fact-finding and on expert advice.[325] He had recruited many top industrialists such as Charles Allen the steel magnate, Sir Vincent Caillard – a financier who had helped found the national Bank of Egypt, Sir Alfred Hickman, a leading iron and steel executive, and Sir Alfred Jones who headed up a great shipping firm. They were joined by men who spoke for agricultural interests such as Henry Chaplin and by someone who had a deep understanding of working-class sociology, Charles Booth, the famous author of an important study of London life. Sir Robert Herbert, former Permanent Under-Secretary to the Colonies, was to chair the body. Professor Hewins would be its secretary. That they were distinguished and that they evidently took Chamberlain's proposals seriously added lustre to the campaign he had launched. Their distinction greatly assisted the raising of funds to sustain the inquiry. Sir Harry Brittain later reminisced: 'We started off funds for the Tariff Commission with a Dinner and we took the hat round, collecting nearly £27,000 in the evening.'[326]

The Times reported just prior to the Commission's first meeting, a month after its inception was announced, promising 'the fullest opportunity to members of every trade to state their views before the Commission. Already hundreds of firms and individuals representing business of all kinds have stated their wish to appear before the commissioners as witnesses.' Clearly there was a degree of urgency for the report concluded – rather optimistically in the light of subsequent events: 'It would be of the utmost service that the preliminary investigation into tariff arrangements should have been made before a new government takes over committed to tariffs.'[327] From the very beginning the Commission reiterated time and again the mantra that this was to be a scientific inquiry, hearing views both for and against protection. Chamberlain was happy enough that it had the trappings of impartiality and balance, provided in the end it furnished him with the statistics he needed to underpin his arguments for tariffs.

Even though the Tariff Reform Commission was based in London and was intended to be independent of Chamberlain and his Birmingham campaigning headquarters, it was subject to regular Chamberlainite pressure. William Hewins was a linking component in the bigger Machine. Not only was he secretary of the Tariff Reform Commission but he was also economic adviser to the Tariff Reform League. He became Chamberlain's able, and usually unquestioning, lieutenant. It was through Hewins that Chamberlain chivvied the Commission to set out a schedule of preferential tariffs once it had completed its investigation in 1905. So far under Chamberlain's spell did he fall that he was even prepared to step out of his academic comfort zone that year to travel to Canada, and to conduct *ultra vires* negotiations with their commissioners on preferential tariffs.

Birmingham contributed to the debate over economic statistics in another way. Even as he prepared to make his fateful speech of 15 May 1903 Chamberlain had commissioned Professor William Ashley, the economist he had recruited from Harvard to found a commercial faculty in his new University of Birmingham; he asked him to write a book on Tariff Reform. The resultant publication, *The Tariff Reform Problem*, remained the most convincing and readable statement of the arguments for a fiscal revolution, and appears to have been the distillation of discussions between the two men across the summer of 1903, pre-dating and then giving place to the Commission which was founded to add weight to the case in the winter of 1903. Ashley also served the Commission, but he continued to be based in Birmingham, being Professor of Commerce, founding the first business school in Britain in the process, as well as later becoming Dean of the University. Chamberlain regularly called him in to Highbury to advise him on economic statistics as he prepared speeches and arguments. Ashley was a much-valued cog in this last incarnation of the Birmingham Machine.

All we have seen so far illustrates the imaginative, at times even febrile, nature of Chamberlain's response to the crisis he had brought about in 1903. The Birmingham Tariff Committee and the Tariff Reform League were squarely aimed at winning support for his radical new fiscal position. Beyond that they were part of an attempt to rejuvenate flagging Unionist politics.[328] They sought to widen popular participation as local League organisations proliferated, and as his gift for communicating his message harnessed the latest technologies. Nor were these bodies the end of it. Chamberlain was determined, first, to conscript working men to the cause. He recognised from the beginning of his tariff campaign that 'if I do not convince the working-class I am absolutely powerless. I can do nothing.'[329] Yet trade unions immediately rushed to denounce him, with the Trades Union Congress condemning as blacklegs all who favoured fiscal change.[330]

However, his faithful Tariff Reform League acted – probably with his encouragement – to redress the balance, forming its own Trade Union Committee, which in April 1904 convened a special conference with delegates from as far afield as Newcastle and Seaham joining London trade unionists. Out of this TUTRA was born, the Trade Union Tariff Reform Association. It was reliant for funds and for propaganda materials on the League. And although it never really challenged the hold that the Free Trade-supporting TUC exercised on organised labour, TUTRA had its successes in parts of Britain, especially the North East and – as might be expected – in the Midlands, where by 1905 a district council was established in Birmingham. TUTRA's activities and branch meetings featured regularly in Vince's *Monthly Notes* up to 1913, at which point it was absorbed into the Tariff Reform League. Its fading away was representative of a wider Tariff Reform retreat after the cause had suffered three successive electoral reversals. But for our purpose TUTRA is important; it may not have been his creation but it illustrates the institutional ingenuity Chamberlain prompted in those around him after 1903, as they sought to proselytise his mission cause across the country.

Chamberlain was much more personally involved in the appeal to another key constituent group – women. When the tariff reformer William Bridgeman stood, and lost, in a by-election in 1904 at Oswestry he discovered several things: firstly, that free traders could ruthlessly portray tariff reformers as plutocrats bent on exploiting the poor housewife and secondly, that the help he got from Primrose League volunteers was feeble and unfit for purpose in a boisterous election campaign.[331] He turned to Chamberlain for advice who wrote chiding him that 'you had practically no lady helpers in your recent contest'. He sent his able Birmingham lieutenant, William Jenkins from the Imperial Tariff Committee, to visit the constituency; he confirmed that the absence of women was a key defect in the Oswestry campaign. As a result, Caroline Bridgeman, the candidate's wife, set about rectifying the situation, creating a dynamic local Women's Unionist Association which provided the impetus for a national Women's Unionist and Tariff Reform Association (WUTRA). Its recent historian has concluded: 'It was arguably the most innovative and successful of the auxiliary organisations formed by (Tariff Reform) supporters of Joseph Chamberlain.'[332] What differentiated WUTRA was that it did not treat women merely as decorative adjuncts to the political process but that it set out to educate them in the issues, so that they themselves could effectively counter Free Trade arguments demonising tariff reformers as anti-consumerist parasites. WUTRA members were not just to be wheeled out as canvassers at election time but to engage in continuous political education. Mary Maxse, WUTRA's chairman, noted in 1912: 'The real burden of political work during the quiet time between elections rests upon the sub-committees in the towns and villages, the men and women who go from house to house arousing and keeping alive the interest of the voter.'[333] In some regards, not a great deal had changed since Chamberlain, Harris, Schnadhorst and others had developed these electoral techniques for nursing Birmingham wards over forty years earlier – but what was new was that women were now as prominent as men in the process. For WUTRA women 'contributed to the education of village people…having debates, delivering speeches and giving Tariff Reform plays'.[334]

A movement which stemmed from advice to one candidate in 1904 rapidly grew into being a significant element in Chamberlain's institutional structure, harnessing the potential of women for the pro-Tariff movement and then for the Conservative Party itself. By 1913, 25 of the 33 constituencies in Chamberlain's Duchy had WUTRA organisations. Just as with the Tariff Reform League, Chamberlain had provided opportunities for those previously unengaged, or simply marginalised, to engage in Unionist politics. This was the man who told his wife in the late 1880s that 'policy and action were for men to settle', and of his loathing 'for the odious (suffragist) crew of strong minded women, all of them more or less unsexed'. Expediency evidently educated him.[335] Still, his evolution fits with that theme of organising and structuring, always with the aim of increasing democratic engagement; it runs consistently through Chamberlain's political career, from the late 1860s up to his abrupt departure from the stage in 1906. And throughout that time Chamberlain saw to it that the Machine he inspired was kept energised and motivated by his personal speech-making.

So, with the Tariff Campaign, in addition to the extra-parliamentary bodies he summoned up, he felt the need to make the argument for tariffs himself at meetings right across the country. At great personal cost to his health he poured his energies into a speaking tour that not even Gladstone had attempted. He visited Greenock, Newcastle, Liverpool, Cardiff, London and Leeds among other destinations from 1903 onwards. Each speech was tailored to address local concerns and to accommodate regional economic interests, so that the preparation required was almost as taxing as the oratorical performance itself. In his previous great speaking tours – for example in the 1895 election campaign – his efforts rewarded and revitalised him with palpable electoral success. In this case, nearly every one of his speaking venues rejected his message when it came to vote in the General Election of 1906.

Despite the institutional innovations he conjured, and notwithstanding this sequence of arresting speeches replete with oratorical flights, his tariff message was insufficiently persuasive. The electorate did not believe that the British economy was sliding down a long decline, was frightened by the prospect of food taxes, and further believed that Protection endangered international peace and was a licence for the unscrupulous to exploit the consumer. Tariffs were toxic, not triumphant. A crushing Unionist defeat in 1906, in which Liberals won 400 seats and Unionists slumped to 157 seats, provided a telling commentary on Chamberlain's fiscal policy. The *Manchester Guardian* certainly thought so. In the election aftermath, it editorialised as follows:

> A candidate only had to be a Free Trader to get in, whether he was known or unknown, semi-Unionist or thorough Home Ruler, Protestant or Roman Catholic, entertaining or dull. He had only to be a Protectionist to lose all chance of getting in, though he spoke with the tongues of men and angels…[336]

Defeat for Chamberlain was followed in July 1906 by his stroke and debilitating paralysis. Aspects of his political legacy continued even while its fountainhead was cruelly disabled. His mind remained keen and he took pleasure in the knowledge that much of the Unionist rump returned to Parliament in 1906 supported tariffs. He had succeeded in winning over his party. He might also reflect that – in keeping with his long-standing ambition to engage many more people in the political process – he had succeeded in involving new groups of men and women through the fiscal debate he had unleashed.

Charles Vince

Charles Vince has a somewhat different profile from some of Chamberlain's allies and loyal supporters featured earlier in the book. He spans a later period than most of the others, being born in Handsworth in 1855 and living on right up to 1929 and so experiencing the Great War, the First Labour Government and the onset of the Great Depression.

In one sense he formed a direct link back to the early days of the Chamberlain political operation, for he was the son of Rev Charles Vince (see Chapter 3). He followed his father's Baptist creed, attending the Church of the Redeemer on Hagley Road, the successor church to his father's, on Graham Street. The elder Charles Vince was also a passionate Liberal. His son remembered attending the great Parliamentary Reform demonstration at Brookfields, and the excitements of George Dixon's by-election campaign in 1867. Hitherto a bystander, his introduction to political activism came as a thirteen-year-old in 1868. He later wrote: 'On election day in 1868 my job was to carry the slips on which the alleged state of the poll was printed, from hour to hour, from the All Saints Committee Room to a polling-booth at the bottom of Hockley Hill, and paste them up, amid the applause of the populace.' He was but one very small part in Harris's highly organised grassroots operation. His father was already educating him in the realities of Liberal politics: 'The political creed in which I was brought up was that Mr Gladstone was all very well, but the true savour of Liberal doctrine was to be found only in the utterances of John Bright, Birmingham's hero.'

In many other ways, his subsequent experience differed from the manufacturers, businessmen and lawyers sketched in previous chapters. He was sent to Cambridge (Christ College), where he studied classics. He then followed a school-mastering career, teaching at Repton. He gained promotion as Headmaster of Mill Hill, the Nonconformist school in North London. Yet, chairmanship of the Liberal committee in South Derbyshire when he worked at Repton, then campaigning for the Liberals to defeat George Curzon there in 1885, re-awakened his interest in, and appetite for, political engagement. In 1891, he resigned from Mill Hill and committed himself to Liberal Unionist politics, attracted by what would be a life-long and frank hero-worship of Joseph Chamberlain. Vince memorialised his decision to serve Chamberlain in his Recollections and Reminscences, *where he wrote that: 'I am left with a consciousness of having been fortunate enough to live through the heroic age of Birmingham politics and of having rendered service loyally, if not helpfully, to a very great and very wise man.'*

The thoroughness and professionalism of Chamberlain's operation is evident in the care with which Vince was trained up at the Birmingham Liberal Unionist Association under the tutelage of J.S. Bailey from 1891. He also had help from another quarter. 'When I joined the BLUA,' he recalled, 'Powell Williams (who was moving to succeed Lord Wolmer in the Liberal Unionist Association headquarters) gave me the encouragement and the elementary instructions of which I stood in need. (He had ensured that) in every ward the party had volunteer officers whose zeal and expertise left nothing to be desired'. This training guaranteed that Charles Vince would be the repository of the collective wisdom distilled from the Chamberlain group's twenty years' political involvement in Birmingham. In 1892, he became the BLUA's secretary; and by the end of the year Chamberlain had persuaded him to take up the same role in the new Midlands Liberal Unionist Association. This latter appointment ensured that for much of the 1890s his services were done outside the city, for he was supporting candidates in more than thirty constituencies. On one occasion in an election in Northamptonshire he spoke for one and three-quarter hours without break, holding the platform before the candidate eventually arrived. But his skills were not oratorical, and his value not as a front-line politician. The role of secretary suited him perfectly; the Birmingham Post in his obituary of January 1929 contended that: 'He was a brilliant success for under him the organisation of the party was at least as efficient as it had been in Schnadhorst's day – and a good deal more pleasant.' Vince's contemporary, Byng Kenrick, was not as uncritically enthusiastic as that (according to Julian Amery), thinking him 'a fat, comfortable, literary-looking gent, good at slogans and pamphlets, though not such a great organiser'. Kenrick was unusual in finding fault with his organisation skills, but all parties agreed that Vince's particular genius was as a writer and publicist, a reflection of his early talents as a scholar at Cambridge and as a distinguished school-master.

He came into his own when Chamberlain converted to Tariff Reform in May 1903 and he followed suit. Vince immediately wrote an authoritative series of articles for the Birmingham Post, a paper for which he had been a leader writer for many years and which continued to haver in its loyalty to Chamberlain on the issue right up to the end of 1905. Vince was Chamberlain's leading interpreter in the local Press.

Chamberlain contracted him to create his own loyal pro-Tariff organisation, firmly based on the existing BLUA. In generating millions of leaflets, handbills and pamphlets and hundreds of thousands of posters for the Birmingham Tariff Committee (later the Imperial Tariff Committee), Vince excelled. Many of the pamphlets he himself authored; as a result, with Ashley and Hewins, he developed an almost unrivalled command of fiscal statistics.

Whilst masterminding the publicity blitz emanating from Congreve Street in Birmingham, he did not lose sight of the need to sustain the Liberal Unionist organisation, both in Birmingham and in the Duchy. That Birmingham and its immediate environs bucked the national swing against the Unionists, in the tsunami of the 1906 election, was in no small measure thanks to Charles Vince's efforts.

Chamberlain trusted Vince implicitly; to Chamberlain's end they were very close friends. The Birmingham Gazette *thought Vince 'a power behind the scenes', a recognition that Chamberlain valued Vince's advice and capacity to get things done.*

Beyond the cut and thrust of electoral politics, Vince followed his bent for scholarship, serving as a committee member on the Birmingham Library Committee (of which he was twice president) and on the Central Library Committee. Many of Chamberlain's team shared the vision George Dawson had articulated, that Birmingham's citizens had the right to cultural elevation, and that access to great public libraries was the means by which enlightenment could be achieved. Vince went further than many of that team; he moved on to write substantial works of scholarship himself, authoring a monograph of his father's hero John Bright, and adding volumes III and IV to Bunce's monumental History of the Corporation of Birmingham.

Vince outlived many of those who had been engaged in the 'heroic age' of Birmingham politics. Even when he died in 1929 the Unionists still held (just) an unbroken monopoly of electoral representation in Birmingham, to the maintenance of which two Chamberlains, Austen and Neville, still contributed. Vince had not lived so long that his legacy had been forgotten. The Gazette *wrote that 'he was a potent organiser whose fame as such had become legendary; he was a well-liked and marvellously dutiful citizen'.*

William Hewins

W.A.S. Hewins was a late-comer to Chamberlain's inner circle, like William Ashley, a man with economic expertise which answered to Chamberlain's needs in the challenging period after the great Tariff Reform speech of 1903. A generation earlier Chamberlain would not have felt the need for economic advice, indeed the discipline barely existed. But it is also the case that a generation earlier Chamberlain would not have been recruiting distinguished Oxbridge-trained academics with a long history of scholarship and educational leadership. The great majority of the profiles in this book are of men who made their names in Birmingham and then served the municipality and Chamberlain's party with distinction. W.A.S. Hewins differed in this regard, as did Ashley, his fellow economist.

William Hewins was in fact born in what would become part of Chamberlain's Duchy, near Wolverhampton in 1865. Schooling at Wolverhampton Grammar School was followed by an honours degree in mathematics from Pembroke College, Oxford. He soon became thoroughly versed in the new economic theory espoused by Dr Cunningham and several German followers which placed economics firmly in the general history of political and social development rather than treating it as an abstraction. He first became an Extension lecturer, teaching and writing in Lancashire and Yorkshire before being appointed in 1895 as the organiser and first Director of the London School of Economics. He was a marked success; he presided over the School's impressive growth and negotiated its inclusion in the University of London. His academic prowess was recognised at the same time by his appointment to the Tooke Professorship of Economic Science and Statistics at King's College, London.

Yet despite appearing well-set as a successful university don in 1903 he abruptly threw over a career in academic life for the rough and tumble of engagement in a highly controversial political campaign. He was prompted by outrage at the condescension shown by some 14 professors and lecturers of economics in a letter to The Times *in which they anathematised Joseph Chamberlain's Tariff Policy, days after his speech. Hewins came out fighting in a series of articles for* The Times *in which he supported Chamberlain's ideas of Imperial Preference and on the rigidities of current Free Trade orthodoxy. The clarity of his exposition attracted Chamberlain, who asked him a few months later to be secretary of the Tariff Commission, the non-party, fact-gathering inquiry set up to provide the statistical evidence to support the case for tariffs. Chamberlain went on to appoint Hewins as economic adviser to the Tariff Reform League whose c.600 branches campaigned all over the country for the adoption of tariffs. Hewins and Ashley became Chamberlain's in-house advisers, called in to check facts, to discuss policy initiatives and at times to educate the great man in economics.*

In time Hewins found he so much enjoyed political involvement that he sought a Commons seat of his own and in 1912 he was returned as MP for the City of Hereford. His economic understanding and experience led to his appointment as Under-Secretary of State to Walter Long at the Colonial Office; there was a nice synergy in this, for his former master had been a most distinguished Colonial Secretary, a post which crystallised those ideas on Imperial Preference which so appealed to Hewins.

Successive electoral reverses in 1906 and 1910 for a Unionist party promoting Tariff Reform did nothing to deter Hewins, who remained a convinced tariff-enthusiast. Although he failed to get back into the House of Commons after 1918 he dedicated his time to chairing the Empire Development Union (a successor body to the Tariff Reform League and the Tariff Commission) and in 1923 the Prime Minister, Stanley Baldwin, drafted Hewins in to a committee chaired by Lord Milner tasked with preparing the way for the introduction of tariffs by a future Conservative government, should the party win a majority in the General Election that Baldwin had called on the issue. To Hewins' intense frustration it did not win. Instead he continued to write, producing various polemical works on tariffs culminating in his Apologia for an Imperialist, *in 1929. He also did much valuable work on 'a scientific tariff' which would be of use to Neville Chamberlain. Sadly Hewins – dying in 1931 – did not live to see the tariff case triumph in 1932 when Joseph Chamberlain's son Neville introduced the Import Duties Bill, which overthrew decades of Free Trade orthodoxy.*

William Hewins' significance was as a man who provided academic ballast to Joseph Chamberlain's campaign. He made it respectable. Beyond that he continued to fight for the Chamberlain vision long after Joseph himself had passed on; like so many of the Chamberlain team we have examined, he showed an impressive loyalty to his leader's memory for the rest of his own life.

AFTERWORD

Three years of political intriguing after 1903, of often bitter and vituperative abuse, of a ceaseless round of travelling followed by speech-making, exhausted Joseph Chamberlain. His younger son Neville, observing signs of failing health in January 1906, tried to have a 'serious talk' with his father to persuade him to slow down. He was predictably stubborn, telling Neville that he could not go 'at half speed' and that he would rather take the risk.[337] In July that year 'Joe' celebrated both his 70th birthday and 30 years as an MP representing Birmingham. Huge crowds marked the occasion as factories and shops closed; they cheered ten-deep on Birmingham's heavily decorated streets as Chamberlain quartered the city in a motorcade. A civic luncheon, fireworks displays across the city's wards, a torch-lit procession and a huge rally at Bingley Hall added to the sense of a very special occasion. His Bingley Hall speech, witnessed by thousands, was both the distillation of his political philosophy and an emotional declaration of his love for his adopted city.[338] It was a fitting climax to a unique relationship between a politician and his heartland. Never before, or since, has there been this deep and enduring bond between a British statesman and a municipality, or indeed with a wider bloc of parliamentary constituencies beyond that, like the Duchy.

It was truly a climax. The adrenalin of the occasion, the exhaustion brought on by delivering a long speech, the plentiful and habitual wine and cigars, all conspired to induce a savage stroke days later. It irretrievably paralysed his right side and blurred his speech. It was the end of Joseph Chamberlain's active political career, but not an immediate end to the causes for which he had fought.

His sons kept the flame of Chamberlainism alive. Austen continued to prosecute the battle for Tariff Reform after 1906 as a member of the Tariff Reform League Council but his leadership was compromised by a feeling that, while his father struggled on and clung tightly to the vestiges of power, the movement was doomed to stall. Austen could occasionally demonstrate all Joseph's intolerance of dissent, at one time launching an attack on remaining free-fooders in the Unionist Party which echoed his father's purges of 1904-5, but at heart he was not belligerent. Garvin thought Austen 'wrapped deep in the cotton wool of platitudes'; like many tariff reformers, Garvin became frustrated at Austen's lack of the kind of charismatic leadership to which he had become used with Joseph.[339] The diplomat who would later triumph at Locarno in the 1920s showed from the outset a natural predisposition to temporise and seek accommodation. His lack of ruthlessness was illustrated when he failed to grasp the leadership of the Unionist Party in 1911 on Balfour's retirement when it seemed his for the taking.

Still, it was not his fault that the Unionists, and by extension Tariff Reform, failed to convince the electorate in 1910. David Lloyd George, the incumbent Liberal Chancellor had offered an attractive alternative (many thought, socialistic) approach to raising money to pay for social reform through higher taxation, especially of the better-off. Furthermore, the economy had failed to decline in the Edwardian years as Joseph Chamberlain had predicted it would if Free Trade prevailed. By 1914 it was clear that Tariff Reform was more of an impediment than a benison. Also, Austen Chamberlain – as a Unionist himself, and as heir to the man who helped found Unionism in 1886 – had to recognise that there was a higher priority, that of forestalling Home Rule, a serious proposition again after the road-block of the Lords had been cleared by the Parliament Act of 1911.

These setbacks were reflected in the way that the Tariff Reform apparatus so painstakingly erected by his father was steadily dismantled. The *Monthly Notes* ceased circulation just before the outbreak of the War in 1914. The League and the Tariff Commission metamorphosed with the war into the Empire Development Union.

The real irony was that Neville, deemed unpromising by his demanding father after an early failure as a sisal grower, was to prove his true political heir, not his establishment-minded brother Austen. He it was who carried tariffs onto the statute book as Chancellor in 1932. The occasion made him deeply conscious of the family legacy, for he said in the Commons debate: 'My father would have found consolation for the bitterness of his disappointment if he could have foreseen that these proposals, the direct and legitimate descendants of his conception, would be laid before the house in the presence of one (Austen) and by the lips of the other of the two immediate successors to his name and blood.'[340]

Even when he was active Joseph Chamberlain had been aware of the pressures to fuse the two branches of the Unionist family. Austen Chamberlain succeeded Joseph on the Liberal Unionist Council and could see the logic in a national merger which was effected in 1912. Birmingham, however, remained the exception. Its BLUA continued as a separate entity through the First World War. By now Birmingham Unionists marched under the banner of a new and more assured leader, Neville. For while Austen was from 1903 a national politician of Cabinet rank, living in London and Sussex, Neville was building a substantial reputation as a local politician. He followed his father in carving out a career on Birmingham's Town Council from 1911, where he specialised in town planning and in working-class housing. When he wrote that 'a large proportion of the poor are living under conditions of housing detrimental both to their health and morals,' he was directly echoing his father's sentiments from his Mayoral term in the 1870s.[341] In 1915, just as his father before him, he became Mayor of Birmingham, now a greatly expanded city after the creation of Greater Birmingham in 1911. With the crisis of war upon him he showed all his forebear's energy and imagination to devise solutions to coal and food shortages, to provide antenatal care for young mothers and to plan for transport and new housing in the city. The municipal mission first articulated by George Dawson but acted out by Chamberlain and his allies (chapter 3) had proved by its transmission to Neville to be an enduring legacy.[342]

In time Neville would seek to join his brother at Westminster. It was Charles Vince, the veteran secretary of the BLUA whom he consulted, and Vince and another Liberal Unionist who effected Neville Chamberlain's adoption for Birmingham Central (later Ladywood) for the 1918 General Election. Thereafter he once again proved to be a chip off the old block. He turned to reviving the local party Machine which had atrophied during the War. It was Neville Chamberlain who in August 1918 masterminded the complete amalgamation of Birmingham's two Unionist parties with a single central office under joint presidents. Sir Arthur Steel-Maitland and he would fill the roles, but there was never any doubt who would run the show. He boasted to his sisters, in a tone and manner uncannily echoing that of his famous father a generation earlier: 'This decision practically places the direction of Unionist policies in Birmingham in my hands.' Over the course of the next few years he energised the Ladywood, Birmingham and Midland organisations, running meetings and social gatherings and launching a Unionist Workers' League and a Junior Unionists group while his wife, Annie, founded four Women's Unionist Institutes in Ladywood. Neville Chamberlain nursed the constituency diligently by 'slumming', calling on the many poor Ladywood constituents in their homes, to gauge constituency feeling.[343]

Neville Chamberlain, just as his father before him, took responsibility for organising Birmingham's Unionist battalions at election time. When all twelve constituencies were held in 1922 and 1924, despite the advance of Labour in recent municipal elections and the arrival of Oswald Mosley, Neville might have echoed Joseph in 1906; then Unionists had unexpectedly taken all the available seats, and immodest postcards had celebrated with the slogan 'We Are Seven'. Neville could have legitimately crowed: 'We Are Twelve'. Only 1929 broke the spell; Labour won six Birmingham seats. Austen Chamberlain barely survived. Yet it proved an aberration. The fall of MacDonald's Labour Government in 1931 and the consequent party split gifted Birmingham back to the Unionists. That continuing domination was paralleled at municipal level, although there it was not quite as complete. As early as 1911, when the city and its Council expanded under the terms of the Greater Birmingham Act, Liberals and Socialists had made some inroads on the Unionist redoubt, taking around a quarter of the seats. Yet at the last municipal elections before the Second World War the Labour Party gained only 22 out of the 136 seats. Unionist hegemony, over which Joseph Chamberlain had presided in the late 1880s, once again prevailed.[344]

Neville Chamberlain's masterly organisation was not the only explanation for Unionist domination of the city. As persuasive is contemporary testimony about the enduring sway of Joseph Chamberlain and his Machine. Even in 1935 a visiting journalist from the *Observer* wrote: 'Labour campaigners are still told: "My father voted for Joe and what was good enough for him was good enough for me."'[345] Throughout the inter-war years, the Electoral Machine he had created continued to outperform its Birmingham Labour Party challengers. The permanent organisation he had inherited from Harris and Schnadhorst continued in place; just as in the heydays from the 1870s to 1906 the party drew on ample business funding; similarly, the professional agents on which he had insisted in every ward, the body of canvassers, the team of people to bring voters out to the polls at election time (with the modern addition of fleets of cars to transport them) – all these electoral devices reveal the continuously smooth working of the Machine he had helped to build. It was only the Second World War which shifted the tectonic plates in Birmingham, ushering in a new era of Labour control of the edifice erected by Chamberlain and his Unionist successors.

However, Birmingham's standing as 'the best governed city in the world' has not survived into the twenty-first century.[346] Near bankruptcy and the 'Trojan Horse' (Islamic infiltration) scandal in its schools have sullied its reputation. It is not surprising then that, in the 2017 contest for the new position of West Midlands 'metro mayor', candidates and commentators should have looked back to an era when Birmingham led the world in civic governance and should have invoked the name of Joseph Chamberlain. The journalist Matthew d'Ancona, in the pages of *The Sunday Times* in April 2017, lauded his 'combination of social compassion and political ruthlessness' which proved to be the impetus for all Conservative social reform in the 20th century. D'Ancona went on to call for central government to cede power and responsibility to regional leaders like the new 'metro mayors' so that they might be freed to implement the sort of radical change which Joseph Chamberlain made his hallmark over a century ago.[347] Yet it seems unlikely we will ever see the revival of a Political Machine of the influence and reach that characterised that created by Chamberlain and his allies; it was of its time, less complex, more personal and more reliant on voluntary commitment and on the remarkable coincidence of a generation of protean talents than appears possible in today's multi-layered local and national administrations.

TIMELINE

1829   Thomas Attwood founds the Birmingham Political Union.

1842   Joseph Sturge establishes the Complete Suffrage Union.

1847   George Dawson inaugurates the Church of the Saviour in Edward Street.

1853   Robert Dale becomes Minister of Carr's Lane Congregational Church.

1857   Birmingham Liberals invite John Bright to represent Birmingham in Parliament.

1858   Formation of the Birmingham Reform Association.

1865   Creation of the Birmingham Liberal Association.

1867   Second Reform Act.
George Dixon's successful by-election campaign in Birmingham.

1868   General Election; Harris and the Caucus direct Liberals how to vote.
Birmingham Education Society formed at Dixon's home, 'The Dales'.

1869   National Education League established.
Joseph Chamberlain elected to the Town Council.

1870   Forster's Education Act.
Birmingham School Board established after elections in which Conservatives/Anglicans secure a majority of the seats.

1874   General Election. Disraeli displaces Gladstone.

1875   Gas and water reform initiated by Birmingham's Town Council.

1876   Birmingham Improvement Scheme.
Chamberlain becomes a Member of Parliament for Birmingham; Dixon succeeds him as Chairman of the School Board.

1877   Chamberlain's National Liberal Federation (NLF) inaugurated; Gladstone attends Bingley Hall celebrations to mark the event.

1880   General Election; Gladstone defeats Beaconsfield. Chamberlain joins the Cabinet as President of the Board of Trade.

1884   Third Reform Act (Franchise). Aston Manor riots in Birmingham.

1885   Third Reform Act (Redistribution). Chamberlain launches his 'Unauthorised Programme'. General Election which Gladstone wins but the Irish hold the balance in the Commons.

1886   Chamberlain in Cabinet as President of Local Government Board. Gladstone reveals his conversion to Home Rule. Chamberlain resigns in protest. Home Rule defeated in Commons, opponents led by Chamberlain and Hartington. Gladstone loses General Election. 77 Liberal Unionists are elected.
Hartington creates LUA (Liberal Unionist Association); Chamberlain creates his own NRU (National Radical Union) in Birmingham when the Caucus splits because divided over support for Gladstone or Chamberlain. Schnadhorst takes the NLF to London and adheres to Gladstone.

1887 Abortive Round Table talks over Liberal reunion. Chamberlain heads Fishery Commission to America.

1888 Chamberlain creates the Birmingham Liberal Unionist Association. Birmingham Women's Liberal Unionist Association founded.

1889 By-election in Central Birmingham; Albert Bright and the Liberal Unionists are triumphant. Start of Liberal Unionists hegemony in Birmingham.

1892 General Election. Chamberlain now leads Liberal Unionists in the Commons. Powell Williams takes reins of Liberal Unionist Association after direction-less amateurism of the Devonshire years. Chamberlain creates a new body to organise the 'Duchy' over which he has sway – the Midlands Liberal Unionist Association.

1895 General Election; Chamberlain's dynamism brings an impressive increase in the number of Liberal Unionist MPs. Chamberlain becomes Colonial Secretary in Salisbury's government. Jameson Raid in Transvaal implicates Chamberlain.

1899 Boer War starts.

1900 Khaki Election; in many areas a jingoistic endorsement of Chamberlain's policies.

1902 Boer War ends; Chamberlain to South Africa to help re-building. Balfour's Education Act upsets many Nonconformists and Liberal Unionist supporters.

1903 Chamberlain stuns political world by publicly embracing fiscal reform – tariffs and Imperial Preference. Birmingham (later the Imperial) Tariff Committee & the Tariff Reform League established.

1904 Tariff Reform Commission and TUTRA founded. Chamberlain ousts Devonshire (formerly Hartington) for national leadership of the Liberal Unionist Association. Chamberlain trains the sights of his Machine on Free-Fooder Liberal Unionists.

1906 General Election; stunning Liberal victory and equally comprehensive Unionist defeat. But Birmingham remains true to Unionists.
In July Chamberlain suffers a catastrophic stroke.

1910 Tariff Reform Unionists fail to win public endorsement for their policy at two General Elections this year (Edward VII dies in the course of the year; tradition dictated that there should be a fresh election).

1914 Chamberlain dies.
First World War breaks out.

GLOSSARY – ACRONYMS AND DEFINITIONS

BES Birmingham Education Society founded by George Dixon in 1868.

BLA Birmingham Liberal Association created in 1865; a model for others nationwide.

BLUA Birmingham Liberal Unionist Association founded by Chamberlain in 1888.

BPU Birmingham Political Union, founded by Thomas Attwood and others in 1829, the first nationally important Birmingham political organisation.

BTC (changed its name to ITC – Imperial Tariff Committee – 1903) Birmingham Tariff Committee formed in 1903 in Birmingham straight after his 15 May speech to be Chamberlain's own trusted organisation propagating the tariff argument round the country.

Clause 25 This was a clause in Forster's Education Act (see below) which permitted local authorities to use rates to fund places for children at Anglican schools in areas where there were no School Boards established.

Caucus A term borrowed from American politics to describe a highly organised and controlling party political system. Applied in Britain first to Birmingham's Liberal Party which became notorious for its close management of elections and of its voters.

Duchy A term applied by contemporaries to the Parliamentary mini-Empire over which Chamberlain ruled in the West Midlands from 1889.

Elections: General called at intervals of up to 7 years until the 1911 Parliament Act changed the maximum term of a Parliament to 5 years. Constituencies in Birmingham: from 1868, there were 3 Birmingham MPs, with voters having 2 votes each; from 1885, there were 7 defined Birmingham constituencies (e.g. Birmingham East; Birmingham West etc.).

Elections: Municipal Elections were held annually with one third of councillors retiring each year. A large borough like Birmingham was divided into wards, which were the municipal constituencies.

Elections: School Board These were established by the Forster Education Act which permitted local areas to constitute a school board to be elected by all ratepayers. Elections took place every 3 years. Every ratepayer had the same number of votes as there were vacancies to be filled on the Board – in Birmingham, therefore, each voter could cast 15 votes. A voter could cast all his votes for one candidate, known as 'plumping'.

Fair Trade was a policy and an organisation supported by – largely Conservative – enthusiasts. It argued that the slump which hit Britain from 1877-8 was caused by unfair foreign competition, for other countries were employing tariff walls, and unloading cheap surplus goods on Britain's domestic market. Birmingham metal manufacturers proved enthusiastic disciples of this message from the early 1880s.

Forster's Education Act 1870 Although contentious it sought to make elementary education in Britain available for all. Nonconformists hated the fact that it did nothing to end the grip of voluntary (Anglican) schools on educational provision. But they did welcome the Act's encouragement to local authorities to found School Boards in areas where voluntary schools manifestly were inadequate for the task of educating all local children.

LUA Lord Hartington, leader of the Whigs in the Liberal Party up to 1886, headed the national break-away group of Liberals who rebelled against Home Rule. He set up a national organisation that year – the Liberal Unionist Association. Chamberlain joined it, though he had his own group, the NRU (see below), as well. He felt the LUA to be amateur and lacking in energy – too often this was an accurate reflection of Hartington himself. From 1892 Chamberlain and Powell Williams asserted increasing control over the LUA's management.

MLUA The Midlands Liberal Unionist Association, founded by Chamberlain in 1892 to organise his 'Duchy' of over 30 West Midlands seats to contest future elections efficiently.

NEL The National Education League formed in Birmingham in 1869 by George Dixon, Jesse Collings and Joseph Chamberlain, among others, to campaign for national, free, compulsory and non-denominational education for all children.

NLF National Liberal Federation, formed in Birmingham by Chamberlain in 1877 to democratise the Liberal Party by organising Liberal members nationally so that policy at Westminster reflected the wishes of the Liberal electorate.

NLU National Liberal Union, a re-branding in 1888 of the NRU (see below).

NRU National Radical Union, founded in 1886 in Birmingham to be Chamberlain's own organisation, espousing across the country a much more Radical agenda than Hartington's LUA (see above) was prepared to endorse. The NRU was intended to be the vehicle for propagating Chamberlain's Unauthorised Programme ideas.

Reform Acts: 2nd Reform Act 1867 Disraeli's Act conferred the vote on many urban householders as well as establishing a number of new borough constituencies (Birmingham receiving an extra MP). Fear of the impact of unlettered voters on the political system was a powerful motivation for education reform.

Reform Acts: 3rd Reform Act 1884-5 The first of the two Acts in 1884 comprising the 3rd Reform Act was concerned with the Franchise. It extended the householder vote of 1867 to rural householders – agricultural labourers would now be enfranchised. This explains the attention that Chamberlain and Collings paid to rural/land issues in the 1880s and 1890s. The second Act was the Redistribution Act in 1885; it dramatically re-drew the electoral map, establishing in most places a pattern of single member constituencies. Birmingham, like a number of large cities, gained more MPs (rising from 3 to 7).

Tariff Reform was the policy advocated by Joseph Chamberlain from 1903. He called for tariffs to create a system of Imperial Preference whereby Britain's colonies would be advantaged in Britain's markets while foreign importers paid a penalty. He also saw tariffs as a means to protect struggling British industry and farmers.

TRC Tariff Reform Commission, founded in 1904 and consisting of economists to provide reliable statistical information for Chamberlain to use when advocating Tariff Reform. W. Hewins and W. Ashley were leading lights.

TRL The Tariff Reform League, a national body established in London in late 1903 and intended to be non-party political, appealing to Liberals as well as Unionists. It was supported by a number of wealthy and influential Edwardians – politicians, aristocrats, businessmen, manufacturers and agricultural spokesmen.

TUTRA The Trade Union Tariff Reform Association formed in 1904 to champion tariff reform among the working classes.

WLUA The Women's Liberal Unionist Association formed 1888 – with Birmingham an early and notably flourishing branch. It aimed to organise women for an important electoral role in canvassing, pamphleteering and advocating policy on behalf of the Liberal Unionists.

WUTRA Women's Unionist and Tariff Reform Association (1906) formed by the amalgamation of the Women's Tariff Reform League (1904) with WLUA to promote political education, support Tariff Reform, advocate social reform and oppose Irish Home Rule. WUTRA's members in Birmingham in 1906 were notably significant in campaigning for Chamberlain and the other Unionist candidates.

NOTES

1   JC 5/8/16.

2   Crosskey, H., 'The Liberal Association – the 600 – of Birmingham', *Macmillan Magazine*, February 1877.

3   Churchill, W., *Lord Randolph Churchill* (London, Odhams Press, 1905), reprint by General Books LLC, Memphis, USA, 2012. Speech in Birmingham 1884, p. 81.

4   *Yorkshire Post*, 11 December 1884, JC 34/2/1/6.

5   Letter, A.J. Mundella to R. E. Leader, 10 July 1879, quoted by Auspos, P., 'Radicalism, pressure Groups and party Politics', *Journal of British Studies* vol.20 no.1, Autumn 1980, p. 203.

6   Ostrogorski, M., *Democracy and Organisation of Political Parties* vol.1 (ed. Lipset., S.) (Anchor Books and Quadrangle Books, USA, 1964), p. 89

7   *BDP* 24 April 1889.

8   *BDP* 13 January 1891.

9   Buckle, G.E., *The Life of Benjamin Disraeli, Earl of Beaconsfield, vol.6* (Macmillan, London, 1920), p. 535. The term 'caucus' originated in the United States where it was applied to political organisations in a number of states.

10   Letter, Joseph Chamberlain to Jesse Collings, 10 April 1876, JC 5/16/51.

11   *Birmingham Daily Gazette*, 15 November 1882.

12   Garvin, J.l., *Life of Joseph Chamberlain, vol.1* (Macmillan, London, 1932), p. 479.

13   From an article 'The Caucus', by Joseph Chamberlain in *Fortnightly Review* 1878.

14   *Fortnightly Review, op.cit.*

15   Garvin, *op.cit.*, p. 253.

16   Briggs, A., *History of Birmingham, vol. 2* (OUP, Oxford, 1952), p. 167.

17   Moss, D., *Thomas Attwood* (McGill – Queen's University Press, Montreal, 1990), p. 263.

18   Moss, *op.cit.*, pp. 159-161.

19   The People's Charter was launched in Birmingham, in August 1838, by Thomas Attwood; it called for universal suffrage, the secret ballot, equal electoral districts, annual parliaments, no property qualification for MPs and payment for MPs.

20   Reekes, A.E., *Speeches that Changed Britain* (History West Midlands, Alcester, 2015), p. 29.

21   Tholfsen, T.R., 'The Origins of the Birmingham Caucus', *Historical Journal* 11, 2, 1959, pp. 161-184.

22   Tholfsen, *op.cit.*, p. 169.

23   Tholfsen, *op.cit.*

24   *The Bright Celebrations in Birmingham* (National Liberal Federation, 1883), cited by Briggs, *op.cit.*, pp. 165-166.

25   Tholfsen, *op.cit.*, p. 182.

26   Hennock, E.P., *Fit and Proper Persons* (Edward Arnold, 1973), pp. 93-94; Reekes, A.E., *op.cit.*, pp. 52-62.

27   Hennock, *op.cit.*, pp. 95-96.

28   Gardiner, A.G., *The Life of George Cadbury* (Cassell and Co., London, 1924), p.45.

29   Schnadhorst, F., in a speech at Nechells Ward meeting, 23 March 1885, reported by the *Birmingham Daily Post*, 25 March 1885.

30   Dixon, J., *Out of Birmingham – George Dixon, Father of Free Education* (Brewin, Alcester, 2013) p. 55.

[31] Crosskey, H., quoted in Armstrong, R.A., & MacCarthy, E.F.M., *Henry William Crosskey* (Cornish Bros., Birmingham 1895), p. 264.

[32] Schnadhorst, *op.cit.*

[33] Garvin, *op.cit.*, p. 261.

[34] Hennock, *op.cit.*, p. 133.

[35] Dixon's electoral address in 1868 quoted by Langford, J.A., *Modern Birmingham and Its Institutions* (Birmingham 1877), vol.2, p. 370.

[36] William Harris speaking to a Liberal meeting in Edgbaston ward, 20 December 1867, reported in the *Birmingham Daily Post*, 21 December 1867.

[37] Garvin, *op.cit.*, p. 254.

[38] Schnadhorst, *op.cit.*

[39] Ward, R., *City-State and Nation, Birmingham's Political History 1830-1940* (Phillimore, Chichester, 2005), p. 64.

[40] Herrick, F.H., 'The Origins of the National Liberal Federation', *The Journal of Modern History*, Vol.17, No.2 (June 1945), pp. 116-129.

[41] Evans, E., *Parliamentary Reform, c.1770–1918* (London, Longmans, 2000), pp. 61-62.

[42] Dunbabin, J.P.D., 'Electoral Reforms and their Outcome in the United Kingdom, 1865-1900' in *Later Victorian Britain,* ed. Gourvish, T.R., and O'Day, A. (London, Macmillan, 1988), pp. 93-125.

[43] Garrard, J., 'Parties, Members and Voters after 1867', in Gourvish and O'Day, *op.cit.*, pp. 127-150.

[44] Chamberlain, J., 'The Caucus, A New Political Organisation', *Fortnightly Review*, July 1877.

[45] Dunbabin, *op.cit.*, p. 101.

[46] Koss, S., *The Rise and Fall of the Political Press in Britain* (London, Hamish Hamilton Ltd., 1981), p. 1; Vincent, J., *The Formation of the British Liberal Party* (London, Constable, 1966), p. 95.

[47] Evans, *op.cit.*, p. 60.

[48] Vincent, *op.cit.*, p. 100.

[49] Green, C., 'Birmingham's Politics 1873-1891, The Local Politics of Change', *Midland History* (1973) 2:2, p. 87.

[50] Letter from Chamberlain to Collings, 12 September 1875, JC 5/16/47.

[51] Vincent, *op.cit.*, p. 96. See also Reekes, A.E., *Speeches that Changed Britain* (Alcester, History West Midlands, 2015).

[52] Lowe, R., *Hansard* 15 July 1867.

[53] Sargent, W.L., *Essays of a Manufacturer* (Birmingham, J. Allen, 1872), p. 5.

[54] Burgess, H.J., *Enterprise in Education* (London, National Society, SPCK, 1958), pp. 11 and 23.

[55] National Education League pamphlet no. 310, Library of Birmingham Archives MS 4248.

[56] Dixon, J., *Out of Birmingham – George Dixon, Father of Free Education* (Studley, Brewin Books, 2013), pp. 76, 63-64.

[57] Taylor, A.F., 'Birmingham and the Movement for National Education,' (University of Leicester, unpublished PhD Thesis, 1960), p. 32.

[58] Report to the House of Commons by two of HM Inspectors, February 1871.

[59] Taylor, *op.cit.*, p. 53.

[60] Collings, J., *The Life of the Right. Hon. Jesse Collings* (The Mayflower Press, Plymouth, England), p. 20.

[61] Dixon, *op.cit.*, p. 89.

[62] Collings, *idem.*

63 Briggs, A., *History of Birmingham: Borough and City, 1865-1938* (Oxford, OUP, 1952), p. lvii, footnote.

64 MS 4248 National Education League publications, Library of Birmingham; J.MacNaught's letter, November 1869.

65 Letter 15 May 1876 JC 5/16/52.

66 Taylor, *op.cit.*, pp. 113-115.

67 Garvin, *op.cit.*, p. 109.

68 Garvin, *idem.*

69 Dixon, *op.cit.*, p. 138.

70 Taylor, *op.cit.*, pp. 174-180.

71 MS 4248 *op.cit.*

72 JC 6/3/2/28.

73 Dixon, *op.cit.*, pp. 115-117.

74 MS 4248, Library of Birmingham.

75 Letter, Chamberlain to Dilke, 14 November 1871, JC 5/24/278.

76 Taylor, *op.cit.*, pp. 83-84.

77 MS 4248 Library of Birmingham, National Education League pamphlet no. 311, January 1873.

78 *Birmingham Daily Post*, 20 July 1870.

79 *BDP*, 21 October 1870.

80 Armytage, W.H.G., *A.J.Mundella, 1825-97* (London, Benn 1951), p. 215.

81 Auspos, P., 'Radicalism, Pressure Groups and Party Politics,' *Journal of British Studies*, volume 20, no.1, Autumn 1980, pp. 184-204.

82 Taylor, *op.cit.*, p. 226.

83 Garvin, *op.cit.*, p. 12.

84 Garvin, *op.cit.*, pp. 256-7; 129-135.

85 Letter to Morley, 19 August 1873, JC 5/54/13.

86 Letter to Charles Dilke, 17 March 1874, Charles Dilke Papers, Add.MS 43855.

87 Auspos, *op.cit.*, pp. 196-7; H.J.Hanham, *Elections and Party Management – Politics in the time of Disraeli and Gladstone* (London, Longmans,1959), p. 122.

88 Taylor, A.F., 'Birmingham and the Movement for National Education', (unpublished PhD thesis, University of Leicester, 1960), pp. 154-158; also *Birmingham Daily Post*, 21 October 1870.

89 Hennock, E.P., *Fit and Proper Persons* (London, Edward Arnold, 1973), p. 134; Briggs, A., *History of Birmingham Vol.II* (Oxford, OUP, 1952), p. 169; Taylor, *op.cit.*, p. 158.

90 Taylor, *op.cit.*, pp. 159-160.

91 Taylor, *op.cit.*, p. 166.

92 *Birmingham Daily Post*, 2 and 3 December 1870.

93 Adams, F., *History of the Elementary School Contest in England* (London, Chapman and Hall, 1882), p. 255.

94 Garvin, *op.cit.*, p. 125; Taylor, *op.cit.*, p. 169.

95 Armstrong, R.A., and MacCarthy, E.F.M., *Henry William Crosskey* (Birmingham, Cornish Bros., 1895), p. 281.

96 Taylor, *op.cit.*, pp. 182-185.

97 Taylor, *op.cit.*, pp. 189-191.

98 Debate on Regulations on Religious Instruction published as 'Religious Instruction in Board Schools', National Education League pamphlet (London, Simpkin and Marshall, 1872).

[99] *Birmingham Daily Post*, 16 January 1873.

[100] Reprinted as a pamphlet by the National Education League, February 1873.

[101] Hennock, *op.cit.*, p. 135

[102] Armstrong, *op.cit.*, p. 263.

[103] Garvin, *op.cit.*, p. 255.

[104] Taylor, *op.cit.*, p. 200.

[105] *BDP* 19 November 1873.

[106] *Telegraph*, 19 November 1873.

[107] *BDP*, 19 November 1873.

[108] *BDP*, 21 November 1873.

[109] *BDP*, 16 April 1880.

[110] JC 31/2-5.

[111] Dixon, *op.cit.*, p. 179.

[112] Cannadine, D., 'The Chamberlain Tradition and Birmingham', in *Churchill's Shadow* (London, Allen Lane, 2002), p. 121; *Six Years of Educational Work in Birmingham; an Address delivered to the Birmingham School Board by the Chairman, Joseph Chamberlain esq., 2 November 1876*, quoted by Garvin, *op.cit.*, p. 211.

[113] *The Dart* 26 July 1888; Dixon, J., *op.cit.*, p. 188.

[114] *BDP* 16 April 1880.

[115] Armstrong and MacCarthy, *op.cit.*, p. 288.

[116] *School Board Chronicle*, Vol.19, 11 May 1878, p. 445, quoted by Dixon, *op.cit.*, p. 183.

[117] *The Dart*, 11 May 1878.

[118] Armstrong and MacCarthy, *op.cit.*, pp. 288-289.

[119] Armstrong and MacCarthy, *op.cit.*, pp. 294-302.

[120] Dixon, *op.cit.*, pp. 196-199.

[121] Ralph, J., 'The Best-Governed City in the World', *Harper's Monthly Magazine*, June 1890, cited by Briggs, A., *History of Birmingham*, Vol. 11, (Oxford, OUP, 1952), p. 62.

[122] Hennock, *op.cit.*, pp. 104-130; Briggs, *op.cit.*, p. 87.

[123] Boyd, C.W., *Mr Chamberlain's Speeches, vol.1.*, 'State Socialism and the Moderate Liberals', 28 April 1885, pp. 163-5.

[124] *Birmingham Daily Post*, 25 March 1874, reporting Chamberlain's speech to the Council.

[125] Letter JC to Morley, 26 October 1873, quoted by Garvin, *op.cit.*, p. 185.

[126] Garvin, *op.cit.*, p. 188.

[127] Garvin, *op.cit.*, p. 203.

[128] Briggs, *op.cit.*, p. 119.

[129] Bunce, J.T., *History of the Corporation of Birmingham*, volume 2, (Birmingham, Cornish Bros., 1885), p. xxxiii.

[130] Armstrong, R.A., & MacCarthy, E.F.M., *Henry William Crosskey* (Birmingham, Cornish Bros., 1895), p. 261.

[131] Briggs, *op.cit.*, p. 67.

[132] Rosenthal, L., 'Joseph Chamberlain and the Birmingham Town Council 1865-1880', *Midland History* (2016) 41:1, pp. 84-8.

[133] Hennock, *op.cit.*, p. 135; Crosskey in Armstrong and MacCarthy, *op.cit.*, p. 263.

[134] Rosenthal, *op.cit.*, pp. 87-89.

135 Ashby, A.W., 'Jesse Collings', *Oxford Dictionary of National Biography*; Eagles, S., 'Past Masters: A Builder of Birmingham, George Baker (1825-1910)', *The Companion*, Summer 2016, pp. 53-57.

136 *Birmingham Daily Post*, 16 December 1909.

137 *Birmingham Daily Post*, 31 July 1919.

138 Pettit, Scott, 'William White', *Oxford Dictionary of National Biography*.

139 *Birmingham Daily Post*, 21 October 1905.

140 Roberts, S., *Joseph Gillott and Four Other Birmingham Manufacturers* 1784-1892 (Create Space 2016), pp. 53-58; *The Dart*, 29 May 1885.

141 Marsh, *op.cit.*, p. 99.

142 Hennock, *op.cit.*, p. 138.

143 Letter JC to Jesse Collings, 12 March 1876, JC 5/16/49.

144 Armstrong and MacCarthy, *op.cit.*, pp. 251-2.

145 *Inaugural Address by George Dawson, MA*, Borough of Birmingham, Opening of the Free Reference Library, 26 October 1866 (Birmingham, E. C. Osborne, 1866).

146 Dale, R.W., *Weekday Sermons*, pp. 175-6.

147 Armstong and MacCarthy, *op.cit.*, p. 207.

148 Armstong and MacCarthy, *op.cit.*, pp. 261-265.

149 Garvin, *op.cit.*, pp. 189-190.

150 Marsh, *op.cit.*, p. 87.

151 Garvin, *op.cit.*, p. 191; Hennock, *op.cit.*, p. 122.

152 Garvin, *op.cit.*, p. 192.

153 Hennock, *op.cit.*, p. 112.

154 *Birmingham Council Proceedings*, 2 December 1873; 9 June 1874, L34/3.

155 Letter JC to Jesse Collings, 12 March 1876, JC 5/16.

156 *Borough of Birmingham, Proceedings on the Adoption by the Council of a Scheme for the Improvement of the Borough* (1875), p.19.

157 Reekes, A.E., *Two Titans, One City* (History West Midlands, Alcester, 2017), chapter 3.

158 Hennock, *op.cit.*, p. 126.

159 Bunce, *op.cit.*, pp. 462-3.

160 *Proceedings, op.cit.*, p. 30.

161 *Birmingham Daily Post* obituaries, February 1904.

162 Reekes, *Two Titans, One City, op.cit.*, chapter 3.

163 Both Crosskey and Bunce quoted by Ward, R., *City State and Nation, Birmingham's Political History, 1830-1940* (Chichester, Phillimore, 2005), p. 77.

164 Ward, *op.cit.*, p. 78.

165 Rosenthal, *op.cit.*, p. 90.

166 Ward, *op.cit.*, pp 78-79; 111-113.

167 Letters JC to F. Schnadhorst and to J. Powell Williams, 11 September 1882, MS 170/2.

168 Ostrogorski, *op.cit.*, p. 89.

169 *Yorkshire Post*, 11 December 1884.

170 Letter A.J. Mundella to R.E. Leader, 10 July 1879, quoted by Auspos, P. 'Radicalism, Pressure Groups and Party Politics', *Journal of British Studies* vol. 20 no.1, Autumn 1980, p. 203.

171 Briggs, *op.cit.*, p. 175.

172 Hamer, D.A., *Liberal Politics in the Age of Gladstone and Rosebery* (Oxford, OUP, 1972), p. 45.

173 Garvin, *op.cit.*, p.254.

174 McGill, B., 'Francis Schnadhorst and Liberal Party Organisation', *The Journal of Modern History*, Vol. 34, No. 1, 1962), p. 20.

175 Hanham, H.J., *Elections and Party Management* (Sussex, The Harvester Press, 1978), p. 126.

176 Hanham, *op.cit.*, p. 391.

177 Chamberlain, J., 'A New Political Organisation', *Fortnightly Review*, n.s. XXII, July 1877, p. 126.

178 Crosskey, H., 'The Liberal Association – the 600 – of Birmingham', *Macmillan Magazine*, February 1877.

179 *Proceedings attending the formation of the National Liberal Federation of Liberal Associations* (Birmingham 1877), p. 16.

180 Chamberlain, J., 'The Caucus,' *Fortnightly Review*, n.s. XXIV, November 1878, pp. 721–741.

181 Chamberlain, J., 'A New Political Organisation', *op.cit.*, p. 134.

182 Auspos, *op.cit.*, p. 199.

183 Letter Chamberlain, J., to Jesse Collings, 8 February 1877, JC 5/16/59.

184 Garvin, *op.cit.*, p. 262.

185 Letter Chamberlain, J. to Morley, J., 6 February 1877, JC 5/54/158.

186 Letter Chamberlain, J. to Collings, J., 22 March 1877, JC 5/16/64.

187 Garvin, *op.cit.*, p. 257.

188 Larry Mark was that month under arrest as one of a number of thugs detained after the Aston Manor *fracas* in October 1884.

189 *Yorkshire Post*, 11 December 1884.

190 Ostrogorski, *op.cit.*, pp. 209-210.

191 Garvin, *op.cit.*, p. 257.

192 Garvin, *op.cit.*, p. 260.

193 Beaconsfieldism was the term applied by Liberal opponents to Lord Beaconsfield's 'cynical' foreign policy (as they deemed it) which supported Turkey, the oppressor in the Balkans, to prevent Russia (a Christian champion of oppressed Balkan peoples) from extending her influence in the Near East.

194 Quoted by Morley, J., *Life of Gladstone*, vol. II (London, Macmillan, 1903), p. 570.

195 *Ibid.*

196 Quoted by Ostrogorski, *op.cit.*, p. 183.

197 Letter Morley, J., to Chamberlain, J., 26 January 1880, quoted by Garvin, *op.cit.*, p. 289.

198 Letters, Harcourt, W., to Chamberlain, J., 15 and 24 January 1880, quoted by Garvin, *op.cit.*, p. 288.

199 Churchill, W., *Lord Randolph Churchill* (London, Odhams Press, 1905), reprint by General Books LLC, Memphis, USA, 2012. Speech in Birmingham 14 October 1884, p. 81.

200 Speech by Lord Randolph Churchill, 2 October 1883, quoted in Churchill, *op.cit.*, p67.

201 Letter Chamberlain, J. to Harris, W., 16 November 1878, JC 5/39/8.

202 Letter Chamberlain, J., to Harris, W., 18 January 1878, JC 5/39/3.

203 NLF Annual Report, January 1879, quoted by Hamer, D.A., *op.cit.*, p. 81.

204 Hamer, *op.cit.*, pp. 82-86.

205 Schnadhorst, F., 'The caucus and its critics', NLF pamphlet January 1880, pp. 18-19.

206 Letter, Chamberlain. J., to *The Times*, 13 April 1880.

[207] McGill, *op.cit.*, pp. 21-23.

[208] Hamer, *op.cit.*, p. 90.

[209] Speech by Schnadhorst, F., 6 June 1882, Brighton.

[210] Speech by Lord Hartington, Accrington, 1 December 1883, quoted by Garvin, *op.cit.*, p. 401.

[211] Ostrogorski, *op.cit.*, pp. 209-210.

[212] NLF letter to Liberal Associations, 1 March 1884, JC 5/63/6.

[213] Ostrogorski, *op.cit.*, p. 106; p. 233.

[214] NLF Circular 29 June 1881.

[215] Letter in *The Spectator*, 9 November 1878, JC 34/2/1/1.

[216] Garvin, *op.cit.*, p. 264.

[217] *Manchester Guardian*, 20 December 1882; Hanham, *op.cit.*, p. 152.

[218] Churchill, W., *op.cit.*, p. 80.

[219] *The Times*, 31 October 1884.

[220] Garvin, *op.cit.*, p. 479.

[221] Article, 'Our True Nobility', *Ipswich Free Press*, 5 June 1880, JC 34/2/1/5.

[222] Ostrogorski, *op.cit.*, p. 187.

[223] Letter Chamberlain, J to Schnadhorst, F., 25 April 1879, Schnadhorst papers, University of Birmingham Special Collections, MS170/2.

[224] McGill, *op.cit.*, pp. 27-29.

[225] Hamer, *op.cit.*, pp. 115-123.

[226] Letters, Schnadhorst, F., to Chamberlain, J., 13 February 1886; April 15th1886, JC 5/63/9+15.

[227] Letters, Powell Williams, J., to Chamberlain, J., 27 April 1886, 11 May 1886, 3 June 1885. JC 5/72/3-6.

[228] Ward, R., *City State and Nation, Birmingham's Political History* 1840-1940 (Chichester, Phillimore, 2005), p. 101.

[229] Letters, Chamberlain, J., to Chamberlain, A., 7 June 1886, JC 5/11/11-13.

[230] *Birmingham Daily Gazette,* 1 July 1886.

[231] *Birmingham Daily Post*, 29 April 1889, quoting a speech by Chamberlain given at a mass meeting of the Birmingham Liberal Union at Bingley Hall.

[232] *Liberal Unionist,* June 1886 quoted by Cawood, I., *The Liberal Unionist Party* (London, I.B.Tauris and Co., Ltd, 2012), p. 108.

[233] Quoted by Cawood, *op.cit.*, p. 120.

[234] Hurst, M.C., 'Joseph Chamberlain, the Conservatives and the succession to John Bright, 1886-1889', *Historical Journal* VII, 1, pp. 64-93.

[235] Hurst, *op.cit.*, pp. 84-5.

[236] Ward, *op.cit.*, p. 115.

[237] Report on the meeting of the Grand Committee, BLUA, 1 September 1889, *BDP* 2 September 1889.

[238] Letter Chamberlain, J., to Mary Endicott, 21 April 1888, JC 28/A1/14.

[239] Letter Chamberlain, J., to Bunce, J.T., April 1888, JC 5/8/90.

[240] Quoted by Marsh, *Joseph Chamberlain, Entrepreneur in Politics* (New Haven/London, Yale University Press, 1997), p. 300.

[241] *BDP* 29 October 1889.

[242] *BDP* Report on Birmingham WLUA meeting in January 1891, 13 January 1891; Cawood, *op.cit.*, p. 150.

[243] *Birmingham Daily Mail*, 18 January 1906.

244 Cawood, *op.cit.*, pp. 155-7.

245 Powell Williams, 'The Rise and Progress of the National Liberal Union' in *Liberal Unionist 45*, October 1889, quoted by Cawood, *op.cit.*, p. 118.

246 *BDP* 24 April 1889.

247 Hurst, M., 'Joseph Chamberlain and West Midlands Politics, 1886-1889', *Dugdale Occasional Papers* No.15, 1962, p. 46.

248 Letter, Chamberlain, J., to Chamberlain, J.A., 3 December 1888, JC 5/12/2.

249 Hurst, *op.cit.*, p. 47.

250 Letter, Chamberlain, J.A., to Chamberlain, J., 10 April 1889, JC 6/2/1/17.

251 Letter, Powell Williams to Chamberlain, J., 10 April 1889, JC 6/2/1/18.

252 Letter, Chamberlain, J.A. to Chamberlain, J., 11 April 1889, JC 6/2/1/20.

253 Letter, Powell Williams, to Chamberlain, J., 12 April 1889, JC 6/2/1/22.

254 Hurst, *op.cit.*, p. 50.

255 Cawood, *op.cit.*, p. 179.

256 Green, C., 'Birmingham's Politics, 1873-1891: The Local Basis of Change', *Midland History*, 2/2 (1973), pp. 84-98.

257 Hurst, M., 'Joseph Chamberlain, the Conservatives and the successor to John Bright, 1886-1889', *Historical Journal*, VII, 1, p. 70.

258 Cawood, *op.cit.*, p. 194.

259 Quoted by Marsh, *op.cit.*, p. 343.

260 Report of the Committee of the Midlands LUA, February 1894.

261 *Ibid.*

262 *Ibid.*

263 Cawood, I., 'Joseph Chamberlain, the Conservative Party and the Leamington Spa Candidature dispute of 1895', *Historical Research*, 2006, Vol.179, no.206, pp. 554–578.

264 *The Times*, 9 March 1892.

265 Cawood, *The Liberal Unionist Party, op.cit.*, pp. 198ff.

266 *Ibid.* Also, Thompson, J., 'Pictorial Lies? – Posters and Politics in Britain, *c.*1880-1914', *Past and Present*, 197 (2007), pp. 177-210.

267 Cawood, *op.cit.*, p. 124.

268 *Birmingham Daily Post*, 20 February 1904.

269 Pelling, H., *Social Geography of British Elections, 1885-1910* (London, Macmillan, 1967), 9.202.

270 Cawood, *op.cit.*, p. 559.

271 Cawood, *op.cit.*, pp. 214-221.

272 Ward, *op.cit.*, p. 139.

273 Cawood, *op.cit.*, p. 230.

274 Letter, Chamberlain, J., to Devonshire, 26 October 1903, JC 18/18/48.

275 *Birmingham Daily Post*, 19 December 1901.

276 *The Times*, 21 December 1901, from a report on 'The Riots at Birmingham,' which quoted Mr W. Finnemore, the secretary of the Birmingham Liberal Association, extensively.

277 Rix, K., 'The Elimination of Corrupt Practices in British Elections', *English Historical Review*, (February 2008, vol. 123, No. 500), pp. 65-97; Ballard, P., 'Rus in Urbe: Joseph Chamberlain's Gardens at Highbury, Moor Green in Birmingham, 1879-1914', *Garden History*, vol.14, No.1, Spring 1986, pp. 61-76.

278 *The Times*, 18 November 1902.

279 Churchill, W.S., *Great Contemporaries* (London, Thomas Butterworth, 1937), p. 57.

280 Amery, J., *Joseph Chamberlain and the Tariff Reform Campaign – The Life of Joseph Chamberlain, Volume Five 1901-1903* (Macmillan, London, 1969), p. 192.

281 Amery, L., *My Political Life, Vol. 1: England before the Storm, 1896-1914* (London, Hutchison, 1953), p. 236.

282 Trentmann, F., *Free Trade Nation* (Oxford, OUP, 2008), pp. 35-64.

283 Thompson, A., *Imperial Britain* (Harlow, Pearson Educational, 2000), p. 82-84.

284 Boyd, C., *Mr Chamberlain's Speeches, Vol. ii* (London, Constable, 1914), p. 294.

285 Cain, P., 'Political Economy in Edwardian England: The Tariff Reform Controversy,' in *The Edwardian Age, Conflict and Stability, 1900-1914*, ed., O'Day, A. (London, Macmillan, 1979), p. 36.

286 Marsh, *op.cit.*, pp. 520; 541.

287 *Ibid*, p. 561.

288 Wright, G.H., *Chronicles of the Birmingham Chamber of Commerce, AD 1813-1913* (Birmingham, 1913), p. 444.

289 Judd, D., *Radical Joe* (London, Hamish Hamilton, 1977), pp. 241-2.

290 Green, E.H.H., *The Crisis of Conservatism* (London, Routledge, 1995), p. 145.

291 Reekes, A.E., *Speeches that Changed Britain* (Alcester, West Midlands History, 2015), pp. 76-78.

292 Reekes, A.E., 'Birmingham Exceptionalism, Joseph Chamberlain and the 1906 General Election', unpublished M. Res. Thesis, University of Birmingham, 2014, pp. 42-53.

293 *Hansard*, 28 May 1903.

294 Letter Chamberlain, J. to Collings, J., 18 July 1903, quoted by Amery, *op.cit.*, p. 307.

295 Amery, *op.cit.*, p. 301.

296 *Ibid*.

297 *The Westminster Gazette*, 10 July 1903. JC 34 1/3/5.

298 Letter W.S. Churchill to Devonshire, 1 September 1903, quoted by Amery, *op.cit.*, pp. 302-303.

299 *Daily Mail*, 18 July 1903.

300 *The Times*, 24 August 1903.

301 Thompson, J., 'Pictorial Lies…' *op.cit.*; Mathew, S., 'Collecting Colonial Postcards,' in *Gender, Sexuality and Colonial Modernity*, ed. Burton, A. (London, Routledge, 1999), pp. 95-115. The picture postcard craze was prompted by the Post Office in 1902, permitting an image to occupy the whole side of a postcard. In 1908 860 million cards were sent through the post.

302 *BDM* 21 November 1905.

303 Ward, *op.cit.*, p. 170.

304 *BDP* 18 January 1906.

305 Lawrence, J., *Speaking for the People* (Cambridge, CUP, 1998), p. 181.

306 *BDP* 11 November 1903; *The Times*, 12 January 1906 and 15 January 1906.

307 Amery, *op.cit.*, p. 308.

308 Zebel, S.H., 'Joseph Chamberlain and the Genesis of Tariff Reform', *Journal of British Studies* 1967, Vol. 7, No. 1, p. 153.

309 Ward, *op.cit.*, pp. 163-4.

310 Zebel, 'Joseph Chamberlain and the Genesis of Tariff Reform,' *Journal of British Studies* 1967, vol. 7, No. 1, November 1967, pp. 152-3; Amery, *op.cit.*, pp. 304-7.

311 Thompson, A., *Imperial Britain* (Harlow, Pearson Education Limited, 2000), p. 42.

[312] Rix, K., 'The Elimination of Corrupt Practices in Elections?' *English Historical Review, cxxiii*, 500 (February 2008), pp. 65-97.

[313] Thompson, A., 'Tariff Reform: An Imperial Strategy, 1903-1913', *The Historical Journal* 40, 4 (1997), p. 1040.

[314] Thompson, *Imperial Britain*, *op.cit.*, p. 43.

[315] *Monthly Notes on Tariff Reform* volume I (July 1904), University of Warwick Records Centre.

[316] *Monthly Notes* volume III (21 November 1905).

[317] The 'electrophone' was then a new distributed audio system which used conventional telephone lines to relay live performances of speeches, theatres and music halls to subscribers with head-sets. In this case, Chamberlain's speech was transmitted to several listening receivers who concurrently read out to audiences the words of Chamberlain's speech they were hearing transmitted down the telephone wire.

[318] Thackeray, D., *Conservatism for the Democratic Age* (Manchester, MUP, 2013), p. 25; Trentmann, F., *Free Trade Nation* (Oxford, OUP, 2008), p. 92.

[319] 'Dump shops' exhibited cheap foreign goods which undercut honest British labour in an attempt to highlight the extent to which imports were driving up unemployment.

[320] Trentmann, F., *op.cit.*, p. 101.

[321] *The Times*, 13 January 1904.

[322] Memorandum from Lord Robert Cecil to A. Balfour, February 1905 quoted by Sykes, A., *Tariff Reform in British Politics, 1903-1913* (Oxford, OUP, 1979), pp. 90-91.

[323] Marsh, *op.cit.*, p. 592.

[324] Amery, *op.cit.*, p. 283.

[325] *The Times*, 19 December 1903.

[326] Brittain, H., Reminiscences, JC 19/7/2.

[327] *The Times*, 13 January 1904.

[328] Thackeray, *op.cit.*, p. 30.

[329] *The Times*, 28 October 1903.

[330] Brown, K., 'The Trade Union Tariff Reform Association 1904-1913', *Journal of British Studies* Vol. 9 No.2 (May 1970), p. 141 *ff.*

[331] The Primrose League was founded in 1883 to commemorate the Conservative hero Benjamin Disraeli, Lord Beaconsfield. Through a network of local 'habitations' it involved nearly a million men and women in fund-raising, canvassing and other related events. After the Corrupt and Illegal Practices Act (1883) had strictly limited candidates' expenses, the Primrose League represented a new emphasis on voluntary involvement in politics.

[332] Thackeray, *op.cit.*, pp. 27-29.

[333] *Ibid.*

[334] Thackeray, *op.cit.*, p. 41.

[335] JC 28/A1/22.

[336] *Manchester Guardian*, 15 January 1906.

INDEX

Notes: JC = Joseph Chamberlain; bold references indicate major biographical information; italic references indicate images.